MW00784146

Stepping Stones

Stepping Stones

Memoir of a Life Together

Alice Lynd and Staughton Lynd

LEXINGTON BOOKS

A divison of
Rowman & Littlefield Publishers, Inc.
Lanham • Boulder • New York • Toronto • Plymouth, UK

LEXINGTON BOOKS

A division of Rowman & Littlefield Publishers, Inc.
A wholly owned subsidary of The Rowman & Littlefield Publishing Group, Inc.
4501 Forbes Boulevard, Suite 200
Lanham, MD 20706

Estover Road
Plymouth PL6 7PY
United Kingdom

Copyright © 2009 by Lexington Books

All rights reserved. No part of this publication may be reproduced,
stored in a retrieval system, or transmitted in any form or by any means,
electronic, mechanical, photocopying, recording, or otherwise, without
the prior permission of the publisher.

British Library Cataloguing in Publication Information Available

Library of Congress Cataloging-in-Publication Data

Lynd, Alice.
    Stepping stones : memoir of a life together / Alice Lynd and Staughton Lynd.
        p. cm.
    Includes bibliographical references and index.
    1. Lynd, Alice. 2. Lynd, Staughton, 1929- 3. Social reformers—United
States—Biography. I. Lynd, Staughton, 1929- II. Title.
    HN59.2.L95 2009
    303.48'4092273—dc22
    [B]   2008044658

    ISBN: 978-0-7391-2749-0 (cloth : alk. paper)
    ISBN: 978-0-7391-2750-6 (pbk. : alk. paper)
    ISBN: 978-0-7391-3460-3 (electronic)

Printed in the United States of America

∞™ The paper used in this publication meets the minimum requirements
of American National Standard for Information Sciences—Permanence of
Paper for Printed Library Materials, ANSI/NISO Z39.48-1992.

Contents

Foreword

One night when I was a young traveling radical—perhaps it was the early sixties—I slept at the home of Staughton and Alice Lynd, two friends from the early civil rights era in Atlanta. I don't remember the time or town with any exactitude, but there was an unforgettable moment when the lights went off. I couldn't help but hear Staughton and Alice going to bed in the adjoining room.

They were talking quietly, just above a whisper. There was periodic laughter, hushed but hearable. I may have caught a few words about their little boy Lee, but otherwise didn't hear anything that passed between them. It was a tone that struck me, an impression of a deep relationship, of a kind that I hadn't found anywhere in my life, nor in my parents' lives, nor in the spontaneous free love of the movement days.

Staughton and Alice were "a two-person community," as they write in this book, *Stepping Stones*. It has been that way for fifty years, as their moving narrative reveals to us.

That their relationship has been exemplary doesn't mean it has been without upheavals and stress. There was a separation, for example, when Alice was tempted to join the Woodcrest *bruderhof* in the late fifties. And Staughton became so caught up in the height of the sixties that Alice felt the Movement came first, the kids an occasional second, leaving her alone in third place.

But they triumphed over all manner of trials, now giving us a unique prism into history through personal story, very much the kind of oral histories of labor (*Rank and File*) and draft resistance (*We Won't Go*) they themselves have written about others.

I met the Lynds when, with Howard and Roz Zinn, we lived in Atlanta, all of us northerners drawn to the center of the student civil rights movement. Staughton, a meticulous scholar whose parents were the eminent sociologists Robert and Helen Lynd, made an important moral choice to teach at Spelman, a black women's college, instead of the Ivy League, following Howard's path before him. Having just left the University of Michigan at age twenty-one, and ten years younger, I considered them as role models. Staughton would become the principal administrator of the historic Mississippi "freedom schools" in 1964. Soon after that, all of us plunged into the antiwar and draft resistance movements, with Staughton and myself traveling to North Vietnam in December 1965 and writing a book, *The Other Side*, about our disobedient diplomacy.

Our differences, such as they were, were experiential. I was more unformed and raw, sifting my daily experiences into evidence to improvise a concept we called "participatory democracy." There had been two life-changing experiences in my case; first, a youthful baptism from campus apathy to activism and, second, the transforming example of direct action by the freedom riders and sit-in leaders. The philosophical notion of participatory democracy itself came from John Dewey, whose writings many of us read in the universities.

The Lynds and the Zinns were from the earlier generation of World War II and Korea, and already were young professionals with families as the sixties began. For them, the sudden emergence of the sixties revolt reinforced previously held ideological and moral doctrines, a blend of Quaker, anarchist, and Marxist traditions. Inherent in their tradition was a moral imperative to "witness," to "speak truth to power," through direct nonviolent civil disobedience, carrying a strong sense of abstention from electoral politics. Our new youth movement arising from below confirmed their ideological hopes for a New Left beyond the rigid dogmas and structures of the past. For myself, the awakening of my generation came first, the search for ideological explanations immediately after.

The historic anti-Vietnam protests flowed directly out of the civil rights and student movements in 1964–1965, with Staughton again in the middle, a trusted, smart, eloquent speaker with an instinctive empathy toward our new movements learned in Mississippi. When Students for a Democratic Society (SDS) organized the first anti-Vietnam protest in Washington, D.C., in April 1965, I remember admiring Staughton as he chaired the event with authority and transfixed us with a comparison between suffering Vietnam and the Crucifixion. As we gazed at the unexpected crowd of twenty-five thousand, I remember Staughton dreaming out loud that some day such a massive crowd would flow over the Capitol and take the government back. He and others imagined a parallel Congress of unrepresented people. It was in keeping with an earlier comment he once made about the Mississippi freedom schools: these were "parallel institutions," embryos of a new society that might emerge from within the womb of the old.

At the time, if the truth be known, I was not 100 percent convinced of the antileadership ethos of our movements. It was true that a consensus process was necessary when people were about to risk their lives. It was true that greater unity became possible when every single person had their voice heard. It was true that human skill levels were increased through trainings, workshops and empowering participation. Nonetheless, there were de facto leaders to whom people gravitated, based on charisma and self-confidence, even in the absence of accountable structures. I believed that Staughton could be, and should be, the leader of an organized national antiwar movement.

My thinking was as follows. First, SDS didn't have the capacity to sustain a single-issue focus on Vietnam; it was a swirling, youthful cauldron of multiple emerging issues. Second, in the absence of SDS leadership, the growing antiwar movement would become a contentious bureaucracy dominated by sectarian and dogmatic groups, tenacious infighters little able to identify with either the new movements, the mainstream public, or the media. Third, the *New York Times* had selected Staughton as a credible, charismatic, quotable and qualified leader. He was perhaps the only person who could unite the New Left and Old Left, speak truth to power, and also be a persuasive advocate within the mainstream.

I still regret that it was not to be. From Vietnam to Iraq, the peace movement has lacked the sort of permanent institutional leadership so common among other single-issue causes. But now I understand how contrary it was to Staughton's nature, beliefs, and relationship with Alice and their family. He was and has remained a leader of another sort, a leader from below, a leader in a process, a leader in thought. Leadership from "above" meant immersion in a hothouse realm of power competition between egos, factions and organizations. Most people from the new movements would simply wilt under these pressures. Only those with hyper-competitive egos, those whose blood heated in the atmosphere of combat, could flourish.

Staughton was combative enough, earning the nickname "Scrapper" at some point. But his nature was far more Quaker than Leninist and, in his own words, he came to suffer from a Post-Traumatic Stress Disorder (PTSD) as a result of the factional disintegrations of both Student Nonviolent Coordinating Committee (SNCC) and SDS. ("National gatherings, and proposals for national organizations, frighten me," he still writes forty years later.)

He also suffered through little-remembered rejections from cowardly administrators at Yale and the University of Chicago, traumas that leave him today with "a deep need to clarify the record" even forty years later.

There was no question about his scholarly credentials. My battered copy of his *Intellectual Origins of American Radicalism* (1968) is one of the finest volumes on my history shelf. Yet the door was closed to an influential intellectual career within established institutions.

Meanwhile, Alice, who came from a Quaker tradition, through Radcliffe, was a listener, a counselor, a seeker, an artistic sort, always knitting or gardening, perhaps as metaphors for cultivating movements from the bottom up. Staughton was freed to embark with Alice in search of a very different model. They decided in the seventies to become lawyers in solidarity with Ohio workers facing layoffs and wage losses due to corporate deindustrialization. They organized and wrote about the rank and file who often lacked support from their own unions. They would be involved in Nicaragua's Sandinista villages, interview and support displaced Palestinians, and devote years to the legal defense of Ohio prison inmates. There were echoes of community organizing and liberation theology in these choices, branches of the same quest that led Staughton and Alice to Atlanta.

I have described the varieties of established Quakerism, Marxism, and sociological thought which shaped their early thinking. But I believe it was the concrete encounter with the activist New Left which gave rise to their original, creative, and lasting approach to the revolutionary process.

First, they took from SNCC, SDS, Quakerism, and liberation theology the core idea of listening to people's stories as the source of direction. "Letting the people decide" is how we phrased it. This was not a blind populism, but a more Socratic approach to listening. In this approach, the key notion is to help people discover their human potential smothered under feelings of helplessness and inferiority. The role of the organizer/leader is catalytic, transitional, aiming to foster and transfer leadership to a decentralized grass-roots level. In the Lynds's phrase, borrowed from Catholic populism, the role of the organizer is to "accompany" people through the process of their liberation. One remarkable example, among many, was their direct correspondence with six hundred inmates in Ohio prisons in preparing and litigating a landmark lawsuit.

This approach was a radical reversal of traditional organizing. In Marxism and traditional religion, the organizers were a vanguard disseminating a correct line, or catechism, to the masses. In the community organizing model popularized by Saul Alinsky, the organizers chose goals for their meetings and campaigns based on an assessment of least-common-denominator issues, like better garbage collection, rather than issues like Vietnam that divided their parish bases. The personification of the pure bottom-up style in the early sixties was SNCC's Bob Moses, although the organization was divided over various organizing approaches. The Lynds followed Moses's approach.

I wonder too if Staughton's mother, Helen Lynd, was an important influence on this eventual orientation. Her book *On Shame and the Search for Identity* explored the same terrain of individual transformations "by means of which an individual can change so fundamentally as to be able to bring something new into the world." The Lynds witnessed the amazing human results of this approach, for example in the emergence of an entire stratum of black women like Fannie Lou Hamer from the invisible realms of plantation life. Here were solutions to two of Staughton's lifelong dilemmas. First, could a new socialist society arise from within the old, not by reforming status quo institutions but possibly through parallel ones, like the New England farmers who created their own courts and militias as British colonialism decayed? Second, could the revolution be betrayed by its own organizations and parties developing bureaucratic interests of their own, as happened with the Soviet Union? Staughton and Alice discovered the possibilities inherent in bottom-up democratic structures from the Mississippi Freedom Democratic Party in 1964 to the Zapatista communities in Chiapas thirty years later. The solution, it seemed to them, was a decentralized horizontal model of social change instead of a hierarchal one.

However, by their own account, all their many organizing efforts, after temporary growth, broke apart or failed to last. These included intentional communities like Macedonia in the fifties, the full-time organizers of SNCC, SDS, a painful factional split with David Dellinger (National Mobilization to End the War), rank-and-file labor organizing in Youngstown (the Workers' Solidarity Club, Solidarity USA, Workers Against Toxic Chemical Hazards, Visiting Nurses Solidarity), the Sandinista communities in 1980s Nicaragua. As these words are written, Staughton is finishing a work on the Zapatista approach to these same questions of leadership and organization.

There are patterns to much admire here, and lessons for many others who wish to sustain themselves personally as well as politically for the long haul.

My own experience over fifty years has been surprisingly similar to that of my friends, from SNCC and SDS to Chiapas and Iraq today. In my organizing roles, again and again I have counted on "ordinary people" to rise, transform, and organize from their fields, the inner cities, and prison cells. I have witnessed the courage of people with everything to lose. For me, the margins always will be the source of creative imagination and rebellion.

At the same time, however, I chose to campaign for elective office and served in the California legislature for eighteen years. While my journey has not been contradictory to the Lynds, my experience has produced somewhat different lessons that I share here. Theoretically, I first would revise the image of the new society emerging from the old. Any "new" society will bear the scars, the birthmarks, of the process through which it passed. Though it will first appear "out of nowhere," it will pass through gradual stages. Whether the process ends in revolution is a possibility I have not seen myself, but the process seems consistently to end in a combination of higher consciousness and significant reform. The dreams of the early communists, including Karl Marx, led in the west to the eight-hour day, trade unions, and the welfare state, not a new society. Where direct communist revolution *was* possible, as in Russia and China, intermediate reforms were bypassed, whole "sectors" of people were suppressed, and the revolutions failed.

Real reform, I believe, means the rise of a new consciousness, the empowerment of powerless constituencies, openings in old institutions, and the restructuring of power relationships. But it usually begins with something like a hamburger denied. From there it begins to confront the systems behind the lunch counter. It may begin with the denial of a vote, and from there inspire dreams of greater participation. Without radicals like the Lynds, there might have been no American Revolution, no Abolition, no Suffrage, no New Deal, no environmental laws and so on. Each of these reform movements began on a human scale, for example, with boycotts of British tea and linen. Yet these historic reforms are sometimes dismissed on the Left as merely "stabilizing" the status quo. The Revolution left the privileged colonists in power. Abolition was achieved; Reconstruction was undermined. Labor rights left workers regulated under capitalism. Winning the right to vote left no one to vote for. Ending the Vietnam War was not a success because imperialism and future wars continued.

A true fidelity to "the people" based on community organizing cannot treat real reform as meaningless.

The Lynds's own experience reveals the tension. The freedom schools became the embryo of Head Start. Draft resistance ended compulsory conscription but led to the "voluntary" draft. The workers' solidarity organizing in Youngstown and Lordstown forced employers to meet their contractual obligations, and lessen exposure to toxic chemicals. The visiting nurses solidarity organizing led to tote bags with organizational logos carried on home visits, and so on.

What does this mean for today? I would argue that the sixties opened up space for organizing and politics that didn't exist when we began. I have adopted an "outside-inside" view of strategy, as opposed to a purely oppositional one. I believe that small reforms sometimes are the eggs that open new possibilities. I think that third party advocates should have worked for Ralph Nader in safely Democratic states, and for Al Gore in the close states like Florida in 2000. To take another example, the Zapatista "*otra campagna*" in 2006, which denounced the larger Mexican parties as essentially the same, resulted in the defeat of a presidential candidate who was pledged to revise North American Free Trade Agreement (NAFTA).

At stake were huge national and global issues, but at the community level it was about protecting the voting rights won by our movement forty years ago and, in Mexico, supporting small communal plots of land won in the Mexican revolution against the siege of corporate globalization.

These are not intended as criticisms of the Lynds, but questions stimulated by their long and distinguished story. Reading their book takes me back to where it all began when I met them in Atlanta, when we plunged into the great questions of life with our whole selves, when it seemed possible that the pure force of our movement would make the Powers do the right thing, or stand down.

It might have been different if the Kennedys, Dr. King, and Malcolm X—all of whom I somehow knew—had lived. I don't remember anyone teaching us how to respond to conspiracies or chaos.

Through all the storms, Staughton and Alice have represented the basic blend of moral force, critical inquiry, and trust in the evidence of things unseen that have helped rank-and-file people become the driving force wherever great social reforms were achieved.

> Tom Hayden, Principal author of *The Port Huron Statement*,
> founding document of Students for a Democratic Society.

Acknowledgments

We wish to recognize and thank a few of the many persons who have helped to make this book possible.

We met Frances Goldin more than fifty years ago when she ran a clinic for tenants at the University Settlement House in New York. Later she became a literary agent and ran interference for a number of books by one or both of us, including *Stepping Stones.*

Mary Susannah Robbins has edited books on the Vietnam and Iraq wars, to which Staughton contributed. She suggested to her publisher that he might be interested in our memoir. He was.

Tom Hayden was a logical person from whom to request a foreword. We have known him since the early 1960s, when he and Todd Gitlin of Students for a Democratic Society visited us in Atlanta. His organizing work in Newark paralleled some of our later efforts in Chicago and Youngstown. Together with Herbert Aptheker, Tom and Staughton made a trip to Hanoi in 1965 that impacted both Tom's life and that of the Lynds. And Staughton sought to testify as a defense witness when Tom and others of the Chicago Eight were tried for their alleged actions in planning protest demonstrations at the 1968 Democratic Party Convention. In assessing how our story relates to his own, Tom did what we hope other readers of this book will do as well.

We shared a draft of the manuscript with our younger daughter, Martha, who works with women's weaving cooperatives in Guatemala. She reminded us how much about the 1960s that we take for granted needs to be explained for younger readers and urged us to be more forthcoming about what certain episodes meant to us. A reader to whom the publisher sent a later draft (and who wishes to remain anonymous) expressed similar sentiments. We are grateful to both.

Memory is both a gateway to emotional treasures and notoriously unreliable as to facts. We thank Denis O'Hearn for setting us straight about a word Staughton thought he remembered from "The Wearing of the Green," which he learned as a child: the traditional peasant headdress in which Irish patriots wear the shamrock is a "caubeen," not, as Staughton supposed, a "shibeen," which is an informal drinking establishment. And Bettina Aptheker told Staughton that her father's New York City office was near Union Square, not Tompkins Square.

After forty years in which the reasons for Staughton's nonpromotion by Yale University remained shrouded in contention, Carl Mirra, a young historian, appears to have established the facts so far as they can be known at this time (see the chapter entitled "A Trip to Hanoi").

Four prisoners sentenced to death helped us in different ways, all significant. As explained at the beginning of the chapters on "The Worst of the Worst," at a moment when Alice was under particular stress Jason Robb drew a lovely rose (that we have reproduced with his permission) and captioned it "Smile." George Skatzes and Maurice Mason, unaware of the title we had chosen for this book, sent Alice a card at this same time expressing the hope that all our stumbling blocks might become stepping stones. And Keith LaMar, a.k.a. Bomani Shakur ("thankful mighty warrior"), shared the pain and excitement of creating his own memoir as we struggled to produce our counterpart recollections.

Finally, without Joseph Parry and Michael Wiles of Lexington Books this volume would not have seen the light of day.

All the foregoing friends and colleagues have no responsibility for our errors and deserve to be richly thanked for any good that readers may find herein.

Staughton and Alice Lynd

Introduction

Hello.

Who are you? We assume that this book will be read by our children and grandchildren. Beyond that precious circle, we hope that other young persons who are seeking a better world will find something useful here. Perhaps you are one of those seekers.

The theme of our adult lives together has been the search for a certain kind of community. In our late-seventies it has become clear to us that we have found such community most of all with each other, in our marriage.

And so the project of a joint memoir. You will hear sometimes one of our voices, sometimes the other. At still other points we speak together, as in this introduction.

AUTUMN LEAVES AND STEPPING STONES

Two images come to mind in trying to explain what we want to do in these pages.

In the New York City apartment where Staughton grew up, as you opened the front door a large chest of drawers stared you in the face. The middle drawer of this "high boy" was full of unsorted photographs, lying loosely one on top of the other like autumn leaves.

As a person gets older, the contents of the mind resemble that drawer of loose photographs. There are so many visual images of past experiences. We want to share some of these pictures-in-the-mind as best we can.

Another image comes from hiking in the woods. Sometimes, especially if "bushwhacking" without a trail, one comes to a stream and there is no apparent means to cross it. The hiker looks for rocks above the surface of the water on which to step, one after another, to get to the other side. There is no way to know in advance whether a particular rock will turn under one's foot.

These stepping stones offer a metaphor of life in a time of rapid social change. There are streams to be crossed and often enough no bridges yet constructed. So we step out in faith that there will be enough stable stones to get to dry land on the other side of the stream.

The memories that make up this book are like loose photographs in a bureau drawer, or stepping stones across an unfamiliar brook. We have tried not to say too much about what they mean to us, or might mean to you. As you read, we hope our experience will assist you to contemplate and clarify your own distinctive path.

OVERVIEW: 1950–1959

Precisely because we present our past as separate chunks of experience (like snapshots or stepping stones) it may be helpful to you to have an overview of the basic external facts.

We met in Cambridge, Massachusetts, in the summer of 1950. Staughton, having dropped out of Harvard College and returned, was trying to graduate. Alice had been spending up to a hundred hours a week attempting to keep up with reading assignments at Radcliffe.

We met at an off-campus apartment that Staughton shared with several friends on Story Street, near Brattle Square. (See the chapter entitled "Story Street.") Although we were not then Quakers, we were married a year later at the Stony Run Friends meeting in Baltimore where Alice's parents had recently become members.

There followed a difficult year in Cambridge. Staughton enrolled in the Harvard School of Design to study city and regional planning. Alice had dropped out of Radcliffe in order to have more time for personal relationships and to develop a better sense of what she wanted to study. She went to work as a secretary and took courses at the Nursery Training School of Boston.

The next year we moved to Chicago so that Staughton could study regional planning in a program overseen by Rexford Tugwell, a former New Deal administrator more interested in the social than the architectural aspects of planning. Alice completed an undergraduate degree in Early Childhood Education at Roosevelt College. She was employed as secretary of the Education Department there, while Staughton worked part-time as a stock boy at the Hyde Park Co-op.

In the fall of 1953 Staughton was drafted. He had been granted 1-A-0 status, that is, to serve in the Army Medical Corps as an unarmed conscientious objector. While Staughton was in the Army, Alice lived at Hull House in Chicago. There she encountered an elderly woman from Russia, who, after first pronouncing that it was too difficult for American girls, taught Alice to do Russian embroidery.

Days after he completed basic training, Staughton (and several dozen other soldiers around the same time) received an Undesirable Discharge because of allegations concerning his political beliefs and associations. (See our chapter on the Macedonia Cooperative Community.) It was years before this decision was overturned and Staughton received an Honorable Discharge, so that he was able to attend graduate school with benefits provided by the G.I. Bill.

Meantime, after attempting to resume our lives in Chicago, we decided in the fall of 1954 to join the Macedonia Cooperative Community in Clarkesville, Georgia. This became our version of the critical experience that Catholics call a person's "formation." Although we left the community three years later, when it joined a fundamentalist Christian group, the values to which we committed ourselves at Macedonia are the values we sought to live by thereafter. Leaving Macedonia, with one small child, another on the way, and no means of livelihood, was one of our most painful and difficult experiences.

OVERVIEW: 1959–1973

In 1959 Staughton went back to graduate school, this time in American history. Alice, as so often in this first period of our life together, provided most of the family income as a secretary: in those years, at the Columbia University College of Physicians and Surgeons in New York City. We lived in a small fourth-floor apartment, around the corner from the Central Park West apartment where Staughton's parents lived.

In December 1960, at the annual meeting of the American Historical Association, Staughton met Howard Zinn. Howard invited Staughton to teach at Spelman College, the college for African-American women associated with Atlanta University.

Alice made a trip to Atlanta, was offered part-time secretarial work in the office of the Spelman College dean, and looked over the on-campus apartment offered to the Lynds. Alice was impressed by the artistic flare of the Spelman students, and Staughton was eager to participate in the civil rights movement then burgeoning in the south. We accepted the job offers and moved to Atlanta in August 1961, just when the Atlanta public schools were beginning to integrate by placing several selected black students in formerly all-white high schools.

We became Quakers after our son fell from a window during meeting for worship at Quaker House. The aid we received from members of the meeting led us to recognize that we were, in fact, members of the Atlanta meeting. The Quakers, more formally known as the Religious Society of Friends, are one of the traditional peace churches. Quakers value not only peace but also simplicity, equality, consensus decision-making, opposition to the death penalty, and speaking truth to power. These themes were central to our own trajectory.

There followed some of the better-known years of our journey. Staughton taught history at Spelman College until the spring of 1964, and in summer 1964 served as coordinator of Freedom Schools in the Mississippi Summer Project. (See chapter entitled "We Shall Overcome.") After he accepted a job at Yale, and we moved to New Haven in the fall of 1964, we both were drawn into the movement against the war in Vietnam. Staughton chaired the first rally against the war in Vietnam in Washington, D.C. (April 1965), was arrested there that summer (August 1965), and in December 1965–January 1966 made a controversial trip to North Vietnam with Herbert Aptheker and Tom Hayden. Meantime Alice became a draft counselor, our third child was born, and Alice edited a book of personal accounts of war objectors.

The trip to Hanoi caused Staughton to be no longer welcome at Yale. In 1967 the Lynds moved to Chicago. There, however, five successive university history departments offered Staughton a job, only to have the decision overruled by university administrators. He was "blacklisted." Meantime, Alice contributed to the family livelihood as a draft counselor, and also, discerned in the relationship of draft counselor and potential inductee a model of the "accompaniment" we later sought to practice as lawyers. It was also when living in Chicago that we made our first significant and enduring contacts with men and women in the labor movement.

OVERVIEW: 1973–1996

We decided to go into law in the early 1970s but could not afford to go to law school at the same time. Staughton attended the University of Chicago Law School from 1973 to 1976. After his graduation we moved to Youngstown, Ohio. Staughton helped workers wronged by their employers and inadequately represented by their unions, and was lead counsel in a lawsuit of workers and local unions devastated by U.S. Steel's decision to close its Youngstown mills. After working nine years as a paralegal, Alice went to the University of Pittsburgh School of Law in

1982–1985. Thereafter, until our retirement in 1996, we worked together at Northeast Ohio Legal Services, the local office in Youngstown of the government-funded program that provides legal assistance in civil cases for persons unable to afford a private attorney.

During these same years, beginning about 1985, we made nearly a dozen trips to Nicaragua, Guatemala, Palestine and, with the Youngstown Symphony Chorus, to Eastern Europe. Our most powerful spiritual experiences were among Roman Catholics in Nicaragua who belonged to what they called the Popular Church, that is, the segment of the Catholic community influenced by "liberation theology" and "the preferential option for the poor."

Our introduction to Palestine came through a Palestinian-American in Youngstown, Sam Bahour. With him we spent parts of two summers in Palestine gathering oral histories. They were later published in a book, *Homeland: Oral Histories of Palestine and Palestinians.*

In Mexico we twice attended a summer program for persons from First, Second, and Third World countries created by Maria Adela Oliveros and closely associated with the *Frente Auténtico de Trabajadores* (FAT), a network of independent unions. After our own initial experience we made it possible for eight colleagues from organizing efforts in Ohio to go as well.

Apart from legal cases our work in Youngstown centered on nurturing certain working-class organizations, often connected with local trade unions, but independent of national trade union bureaucracies. These included the Workers' Solidarity Club of Youngstown, Workers Against Toxic Chemical Hazards (WATCH) and, in response to the epidemic of plant closings and bankruptcies in the regional steel industry, an organization of retirees called Solidarity USA. After retirement, Staughton also served as local education coordinator for Teamsters Local 377 during the years that Ron Carey was president of the national Teamsters union.

OVERVIEW: AFTER 1996 AND IN CONCLUSION

Since 1996, when we retired, we have worked out of our home as advocates for prisoners. Staughton believes that Youngstown city fathers deliberately sought out prisons to take the place of the area steel mills, virtually all of which had closed by the summer of 1980.

After the Lucasville prison uprising in southern Ohio in 1993, Ohio decided to build a supermaximum security prison in Youngstown. We got to know the alleged leaders of the uprising who were sentenced to death and subsequently were confined at the "supermax" prison. Later, we and other lawyers filed a lawsuit to ameliorate the conditions under which the highest security prisoners are confined in Ohio.

Our journey has taken us across many stepping stones: the Macedonia community, civil rights activity, antiwar movements, a quarter century among rank-and-file workers, abolition of the death penalty, and advocacy for and with prisoners whom the State of Ohio considers "the worst of the worst."

There is more than one way across the stream. Our children carry forward our values in different directions. Barbara and her family became Catholics. Lee has devoted himself since the age of ten to developing alternative sources of energy. Martha lives in Guatemala where she has worked for many years with women's weaving cooperatives.

At a time in 2004 when Alice was experiencing great stress (see the chapter entitled "Mr. X"), two prisoners on Death Row sent her a message of encouragement. We had not discussed with them either this proposed memoir or what we planned to entitle it. The message was: "Give me the strength to make stepping stones out of stumbling blocks."

Beginnings

SON OF MIDDLETOWN, *STAUGHTON LYND*

I grew up in New York City. Later in life I would become a member of the Society of Friends, or Quakers, but I think part of me has always been a feisty and combative New Yorker. In critical moments I have imagined myself a young person in Hungary in 1956, throwing paving stones at Soviet tanks. Or I have supposed myself a boxer between rounds. The seconds wave smelling salts under your nose and hold up a finger to determine if your eyes still focus; but you answer the bell for the next round. My favorite anecdote from the American Revolution concerns John Paul Jones. Commanding a privateer, Jones encountered a larger, more heavily-gunned British warship. His masts were blown away and the British captain called through a megaphone, "Are you ready to surrender?" Jones is said to have answered, "I have just begun to fight!" Thereafter he prevailed and towed the British warship, a prize of war, into a French port.

I was born on November 22, 1929, thirty-four years to the day before the assassination of President John F. Kennedy. The Great Depression was just beginning. That year my parents, Robert and Helen Lynd, published the book that made them famous, entitled *Middletown: A Study in American Culture.*

Middletown created a situation of security for our family that surrounded me until I left for college. On the strength of that publication my father, who had never taken a graduate course in sociology, was offered a tenured position in the Sociology Department of Columbia University. *Middletown* was permitted to serve as his doctoral dissertation. But before my dad received his Ph.D. he was obliged to go through the book and

7

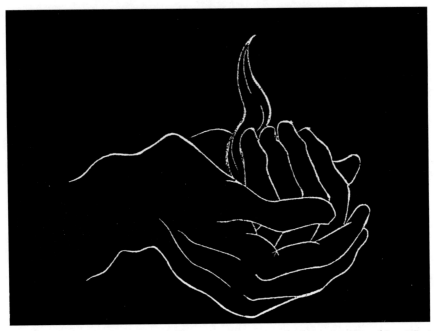

Staughton drew this picture when he was in the army and Alice was visiting him at Fort Leonard Wood, Missouri. When Alice returned to Chicago, she made a linoleum block and the Lynds used the prints as Christmas cards.

cross out every sentence supposedly written by my mother rather than him. My mother commented later: "This was an absurdity, because what we did as we actually wrote it was that we would each write a chapter and then we would exchange and rewrite."[1]

Security and stability took many forms. About the time *Middletown* was published and I was born, my parents moved into an eighth floor apartment in a building at 67th Street and Central Park West. Central Park itself was just across the street. From the living room of our apartment I could watch the sun come up above the skyline of Fifth Avenue on the other side of the park.

Countless times during my childhood, my father and I would get up early, retrieve bicycles (in my case, a tricycle) from a room on the ground floor of our apartment building, and bicycle around Central Park before breakfast. We would count the squirrels, or as I pronounced them, the "hurlas." Other days I would snuggle into bed with him and he would read aloud to me from a book like *The Cruise of the Cachalot*. (A "cachalot" is a whale.)

Where we lived at 75 Central Park West was only four blocks from the midtown elementary school of the Ethical Culture Society. Until I graduated from sixth grade, I could walk to school.

On one occasion our entire family walked up and down eight flights of stairs between the ground floor and our apartment, in support of the building personnel, including the elevator operators, who were on strike.

I have struggled to decide how much to share about the undercurrents of my secure childhood. Let me try to say a few words about class, race, and gender, and about the ways in which the Protestantism in which both my parents were raised encountered these realities.

Class

We are told in the introduction to *Middletown* that two streams of colonists met in the midwest: the Yankees from New England and New York, and the southern stream who, having passed through the Cumberland Gap into Kentucky, went down and, in some cases, across the Ohio River.[2] My parents exemplified these two kinds of colonists.

My father's people were from the upper south. He grew up, first in New Albany, Indiana, and then across the river in Louisville, Kentucky. Later, as a historian of the period of the American Revolution, I made perhaps my most original contribution in trying to understand how, in the anticipations of the Continental Congress that passed the Northwest Ordinance and of the Convention that drafted the United States Constitution, both in the summer of 1787, people like my father's family who brought the culture of the south with them across the Ohio River were expected to interact with people like my mother's family from New England. Still more remarkably, as residents of Ohio after 1976, Alice and I had occasion to confront the difference between the northern and southern parts of states like Ohio, Indiana, and Illinois when Alice was cited for contempt and briefly jailed by a judge in Portsmouth, Ohio, just across the Ohio River from Kentucky. (See the chapter on "Mr. X.")

In the early 1920s my dad gave up a job with the *Publishers Weekly* and enrolled at Union Theological Seminary. I believe that while a student there he sometimes sang at missions on the Bowery. When I was a child there were few obvious traces of this period in his life. We never went to church on Sundays; instead, we would take the IRT subway to Chambers Street, cross the Hudson River on a ferry, and then take the Erie Railroad to one or another stop at the western edge of Harriman State Park, near Bear Mountain. After hiking all day we often ate ice cream at Tuxedo Park, put a penny on the railroad track to see how the train would flatten it, and, as we left the ferry in Manhattan, bought a small bag of roasted chestnuts.

Yet a certain ambience lingered. David Hartley, my father's nephew, went to a Quaker work camp in the late 1930s, joined the Society of Friends (Quakers), and drove an ambulance in Europe during World War II. After the war David took part in reconstruction work in Italy. A few years later my father attended David's wedding to a "birthright" Quaker, and I remember the glow on his face as he recounted the simple ceremony. Another such moment concerned a friend of my dad's named Kermit Eby. Mr. Eby, who became a labor educator, grew up in the Church of the Brethren. Members of the Brethren washed each other's feet before Easter and my dad described it to us with a certain wistful enthusiasm. He also occasionally burst forth with a set of words that I later understood to be quotations from the New Testament. One such was John 15:13, "Greater love hath no man than this, that a man lay down his life for his friends."

It seems that between the first and second years at Union, students were expected to volunteer for summer preaching assignments.[3] My father wound up at a Rockefeller oil camp in Elk Basin, Wyoming. He arrived by stagecoach and located a boarding house. But at dinner the first evening Dad sensed a chill around the table. He concluded that men who worked six days a week for Mr. Rockefeller were not excited about a handsome young man from the east who would spend his days visiting their wives. So my father got a job as a pick-and-shovel laborer, and preached in the school house Sunday nights. It is the single thing about him of which I am most proud. It was a manifestation of a way in which a professional person could relate to ordinary people that Alice and I came to call "accompaniment."

In 1949, when I was twenty, I thought I saw a momentary reappearance of the pick-and-shovel laborer of the early 1920s when my father was invited to address an educational conference of the United Automobile Workers. The speech was printed as a pamphlet because, according to Victor Reuther's preface, "reports of it have circulated through the union with the result that there has been an insistent demand for its publication."[4] I remember my father's face as he came in the door of our family apartment after giving that speech. I had never seen him so happy.

Following his summer at the Rockefeller oil camp in Wyoming, my father and John D. Rockefeller, Jr. exchanged views in the pages of a periodical called *The Survey Graphic*. After my father's death I found reprints of these articles in an envelope on which he had written, "Stau [one of his nicknames for me], save these." My dad was quite critical of Mr. Rockefeller's operation. Moreover, there was an oft-repeated story at the family kitchen table that after his summer in Elk Basin, my father asked John D. Rockefeller for a contribution to a community center there that might ease the isolation and hardship of the daily lives of women. Mr. Rockefeller was said to have declined on the ground that it had been a bad year for Standard Oil.

My parents confronted the phenomenon of class in writing *Middletown* because the Institute of Social and Religious Research that sponsored the study was funded by the Rockefellers. My parents were convinced that any single facet of a community's life, such as religion, could only be understood in the context of the total life of the community. My mother says, "We were very much interested in what it would look like for an anthropological technique to be applied to an American city. We were fascinated with whether this would work."[5]

The anthropological approach struck the sponsoring committee as "formlessness," according to my mother. The committee didn't know where the study was going, and, she confesses, "neither did we. Something would come up, and that would lead to something else, which wasn't on any chart."[6]

My mother states that after she and my father completed the second draft of *Middletown*, it sat around for a year because the "Rockefeller people" didn't want to publish it:

> They told Bob that they had read it and they thought it wasn't any good, it was unpublishable. They thought it didn't cohere. They'd never seen that kind of a book before. They didn't think it was interesting, and they thought it was irreligious.[7]

It was a grim period, my mother continues. "I was about 26, Bob was under 30. It was getting on for four years then, and we had worked long hours and long days. . . . We kept hoping that something would happen that would change their minds."[8]

At some point my dad showed the manuscript to the anthropologist Clark Wissler, who said he liked it and would do an introduction:

> And then, after about a year, Bob asked the Institute people if they would allow him to publish the manuscript if he could find a publisher. They owned it. It was their property. I think the only reason that they said he could was because they were sure he couldn't. They told him so. They said they didn't think he could possibly get it published, but they wouldn't forbid him trying, and if he could get a publisher they wouldn't forbid its publication.[9]

When the book appeared it was reviewed on the front page of the book review section of the *New York Times*.

Middletown placed heavy emphasis on economics, as in the chapter on "The Long Arm of the Job." My mother comments, "It became very clear that there were two classes in the community, which we called the business and working classes."[10] She herself came from a very meager economic background. Her family took in lodgers so as to be able to put three daughters through college. As a student at Wellesley, my mother made sure not to take a nickel with her when she went downtown for fear that she would use it to buy an apple. She also told me of a time when a letter came to the house while her father was at work informing him that he was permanently laid off, and his three daughters sat at the kitchen table trying to decide which of them should break the news to him when he came home.

Race

There is, however, a gigantic qualification one must make to the suggestion that my parents' approach was "anthropological." In a nation of immigrants scarred and significantly defined by the experience of African-American slavery, they chose to study a city where people were almost all white and born in the United States.

Here I must mention a matter that gives me pain and shame. As I said earlier, my father grew up in New Albany, Indiana, just north of the Ohio River, and in Louisville, Kentucky, on the other side. Both settings were saturated with racism, as are geographically comparable communities like Cincinnati, Ohio and Cairo, Illinois.

My dad, although kindness itself to any African-American he encountered, was imperfectly aware of what was implied by jokes and songs that he repeated endlessly. Such a joke concerned the African-American soldier who confronted a German soldier during World War I. Each took a pass at the other. The German said, "Missed me." The black man, armed with a razor, replied, "Just wait till you wiggle yo' haid." Such a song at Princeton contained the lyric, "It takes a long, tall, brown-skinned gal, To make a preacher lay his good book down." Much later, a chapter in DuBois's *The Souls of Black Folk* brought home to me the full horror of those lines.

In truth, I became conscious of these matters slowly and awkwardly. At Harvard, I once left a note at the room of a high-school classmate in which I said that I had not seen him in "a coon's age" (another of my father's expressions). My friend had to explain to me that the word "coon" did not refer to a four-footed animal.

How does *Middletown* justify the decision deliberately to study a city with a "small Negro and foreign-born population"? The introduction states forthrightly:

> In a difficult study of this sort it seemed a distinct advantage to deal with a homogeneous, native-born population, even though such a population is unusual in an American industrial city. Thus, instead of being forced to handle

two major variables, racial change and cultural change, the field staff was enabled to concentrate upon cultural change. The study thus became one of the interplay of a relatively constant native American stock and its changing environment. As such it may possibly afford a base-line group against which the process of social change in the type of community that includes different racial backgrounds may be studied by future workers.[11]

Some of my parents' own findings call this baseline methodology into question. The most recent census at the time *Middletown* was written reported that 2 percent of Muncie's population was foreign-born, a little less than 6 percent were African-American, and "nearly 85 percent in 1920 was native white of native parentage."[12] In the Muncie of the mid-1920s:

The small group of foreign-born mingle little with the rest of the community. Negroes are [not allowed] in the larger motion picture houses or in Y.M.C.A. or Y.W.C.A.; they are not to be found in "white" churches; Negro children must play in their own restricted corner of the Park.[13]

A decade later, when my parents published *Middletown in Transition*, the percentages of foreign-born and African-American families in Muncie remained 2 and 5.5 percent, respectively.[14] But the second book has fourteen index entries under "Negroes" as compared to three in the first. And the authors indicate that when the number of African-Americans increases, or when they compete directly with whites for jobs, white hostility escalates. A few Negroes or Jews may be tolerated, "but as the number increases they may become a 'problem' and mild antipathies may crystallize into antagonism."[15] Similarly:

It may have been true in the past that, as a Middletown employer remarked, "Our Negroes work for the most part at jobs where there is little or no competition from whites. They apply for certain jobs and whites apply for the others"; but in a world of too few jobs such tentative color lines will tend to vanish. And the Negro, always suspect to the whites in a crisis, will tend to receive the full brunt of white resentment as the whites seek to wrest their jobs from them.[16]

Thus the baseline concept of the first Muncie study seems questionable in light of the second study. The attitudes of whites when the number of African-Americans is small do not tell us much about what their attitudes will be when the numbers are more nearly equal. Likewise the benign tolerance of suburban whites who do not compete with African-Americans economically[17] does not throw much light on what will be felt by white workers who compete for the same unskilled jobs that African-Americans hold or aspire to.

I think the baseline rationale should be set aside. A simpler way of accounting for my parents' decision to study a community that was almost all-white and born in the United States is that this was what their life experience qualified them to do. I often heard my father speak of what "religion" meant to him growing up: it was the experience of standing up to sing hymns with his family in the oak pews of the local Presbyterian church, in the midst of a community to which they belonged.

Mother shared with my father the experience of growing up in a community centered on the Protestant church. She wrote about it to a friend after her mother died:

> The nurse who came in for night care was a stranger to me but said she was in Mother's "circle" at the Church and told of letters Mother had written her when she was ill. I asked her if she had known Father and she said, "Oh, yes, I joined Grace Church under Deacon Merrell."

> The man who has done painting and odd jobs for Mother for years came in and looked at her, tears streaming down his face. He said that the first anniversary of Father's death he had turned down a ticket to the World Series so that he could be painting at the house as he knew it would be a hard day for Mother.

> Before the funeral service began as we were sitting in an alcove apart from the "friends" a woman came over, put her arms around us and kissed us— the woman who had done cleaning for Mother my first years in college when Adela and Margaret were in high school. And two of the people whom Mother took in to board to help on expenses when we were going through college.

> The new minister was a well-meaning, banal, boy scout hard to bear. . . . But he, too, took on stature when he read with quiet dignity the passages we selected for the service. . . . I'm glad I grew up with that, and that sort of affirmation of "the length and breadth and depth and height" of love "beyond all that we ask or know" is in whatever world I am trying to work for.[18]

I am convinced that what my parents were trying to do in Muncie was to excavate this experience of genuine religiously based community from the provincialism and crass materialism with which that experience was encrusted. In very much the same way the southern civil rights movement, as I experienced it in the early 1960s, lived, moved, and had its being in African-American churches throughout the south. There people nerved themselves up to dream dreams of a better day and to act on them. To these same churches they returned to lick their wounds after bruising encounters with the entrenched authorities.

Gender

My mother Helen Lynd died from the aftermath of a stroke. When she first experienced the stroke, she lost the ability to speak. Then, somehow, words came again. According to her hospital roommate, the first word that she spoke was: "love."

I believe that Helen Lynd considered that, in the last analysis, social change comes through individuals. A person thinks or acts in a new way; others gather around that breakthrough; soon a new institution confronts the powers-that-be. Somewhere in the social scheme of things there occur mutations, individual mutations, and then everything else follows.

So this was the problem. How do those changes occur in individuals that lead on, in time, to large social transformations? This question pursued Helen Lynd for more than half a century, from the 1920s to her death in 1982.

Where does my mother's book *On Shame and the Search for Identity*[19] fit in? I suggest that there she sought to explicate the detailed process by means of which there could occur the kind of personality mutation that she believed would in the long run lead to a better world.

If I may attempt a paraphrase, I think she was saying: To go forward into the new is to make oneself vulnerable. But that which is exposed in experiences of shame is not only our ridiculous nakedness, our pathetic inability, our disconcerting errors. It is the lineaments of our particular soul and self; it is our pride; it is our glory. He or she who hopes to make a contribution to the better world, to the new day, must be willing to endure what Erik Erikson called repeated experiences of adolescence and to persist despite many failures.

This is a deeply Christian view of things, recalling the suffering servant who was despised and rejected of men before, in the long sweep of history, at least in some sense triumphing in the end. It is also a profoundly Hegelian attitude, because it envisions the possibility of a dramatic dialectical reversal, what Hegel called an *Aufhebung*.

I think that when my mother glimpsed the connection between, on the one hand, the humiliation of what she called the shame experience, and on the other hand, the discovery of identity, it appeared to her like perceiving the structure of DNA. Somehow, I believe it seemed to her, she had laid hold of the intimate mechanism by means of which an individual can change so fundamentally as to be able to bring something new into the world.

However, the question of gender played a less benign role in my childhood about which I must try to say a few words.

My father was to outward appearance the personification of (to use one of his favorite words) "robust" manhood. He took me hiking; he batted baseballs to me on my way to becoming captain of the high school base-ball team. He had a strong baritone voice. At his memorial service, a close family friend remembered how during New Hampshire summers several families would canoe to an island in White Oak Pond for a picnic supper, and then, as we paddled back to shore in the darkness, "Bob's voice would echo across the lake."

My father passed on to me a certain ultimate confidence in finding one's way through difficult situations, at least out of doors. One Sunday, Dad and I went hiking in Harriman State Park with my high school friend, Paul Willen. We stopped to rest near an exposed rock face. There appeared to be a small ledge, diminishing in width as it ran horizontally across the face of the cliff. I found myself halfway along it but unsure whether I could go further. "Go ahead, you can make it!" my father called. Paul exclaimed, "My dad would never let me do something like that!"

But my father also came to feel deeply humiliated as a male. This was partly because his value-oriented style of sociology was out of synch with the statistical sociology that his Columbia colleagues, Paul Lazarsfeld and Robert Merton, championed after World War II. A more fundamental cause was that he felt rejected by my mother. In the intuitive manner of children, I figured out that as she saw things my father had carried into adulthood some of the anxious lower-middle-class values that she strug-gled so hard to overcome in herself. My dad once told me that at some point early in their marriage she pounded the earth in the Alps and said, "What are we going to do about your mind?" For whatever reason, dur-ing the 1930s and World War II she developed lesbian relationships with three of her students, and my father was very, very deeply hurt.

It is not easy to be a sensitive person of the male gender—a gentle man—in the United States of America. On my wife's side of the family, her father and brother-in-law were extraordinarily gentle males married to very forceful women, and her nephew is gay.

Somehow I resolved to try to be a heterosexual male who was also a gentle person. I rejected several opportunities to develop homosexual re-lationships. My father forever told me that I should marry a woman like my mother, but I had a horror of replicating his experience as a husband. To this day I find it difficult to relate to aggressive women.

In the end I found Alice and my problem was solved. That is what this book is about.

WHEN I WAS LITTLE, *ALICE LYND*

When I was getting to know Staughton during the summer of 1950, my uncle, a World War II veteran, was dying of Hodgkin's disease. Staughton asked me, "Are you very close to your uncle?" No one had ever asked me a question like that before! I grew up in an adult world in which neither I nor anyone else knew much about what I was feeling.

Staughton and I both had parents who worked together as equal colleagues. That was most unusual in the 1930s. I remember asking my mother when I was five or six years old, "Why do you work and nobody else's mother works?"

Staughton and I each had one sister. My sister, Cushing, was four years older than I and big for her age, while I was quite slight. Staughton's sister, Andrea, was four years younger than Staughton and, in my opinion, more like me—more interested in music and dancing than in intellectual matters.

A major difference in our childhood years was that throughout the Great Depression, Staughton's parents had steady jobs and mine did not.

A few months before I was born, my father was fired from a life insurance research bureau. He had been asked to survey the pay of insurance agents. He reported that they weren't paid enough to live on. He didn't get a steady job again for more than ten years. My parents took consulting jobs that lasted a few weeks or months, so we moved from place to place several times each year. When they didn't have work, we lived at my grandfather's house.

Metacomet and Mamie

Because our mothers as well as our fathers worked, Staughton and I each had someone else to take care of us. In the summer time, or during jobs that were too short to move the family, my older sister and I would stay at "Metacomet,"[20] my grandfather's summer home in Westerly, Rhode Island.

My grandfather, Dr. William T. Howard, had been a professor of pathology at Case Western Reserve Medical School in Cleveland. Later he became Commissioner of Health for the City of Baltimore. My grandmother died and my grandfather retired before I was born.

In 1902, the Howard family hired a sixteen-year-old girl by the name of Mary Lehnert, a devout Catholic from a working-class family in Massillon, Ohio, to take care of my mother, Mary Cushing Howard, who was then two years old. "Mamie" stayed with the family, living most of her life at Metacomet, until she died in the 1970s. She took care of my mother's brothers when they were children. After they were grown, my mother's younger brother, Bill, continued to live at Metacomet with Mamie. Whenever we were at Metacomet, in addition to her household tasks, Mamie was responsible for the care of my sister and me.

Mamie would play cards with us in the evenings. She taught me to knit. She also insisted that I never make noise going up and down stairs. I was never to let sand fall out of my shoes onto the polished wooden floor that Bill had so perfectly finished. I was never to have more than two dresses in the laundry each week. While Mamie ran the washing machine and the wringer, I would wash the family's socks in a bucket. Mamie showed me how she ironed, but she never let me try ironing myself. When she made apple pie, she helped me to make a little tart with the scraps. She would take me to a neighbor's to buy a chicken for Sunday dinner, and pullet eggs. I liked pullet eggs because they were small, like me. Sometimes the neighbor would give us crabapple jelly in tiny jars.

Letty

Mamie stayed at Metacomet. Someone else was needed to take care of my sister and me and to travel with us from city to city during much of each year. One morning during the summer of 1934, I was introduced to Mrs. Letitia Ambler Smith, a cousin of my mother's best friend. "Letty" became a mother-substitute for me. She was with us from the time I was four until I was almost nine and her health did not permit her to continue.

I think Letty had a profound influence on the person I became. She was a Quaker. In the Quaker manner, she used the familiar word "thee" instead of "you." She said what she thought very directly. She dressed very simply. If I recall correctly, she always wore brown. Her husband was in a mental institution and she had no children. She loved my sister and me as if we were her own.

Letty was observant, inquisitive, resourceful, and knew how to do or could improvise a way to do all sorts of things. She taught each of us a whole range of hobbies with no overlap between what she taught Cushing and what she taught me. Cushing was a tomboy. Letty showed her how to take an old camera, build a photo enlarger, and eventually a dark room. Letty did wood carving.

And Letty could do all kinds of fine needlework. She taught me to sew, to embroider, and to crochet. When I was five years old, we lived for a few months in a house that had an old treadle sewing machine. If I sat at the machine where I could manage the cloth, my feet did not reach the foot treadle, so I would operate the foot treadle while Letty steered the cloth through the machine, or I would steer the cloth while Letty operated the treadle. We made hassocks (a kind of stool), taking six large cans, wrapping them with cardboard and strips of muslin, padding the seat with cotton batting, then sewing a cover out of a sturdy fabric with a bottom of oilcloth. Letty made me a chair out of an old wooden orange crate with a bin for my books and papers.

She would notice something and act immediately on the thought that came into her mind. One time when we were staying in a rented apart-

ment, after gazing at a bureau, she crossed the room and, to my amazement, pulled out what appeared to be a secret drawer with no handles at
the bottom of the bureau!

I took from Letty her Quaker simplicity, her ability to see possibilities
and act on them, and confidence that I could make things. If one way
didn't work, I could try another.

When Letty was not with us, I mostly played by myself. I would string
up blankets and make myself a little hiding place in the corner behind the
bed in my room at Metacomet. I could peek out to see if anyone walked
by but they could not see me, or so I thought. Grandpop loved roses and
I remember him in the evenings watering the garden. Grandpop would
ask me, "What are you making?" (not "What are you doing?"). When I
was about ten, he showed me how he planted lettuce.

Because we moved so much, I was unable to develop any sustained relationships with other children. Cushing was full of energy, boisterous,
and had an explosive temper. I was meek and shy, often called a crybaby
and told to stop whining. If Mother asked me what was wrong, I simply
answered, "Big nothing."

There were rules for everything. Cushing would break a rule, and I
thought it was unfair that I was then expected to abide by that same
rule. I regarded the rule as broken, like a broken cup; you couldn't use
it anymore. But that was not the way others saw it, so I learned to abide
by the rules.

My Parents

World peace, gender, and race were issues in my family as well as
Staughton's.

My father, Henry Edward Niles, was an extremely gentle man, and a
man of very high integrity. He amused me by letting a snake run down his
leg inside his trousers. But I don't think he ever had a clue as to who I was.

My father's father, Alfred S. Niles (who died before I was born), and his
brother, my Uncle Emory, were judges in Maryland state courts. During
World War II gasoline was rationed. It was said of Uncle Emory that he
was not appointed to a higher court because he did not permit the Gov-
ernor's wife to have a B-ration card for gasoline so that she could attend
social events. (I think B-ration cards were issued only to people who had
a particular work-related need for more gasoline than they could get with
an A-ration card).

My father was equally scrupulous. If he mailed a personal package
from his office, he would be sure to pay the postage out of his own pocket.
He would prefer not to go to Friends Meeting if he would arrive late because he did not want to disturb other people.

My father's brother Alfred was known in the family as the "Walking Encyclopedia" and my father, Harry, was known as the "Loose-leaf Supplement" where all the unrelated interesting tidbits were stored. My father wanted to be a farmer. He would notice ripe berries or unusual wild flowers as he drove along country roads. He would find remote streams where he could tease snapping turtles, and he would pick wild grapes into a basket in the canoe. But my mother could not see herself as a farmer's wife!

There is a family story that when my parents met at a dance in 1917, my father asked my mother what she thought about women's suffrage and he got an earful. Throughout her life, Mother believed that men got jobs for which she was better qualified.

In college my mother completed a joint major in piano (at the Peabody Conservatory of Music) and economics (at Johns Hopkins University where they let her into night school). It was shocking to her relatives that a woman would major in economics! Father studied economics (including Veblen) at the London School of Economics, and Mother completed all but the dissertation as a Ph.D. candidate in economics at Columbia University.

In the 1920s, my parents went to Switzerland where the League of Nations was headquartered, searching for a way they could work for world peace. Salvador Madariaga advised them that they should do so among business executives in the United States. In the late 1960s, at least in part due to my mother's instigation, after retirement as president of the Baltimore Life Insurance Company my father organized Business Executives Move for Vietnam Peace (BEM). His activity with BEM earned him a place on Vice President Agnew's list of undesirable citizens. Father regarded his place on that list as his most distinguished achievement!

When Staughton and I told my parents that we were planning to go to Nicaragua during wartime in 1985, Mother told me she had opposed the invasion of Nicaragua by the U.S. Marines in the nineteen-teens and nineteen-twenties!

My parents did not actually join the Society of Friends (Quakers) until the 1940s. My mother's mother was a devout Episcopalian and her father was an atheist. My father's father was Presbyterian but when he was on a committee to select a new Presbyterian minister, he realized that he did not believe in hell fire. He left the Presbyterian Church and joined the Unitarian Church. I remember Mother taking me to Friends Meeting in Westerly, Rhode Island, when I was four years old. For me it was a quiet time to sit beside her or lie on the bench next to her.

During World War I, my father went through basic training in the Army but the war ended and he did not see combat. The hardest part for him was bayonet practice. During World War II he was still of draft age and, I think, seriously considered declaring himself to be a conscientious objector. But he concluded that if his family were attacked he would do what he could to defend us. He registered but was not drafted. Even though women were not drafted for military service in the United States, I later regarded myself as a conscientious objector to war.

My mother's two brothers also contributed to my attitudes toward the military. Pip, a man who loved sailing, enlisted in the Navy out of a sense of "noblesse oblige" (aristocratic obligation). I used to make blueberry pies when he came home on furlough before he was sent to the Pacific. He was in command of two ships. Being experienced at reading nautical charts, on one occasion he determined that if he followed orders his ships would sail into a coral reef so he commanded them to go by a different route. He was reprimanded and, according to family folklore, put the reprimand at the top of his file when he was discharged so that he would never be called back into service. I recall visiting him five years later in a huge ward in a veterans' hospital shortly before he died. In retrospect, I have often wondered whether his cancer resulted from exposure to nuclear radiation or from other toxic exposures during his military service.

My mother's younger brother, Bill, dropped out of high school in eleventh grade and was driving a coal truck when the United States entered World War II. He did not want to go into the military so he figured he had better get a job in an essential industry. Being highly skilled with his hands, he became a superb tool and die maker.

I, like Bill, had a difficult time with school work and I, like Bill, was not a good conversationalist. Both of us stayed on the sidelines and didn't know what to say in any social gathering. But I, like Bill, was very good at making things with my hands and doing detail work. We were not particularly close as I was growing up, but as youngest children in families of fast-talkers, Bill and I had a lot in common.

I have a few positive memories of my paternal grandmother, Mary Waters Niles. When I was nine-and-a-half years old, my father got a steady job in Baltimore and Letty was no longer with us. I had saved up $35 and I wanted to buy a sewing machine that cost $45. My grandmother gave me $10 so I could buy my first sewing machine. I still have it! Every Christmas, Grandmother Niles would make a variety of cookies. When I was twelve, I spent a day with her learning how to make my father's favorite cookies—very thin gingersnaps. Those cookies are still a family tradition.

Beginning a few weeks after I was born in July 1930 until January 1940, my parents worked together as "consultants in management" or "efficiency experts." They concluded that the single factor that made the most difference in efficiency was for people to be treated with respect, for them to understand the relevance of their work, and for their ideas to be taken seriously. They did some of the early writing on human relations in management. However, when Father was offered a job by the Baltimore Life Insurance Company in 1940, Mother consented because she thought the life of moving all the time was not good for me, and she set as a condition that she could take a job in Washington, D.C. She was eventually hired to do personnel policy work for the U.S. government.

When I was a small child, my parents would get home from work by 6:00 p.m. We ate dinner at 6:00 and bedtime was at 7:00. After dinner, Mother would play with me until the alarm clock rang at 7:00. When I was five years old, we lived for a time in a house that had a piano. I remember Mother playing the piano as I was falling asleep. During World War II, around the time I was twelve years old, Mother was working twelve-hour days, six days a week. Father did not want her to work so hard. He said to me that he wished Mother was more like his sister who was on the board of the YWCA and worked only part time. My sister followed our mother's example; I followed more according to my father's wish for his marriage. I worked part time and was home most of the time when our children were not in school, except when full-time employment was necessary to sustain our family and Staughton could be home with the kids before and after school.

Race

There were strong racist undertones in what I heard as a child. Grandpop had an African-American cook named Blanche. Blanche would come from Baltimore to Metacomet in the summers. Blanche, I was told, didn't want children in the kitchen. In the winter, when Blanche was not at Metacomet, Mamie would put out a set of white canisters that she thought Blanche would not keep clean.

There were also Mother's stories handed down from slaveholding days. She told us that one of her ancestors would go to the slave cabins and take care of the sick. And, so she said, a cousin took his slaves to Illinois, told them they were free, and the slaves asked him not to leave them because they did not know how to make it on their own.

After we moved to Baltimore in 1940, my mother hired an African-American woman by the name of Geneva to cook, clean, and do the laundry. I spent a great deal of time with Geneva in the kitchen and eventually I became an advocate for her. She was paid $13 per week. She told me exactly how much she had to pay for each item in her budget. It was not enough. I went to my parents and asked them to pay her more. I don't think they did. I think they did not want to pay her more than the going rate.

By the time I was ten years old I was allowed to take the bus and go downtown shopping by myself. I could go to stores where African-Americans were not permitted to shop. I would buy dresses and other things for Geneva and later for another maid. They didn't like big practical coverall aprons. They wanted dainty white ones. So I bought them dainty white aprons. I visited Geneva in a hospital ward for indigent patients after she had surgery. I did these things completely on my own.

FRIENDS

Staughton

Ethical Culture

I attended the schools of the Ethical Culture Society in New York City from pre-kindergarten through twelfth grade. The words displayed above the stage of the Society's auditorium on West 64th Street were: "The place where men meet to seek the highest is holy ground." (Of course the word "men" was intended in its pre-1960s sense, signifying "human beings." When I found myself in the Philadelphia meetinghouse of the Ethical Culture Society in the fall of 2004 I noticed that the word "men" displayed above the stage in their auditorium had been replaced by the word "we.")

I graduated from elementary school on the stage at 64th Street, and was inducted as student body president of the high school on that stage in 1945. These words have ever since provided the best definition I could provide—for example, to my draft board when I applied for conscientious objector status—of my personal ethics and morality.

I skipped second grade and was always younger than most of my classmates. But in elementary school and high school I had lots of friends.

In the schools of the Ethical Culture Society almost all my fellow students, and therefore almost all my friends, were Jewish. They were also middle-class. When founded in the late nineteenth century, the Ethical Culture schools were intended as "workingmen's schools." They had become something quite different by the 1930s. Brilliant Jewish radicals from well-to-do families such as physicist Robert Oppenheimer and attorney Arthur Kinoy passed through the schools not long before I arrived.

My best friend in elementary school was the late Daniel Newman, son of Rabbi Louis Newman. Danny became an artist. He never ceased to tease me that in first grade we had painted a mural based on the Babar stories, and (according to Danny) I had insisted that he paint only the grass leaving the difficult portrayal of characters to me.

The Jones Boys

In high school I helped to form and belonged to what in retrospect should perhaps be considered a gang. Initially there were three of us: Paul

Willen, whose parents were Trotskyists and with whom I argued end-lessly about the character of the Soviet Union; Phil Brickner, who became a doctor and won my admiration by seeking to serve persons so poor that they did not have Social Security numbers; and myself.

We called ourselves "the Jones Boys" and when we could remember to do so addressed each other as "Jones." The name came about as follows. One summer, preparatory to a hiking trip in the White Mountains, Paul and Phil journeyed to the house in New Hampshire my parents were rent-ing for the summer. We prepared for our adventure by reading comic books. In one of them, a strip about Popeye the sailor, Popeye's friend Wimpy found himself out of meat to make his favorite food, hamburgers. Wimpy thereupon went into a field and began to lead away a cow. A farmer, the cow's owner, angrily confronted Wimpy and asked, "Who are you?" Wimpy replied, "Jones is my name. I'm one of the Jones boys." The die was cast.

The subsequent trip in the White Mountains contributed to Jones Boys' mythology. World War II was in progress and the Appalachian Mountain Club had closed most of the huts where one could stay overnight. It was therefore necessary to backpack our provisions. After the first two days we found ourselves with the following remaining foodstuffs: peanut but-ter; raisins; a loaf of bread that had been carried next to someone's sweaty back; and chocolate, but of the wrong, bitter kind. We spread these items before us and considered what to do. There was only one possible answer. We mixed everything together, christened it "Jones Brothers' mountain brew," and lived on it for the next two days. At journey's end, Phil came down with Rocky Mountain spotted fever, while Paul, who had made the entire trip in ordinary street shoes, had very sore feet. As best I can re-member, I felt fine.

The next summer we made our second hiking trip in the White Moun-tains, with a fourth colleague, Danny Butler. Unfortunately Danny twisted his ankle severely on the first day. The Storm Trooper subculture of our gang then displayed itself. For the rest of the trip, Phil, Paul, and I would sprint ahead, rest until Danny hobbled into view, and then jump up and proceed without giving Danny a moment's rest.

I do not excuse this atrocious behavior. I merely record it as a historian, the more so because we did much the same thing the next summer. This time the aspiring member and victim was David "Duff" Dretzin. Phil, Paul, Duff, and I proposed to bicycle from Albany to Montreal, take the train to Quebec City and back to Montreal, then bicycle to the White Mountains. Duff got sick in Quebec and we left him in a bed at the local YMCA. For some reason Duff did not hold this against the rest of us, and generously made his home available for a "Jones Boys reunion" fifty years later. Duff was wrong. Our behavior was unforgivable. We were young, but that was no excuse.

Lee Hosford

I was a fish out of water among the two thousand members of my freshman class at Harvard. My friends were mostly Communists and Trotskyists, still middle-class and in different ways objectionable as well as attractive. The Trotskyists that I knew were devotees of Paul Goodman and into homosexuality as well as Trotskyism. I kept my distance.

However, I did read Trotsky's *Literature and Revolution* early in my junior year (fall of 1948). It made an enormous impression, especially the end where Trotsky forecast a future in which all human beings would be Aristotles and Goethes, "and beyond these, new peaks will rise." I left college abruptly and took a train across the country to Portland, where Duff Dretzin was attending Reed College. For several weeks I ate at the college cafeteria and I don't remember where I slept. I read certain writings that became touchstones for me ever after, especially Rosa Luxemburg's booklet on the general strike (which I read in German) and the program of the Workers' Opposition in the Soviet Communist Party of the early 1920s. Early the next year, after returning to New York, I "borrowed" from the New York Public Library two huge blue bound volumes containing the bulletins Trotsky published (in Russian) after his expulsion from the Soviet Union. What I found most moving were the obituaries that he wrote about a variety of his former comrades as, one by one, and for different reasons, they died. (After hitchhiking around the country with these monster tomes in my backpack, I returned the books surreptitiously.)

Such readings on the margin of international radicalism became the basis for a friendship when, while still away from Harvard in 1949, I met Lee Hosford. Our son Lee is named for Lee Hosford.

Lee was the son of an engineer for a suburban railroad in Pasadena, California. When Lee was in grade school his younger brother was run over by a truck, apparently leaving Lee with the belief that the son most loved by his parents had been killed.

Lee was a working-class intellectual: that is, he came from a working-class family and was making his way in the world of ideas and radical politics. In my naive eyes it seemed that Lee had tried every kind of radical politics and every variety of addiction. Whereas in my parents' household it was an article of faith to be positive, Lee was disillusioned and cynical. He pointed out to me that the conduct of international war had become less civilized and more barbaric throughout the twentieth century (and this was only 1949). He recited the dialogue between Soviet prosecutor Vyshinsky and defendant Nikolai Bukharin in the Soviet purge trials of the 1930s, when Vyshinsky had called Bukharin every imaginable epithet ("running dog" was a favorite expression back then), and Bukharin, in the depths of his humiliation yet with perverse loyalty had replied, "Citizen Prosecutor Vyshinsky, you have found the word." He drew my attention to poems such as Robinson Jeffers's "Shine, Perishing Republic."

Lee was the most brilliant person I have ever known. He had been disappointed in love as well as politics. Somehow in my innocence he perceived a quality that he could trust, and though his capacity to do so dribbled away over the years, to the best of his ability he held up his end of our friendship. Before Alice and I moved to the Macedonia community in Georgia in 1954, I took a plane to California to visit Lee. I would next see him in 1958 as a prisoner in San Quentin. In an attempt to get money to buy drugs he had robbed a store (I think pretending to have a gun, not with a real one).

Lee Hosford was the first in a long series of working-class friends who have helped to define my adult life. After him came, among others, Walter Smalakis, a disfigured veteran who was a coworker at the Hyde Park Co-op in Chicago and who testified on my behalf when I applied for conscientious objector status; Howard Zinn, who recruited me to teach at Spelman College, and has remained my comrade for over forty years; Ed Mann and John Barbero, steelworkers because of whom Alice and I moved to Youngstown; Bob Schindler, Tony Budak, and Jim Jordan, with whom (along with Ed Mann) we created the Workers' Solidarity Club of Youngstown; and Stan Weir, longshoreman, labor educator and cocreator of a small publishing house that printed books for workers.

I have no certain explanation as to why I, the child of two upper-middle-class professors, found in these men my comrades. It was a puzzle to Howard Zinn as well. There is a chapter toward the end of his autobiography, *You Can't Be Neutral On a Moving Train*, in which Howard describes how he, I, and his children Myla and Jeff, climbed a mountain in New Hampshire together during the summer of 1961. The two families had arranged to spend several days getting to know one another before the Lynds moved to Atlanta. Howard says that as he and I went up and down that mountain we discussed every political topic imaginable and could find nothing about which we disagreed. He wondered how this could be, since he came from a very poor family and my background was one of affluence. Class analysis suggested we should have different outlooks on the world but, so far as he and I could tell then and thereafter, we didn't.

Of course my parents' own radicalism, such as it was, prepared the way for my comradeship with these working-class friends. But there was more to it than that. Somehow, WASP (White Anglo-Saxon Protestant) though I assuredly was and am, I felt myself at the very deepest levels of my being in conflict with members of the U.S. ruling class. I encountered such folks close up as a Harvard undergraduate and, later, as a Yale professor. During my first year of teaching at Spelman College (1961–1962), I was recruited by the Yale History department. The professor who took me around New Haven advised me not to leave my briefcase in the car at lunch time because we were in "Darktown," and not to consider living in a certain suburb because the "sons of Abraham" were very numerous there. (That same professor was later an outspoken opponent of accepting female students at Yale.) I felt that I might be teaching in the academic minor leagues but I had not sunk that low. To the astonishment of the Yale historians I turned them down.

Alice

I made no significant friendships until, at the age of fifteen, I went away to boarding school. The Cambridge School of Weston was located about a mile from a crossroads where a suburban train stopped north of Boston. I, like most of the Cambridge School boarding students, began in tenth grade. I was the oldest of four girls with overlapping friendships: I was born in July 1930, Tilly in September of that year, and Ruth and Bobbie two days apart in April 1931. At the end of tenth grade we spent a weekend together on a farm.

Ruth was my first close friend. She was a day student who boarded during the week in the home of the math teacher. Ruth was a talented violinist with perfect pitch. We learned a Mozart sonata for violin and piano under the guidance of a teacher who impressed on us the interplay between the two instruments, not regarding the piano as mere accompaniment.

Tilly, daughter of the French teacher, was also a day student. In our senior year, Tilly was one of two students in Massachusetts who won four-year Pepsi Cola college scholarships. She later became a professor of English at the University of California in Santa Cruz. I recall being stunned at Tilly's response to something I must have said, "But Allee, that's a value judgment!"

Bobbie was a "five-day boarder," who went home on weekends. Her father taught psychology at Harvard University. Bobbie and I both practiced piano in the same building. At the end of my practice session, I would go and listen to what Bobbie was playing. Then we would walk together to supper. I missed months of school due to illness so catching up on what I had missed was a struggle. Bobbie helped me. She could not understand why anyone who worked as hard as I did did not get good grades.

During the last few months of tenth grade, Bobbie and I were room-mates. We walked through the woods instead of along the road to the house where we lived. On Friday afternoons, her mother would pick her up and sometimes take me as well as Bobbie to their home for the week-end, stopping at a doughnut shop on the way. Bobbie and I had matching skirts; I made matching blouses.

Bobbie was capable of great joy and laughter. She wrote poetry. She cried with me when I was upset. At the end of our senior year, we took an early morning walk up the ski hill behind the school, and watched the mist rise from ponds in the valley below. We went to her house, basked under a sunlamp and listened to records.

She had expectations of herself that astounded me, possibly echoing her father's judgment as to whether what she wrote was good enough to be published. One time she read me a page from Kafka. More than once, after a weekend, she would tell me that she had stopped in front of a car but the car did not hit her. She didn't understand why anyone would love her.

Bobbie, Tilly, and a childhood friend of Bobbie's went to Swarthmore College. I assumed Bobbie was under their watchful eyes. Nobody told me when Bobbie broke a window and used the broken glass to cut her wrist. She survived, but, unknown to me, dropped out of college and was living only a few blocks from where I was at Radcliffe College. She came to see me just before Christmas vacation in our sophomore year. At that time she wore only a dress that I had made for her. She offered me a book. I think it was Elizabethan poetry. I declined, believing I would never have the time to read it.

In February I received a letter from her mother telling me that Bobbie had died from an overdose of sleeping pills. My immediate reaction was, now I have to go on living for both of us. It was maybe twenty minutes before I began to cry. For the next six months I was in a state of shock. I was vulnerable to any little reminder of her.

I met Staughton in July. At the end of July, we took a walk together. I told him that what I really needed was a friend, not a romantic relation-ship. I got both! One afternoon in August, Staughton held me in his arms while I cried for hours.

When I went to see Bobbie's mother shortly after Bobbie died, her mother gave me some of Bobbie's music books. Some years later, I tried to learn the Bach fugue that I particularly loved to hear Bobbie play. Bobbie's mother also gave me two of Bobbie's dresses. One I used until it was worn out; then I sewed pieces of it into a quilt. The other dress was Bobbie's plain white high school graduation dress. I wore that dress twice: on the day I married Staughton and on our fiftieth wedding anniversary.

Our first child, Barbara, was named for Bobbie.

A PREMATURE NEW LEFTIST, *STAUGHTON LYND*

When I met Alice in the summer of 1950 I was too shy, or too scared, to tell her that I was a socialist. (The Korean War had begun in June 1950 and we met in July. Radicals were seeking cover.) So, sitting on the steps of Memorial Chapel in the middle of Harvard Yard one evening, I told her that my parents were socialists. Alice, who had been exposed to Marxism in two of her Radcliffe courses, responded: "What's wrong with that?"

In truth, I had by that time acquired what amounted to a New Left view of the world, a set of beliefs quite different from the outlook of my parents. My dad was persuaded that trained professionals should analyze the world and make decisions for the rest of society. He wanted me to be such a decision-maker. My mother reacted to authority as an outraged individualist. As for myself, a decade or more before the southern sit-ins, the organization of the Student Nonviolent Coordinating Committee (SNCC), or the promulgation of the Port Huron Statement by the newly formed Students for a Democratic Society (SDS), I already believed in walking your talk, that is, putting your body where your mouth is; making decisions in the most decentralized way possible; and combining Marxist analysis with an understanding that individual action requires ethical choice. Like so many young people in the 1960s, I faulted my parents for talking a good game but not letting that disturb their comfortable lifestyle.

I don't find it easy to reconstruct how I came to affirm these ideas. My take on things differed not only from the worldview of my parents but from the prevailing radical culture. As I was growing up, the Communist Party was the largest organized presence on the Left. Since 1935, stung by the triumph of Hitler in Germany, Communist parties everywhere sought to make common cause with liberals in opposing fascism. In the United States that orientation entailed uncritical support for President Roosevelt, and synthetic homage to the so-called tradition of Jefferson, who never freed his slaves, and Jackson, who sent the Cherokee Indians on the Trail of Tears. I spent a good deal of time at meetings, hootenannys, and the like, where the ambience was decidedly Old Left, that is, influenced by the outlook of the Communist Party. Older political persons that I knew were usually friends of my parents. They tended to support the British Labor Party and the Soviet Union.

What caused me to break away from this mindset and become what I think of as a premature New Leftist? I can see moments when something new came into my consciousness. I want to describe several formative political experiences growing up in New York.

Sam Levinger

In every generation there come times when young people feel challenged to act out their beliefs at great personal risk. In 1964 this would mean going to Mississippi, and in the 1980s, traveling to Nicaragua and El Salvador. In 1935–1937 it meant going to Spain to do battle in support of the democratically elected government against General Franco's coup from the Right.

On May Day, 1936, a young man named Sam Levinger carried me on his shoulders in the huge New York City May Day parade. Later that year he went to Spain with the Abraham Lincoln Brigade, and was killed at the battle of Belchite.

For a long time I assumed that Levinger was a Communist, as were most of the volunteers for the Lincoln Brigade, and as I would not have been. Many years later I learned that he was a Socialist. He was also a poet. I am acquainted with his niece and have read through her collection of her uncle's poems.

I believe I came to feel that I was trying to live the life that Sam Levinger might have lived, had he survived the Spanish Civil War and been able to return to the States. By "the life" I imagined nothing very specific. What Sam represented to me was the imperative of acting out one's beliefs.

Ireland

My parents were teachers, and they hired a recent immigrant from Ireland named Mary Bohan to care for my sister and myself while our parents were at work. Mary was from County Tipperary. She taught me all manner of Irish revolutionary songs.

One was called "My Old Fenian Gun." The song describes how a boy observes a gun hanging above the kitchen fireplace, "its barrel long and grim." His father never touches the gun or talks about it. There comes a day when the boy takes down the gun. According to Mary, the father then tells the boy how his mother died when his parents fled from British soldiers through the winter cold. As the song ends the boy, now grown to be a man, has spent "this last long year . . . inside a gloomy English jail." And he reflects: "I've done my part I'll do it still, Until the fight is won, When Ireland's free she'll bless the men, Who held the Fenian gun."

Another song was called "Michael Dwyer." Over the years, working from fragments of the song I remembered, I established that in the 1790s Michael Dwyer had been a guerrilla in the hills of County Wexford in southeast Ireland. In the area there was indeed a river named the Slaney which, according to the song, Michael Dwyer swam to safety. Tom Hayden helped me to locate a complete text of that song. It seems that Dwyer and his companions were trapped in a house by British soldiers, who set fire to the building. A man named McAllister was badly wounded. He told his comrades that he would stand in the door, which they were to open. The Black and Tans would discharge their single-shot muskets, killing him, giving Dwyer and the others the opportunity to escape.

There were also songs better-known in this country, such as "The Wearing of the Green," "The Minstrel Boy," and "Kevin Barry."

"The Wearing of the Green" concerns a British order that the Irish must cease to wear "the green," that is, the shamrock symbolizing Irish independence. The song declares: "When the law can stop the blades of grass from growing as they grow, And when the trees in summertime their verdure dare not show, Then I will change the color that I wear in my *caubeen*, But till that day thank God I'll stick, To wearing of the green."

"The Minstrel Boy," I learn from Denis O'Hearn, "was written by Thomas Moore to commemorate his Trinity College colleagues who left the comfy university life of Dublin to join the United Irishmen in the 1798 rebellion." The last verse, as I remember it, goes:

> The minstrel fell but the foeman's chains
> Could not bring that proud soul under.
> The harp he loved never spoke again
> For he tore its strings asunder.
>
> And said, "No foe shall sully thee
> Thou soul of love and bravery,
> Thy songs were made for the pure and free
> They shall never sound in slavery."

One evening, after hearing "The Minstrel Boy," I asked Mary to telephone my parents and tell them I would never be a soldier.

As for Kevin Barry, he practiced an ethic of solidarity that the Lynds later encountered in five men sentenced to death for their alleged roles in a 1993 prison riot. The song says:

> Just before he met the hangman
> In his lonely prison cell,
> The Black and Tans tortured Barry
> All because he wouldn't tell
>
> The names of his companions
> And other things they wished to know,
> "Turn informer and we'll free you,"
> Barry proudly answered, "No."

ain

There was another formative experience connected with the Spanish Civil War. Seymour Martin Lipset became a rather conservative political sociologist. In the early 1940s, however, he was a graduate student of my father's and a socialist, who wrote his dissertation on the Canadian Commonwealth Federation.

Marty Lipset decided that my political education would not be complete until I had visited the New York City headquarters of the Socialist Party. The office was on the East Side and so we caught the shuttle at Times Square. I have no memory of the Socialist Party headquarters but a story Marty told me on the shuttle changed my life.

It seems that one day during the Spanish Civil War there was a long line waiting for lunch. Far back in the line was a well-known anarchist. A colleague urged him: "Comrade, come to the front of the line and get your lunch. Your time is too valuable to be wasted this way. Your work is too important for you to stand at the back of the line. Think of the Revolution!" Remaining where he was in line, the anarchist leader replied: "This *is* the Revolution."

Burnham's Dilemma

I spent a great deal of time going back and forth to high school on the IRT Seventh Avenue subway. On the subway, I gave myself a political education. I read, for example, Edmund Wilson's *To the Finland Station*, which offered portraits of the great Marxist leaders as human beings. And I read a book by an ex-Trotskyist named James Burnham called *The Managerial Revolution*.

Burnham said that Marxists expected a socialist revolution to replace capitalism in the same way that a bourgeois revolution had destroyed feudalism. According to Burnham, socialists believed that the new proletarian society would grow within the womb or shell of the old until, like a newborn chick, it would come forth fully formed. Burnham argued that there would be no such socialist revolution. In medieval Europe, Burnham contended, the bourgeoisie was able to create a variety of new institutions in the interstices of feudal society. These new institutions included free cities, guilds, Protestant congregations, banks and corporations, and finally, parliaments. Only when the middle class had to a considerable extent brought a new economy and a new institutional world into being, within feudal society, did the bourgeoisie take state power.

Nothing like this has happened or can happen inside capitalism, Burnham wrote. People look hopefully to trade unions but, in fact, trade unions are part of the capitalist scheme of things. Trade unions do not challenge capitalism. They only ameliorate capitalism's burdens and smooth its rough edges.

I cannot be certain but my impression is that when I exited the subway at 67th Street and made my way home, I opened some authoritative source of wisdom such as Emile Burns's *Handbook of Marxism* to find the answer to Burnham. The problem was, I couldn't find an answer. Nor could I find an answer for roughly the next fifty years until, as I describe later on, the Zapatista movement offered an answer expressed in the words, "*Mandar obediciendo*," "To govern in obedience."

Bread and Wine

My growing feeling that the revolution had to be, somehow, both Marxist and ethical, was articulated in a book.

One day on the subway my friend, the late Danny Newman, held up a paperback and asked me if I had read it. It was *Bread and Wine* by Ignazio Silone. I shan't take the time to narrate the whole plot of my favorite novel. Suffice it to say that a Communist revolutionary disguises himself as a priest, and in doing so is forced to consider how these two parts of his experience—the Marxist and the Christian—fit together.

I too felt the need for such a synthesis. I recall an evening at Harvard in the late 1940s when I had supper at Cronin's tavern with several fellow students who were in the orbit of the Communist Party. They baited me with the question, "Do you believe that there are ethical principles that are valid throughout history?" I was supposed to say, "No, the ethics of any particular period of class rule are specific to that society." But I answered, "Yes."

The quest for a synthesis of ethics and Marxism would follow me the rest of my life. Having dropped out of Harvard in the fall of 1948, I enrolled at Columbia in the fall of 1949 only to drop out again. The triggering event was a movie about the life of the French saint, Vincent de Paul.

According to the movie, Vincent was chaplain to the French king. The king liked to amuse himself by galley races. The king's galley, rowed by galley slaves, competed with the galleys of various courtiers.

On the day of a particular race, Vincent was stationed beside the king in the high poop at the rear of the king's galley. As the race became heated, the king repeatedly gave orders to increase the "beat." Vincent began to protest that the oarsmen were being worked too hard. The king responded with words to the effect, "Don't worry. They are different from us. They enjoy it." The beat was increased yet again, and Vincent became more agitated.

Suddenly an oarsman collapsed at his oar, unconscious. Vincent clambered down into the hold of the ship. He himself took up the man's oar.

I left college the next day. I suppose it seemed to me that life in the university was like life in the high poop of the king's ship. However awkwardly, one had to find a way to the place in society where ordinary people toiled at the oars, and assume a position beside them.

Zionism or Socialism?

One of my high-school friends was the late Daniel Lourie. Danny's father, Arthur Lourie, was the representative in the United States of the "Jewish entity" in Palestine before the creation of the State of Israel. One weekend Danny took me to a training farm in Cream Ridge, New Jersey, where young people were preparing to "make *aliyah*," that is, to go to Palestine and work in cooperative farms known as *khibbutzim*. By that time—I was perhaps fifteen years old—I considered myself a socialist. On Sunday morning I was hoeing in the garden with a man probably aged about thirty-five, but who, in part because of a weather-beaten face, I considered old. In my youthful enthusiasm I asked him, in effect, "What's with this Zionism? What happened to socialist internationalism?" My companion put down his hoe, turned, and looked at me. He said, "We've done enough dying on other people's barricades." For several years thereafter I thought of the Jewish presence in Palestine as a model of decentralized socialism.

This was enough for me until I was a sophomore in college. Then a young woman at Wellesley introduced me to a family friend whom I recall only as Jimmy. Jimmy had spent time in the Middle East, I believe at the American University in Beirut. I offered my what-the-Jews-are-doing-in-Palestine-is-decentralized-socialism rap. Jimmy turned to me as had the man in the garden, and said, "You're wrong. The land was stolen from the Palestinians who lived there."

In the 1950s I heard Martin Buber speak at the University of Michigan. A short, stocky man with an enormous white beard, he urged that Palestine should become a single, binational state. (See the chapter below on Palestine.)

The New England Town Meeting

In the years just before I met Alice, I became intensely interested in the New England town meeting. The period of the American Revolution was rich in ad hoc self-governing institutions like the Sons of Liberty and the committees of correspondence and safety. These in turn appeared to have emerged, at least in part, because ordinary people had already had the experience of directing their own affairs in entities like the town meeting.

On our honeymoon in 1951, Alice and I attended a conference of so-called intentional communities (what would later be called "communes") in Yellow Springs, Ohio. Alice recalls clearly that one reason we decided to go there was my interest in town meetings. And it was there that we first met Art and Mary Wiser, members of the Macedonia Cooperative Community that we ourselves would join in 1954.

MUSIC AND DANCE AND DISCOVERING CHILDHOOD,
ALICE LYND

By the time I was nine-and-a-half years old, according to my mother, I had moved forty-five times and attended twelve different schools. (I can remember eleven of them!) Some were private, some were public. The school I liked least was the Little Red School House in New York City. There, I remember a girl stamping on my foot and asking, "Does that hurt?" and doing so several times again, each time harder, and each time asking, "Does that hurt?" In first grade at a public school in Ossining, New York, I recall being caught with a piece of cloth under my desk; I was pulling the threads along the edge of a place mat to make a fringe.

The school I liked best was a formal girls' school in Toronto, Canada. We memorized poetry, and curtsied before and after reciting it to the teacher. I also remember a school assembly when we were told about a man named Gandhi.

Because of moving so often, I had no continuing relationships with other children. I was not good at sports. Music and dance provided me with solace and, over time, gave me my first experiences in being part of a community.

Music

When I was five years old, the local school had no kindergarten and I was too young for first grade. There was a piano in the house where we lived. So I took piano lessons. I was the youngest student playing in a piano recital.

My mother had the scores of Beethoven's symphonies arranged for two piano players. One of the movements began with the repeated notes D, D-D, D, D; then D, D-E, F, F, and so on. I played that simple melody line while she played the accompaniment in the bass clef.

After surviving a deadly hurricane in Rhode Island when I was about seven years old, I described the ferocity of the storm by improvising on the piano. I tried, repeatedly and unsuccessfully, to write my composition on paper.

At about that same age, I remember a teacher at school playing intervals on the piano and asking me what they were. Apparently, I knew them by then.

Between fourth and sixth grades, I took piano lessons at school. I normally learned music by ear. My teacher was determined to make me read, and to break my habit of memorizing. (Neither she nor I recognized then that I had an intractable problem doing any kind of reading.) I completed a four-year "ear training" program in one year. When I was in seventh grade, I was sent to the Peabody Conservatory of Music to take a course in harmony, using the same book my mother had used there decades earlier. But I was too young to master it.

During the summer I turned fourteen, I went to a music camp. Everyone was in the chorus. And every Friday evening, we gave a concert in the nearby town. Among the pieces we performed that summer were "How Lovely Is Thy Dwelling Place" from the Brahms *Requiem*, "*Cum Sancto Spiritu*" from Bach's *Mass in B Minor*, and "*Ruht wohl*" [Rest well] from Bach's *St. John Passion*. (I could hardly believe that Mother had regarded music by Bach as "finger exercises.") Singing in that chorus opened up a whole new world of music for me!

The best musical instruction I ever had was as a member of the "Madrigal Group" for three years during high school under the guidance of Louise Aiken, fondly known as Ouisel. Each year she selected four sopranos, four altos, four tenors and four basses. (If necessary, she would pick several boys and help them learn to sing.) She asked us to listen to each other, to blend our voices and to be sensitive to which musical line should be brought out, to where the parts were pulling in dissonance and where we should be moving in harmony. During rehearsals, she might ask us to sing in a quartet with only one person on each part. Once when I was singing, another member of the group blurted out, "Did you hear that? It sounded like a flute!"

I started out as a soprano but in my second year, Louise asked me to sing alto. It was a challenge. I learned to do it during a prolonged illness. Lying in bed, listening to Christmas music on the radio, in my mind I would try to follow an inner part. When I returned to school, I could do it. To this day, I love to sing second soprano, placing my notes at an interval just below those of the first sopranos! I still prefer ensemble singing to any other way of enjoying music.

I went to Radcliffe College at a time when there were no courses in which one could do hands-on art or music. We could try to infer ancient history from shards and myths, but there were no courses in which a student could make pottery or play an instrument.

Singing in the Radcliffe Choral Society is what got me through several very difficult years at Radcliffe. Especially during the spring semester of my sophomore year, it was the only way I knew to grieve for Bobbie. On the spring tour with the Harvard Glee Club, we sang the Schutz *St. John*

Passion. And upon our return, we performed the Bach *St. John Passion* with the Boston Symphony Orchestra.

At my fortieth high school class reunion with Staughton, the buzz was: "Allee married a wonderful tenor!"

Dance

I remember as a little girl dancing on the grass, and putting on dance performances for the adults at Metacomet. Letty made me a costume from squares of different colored cheese cloth, so that I could swirl the fairylike wings and skirt.

In college, I took modern dance to fulfill the physical education requirement. But it was during our first year of marriage that I discovered Barbara Mettler.

Barbara Mettler taught what she called "creative dance." She might ask beginners to start by making a single movement with one hand. Then another movement. Then a third. Take a few minutes and experiment; then decide on a sequence of three movements. We had each composed a mini-dance. Each student would do her (or his) dance and then every other student would do it.

We went on to make fast and slow movements, abrupt and smooth movements, tense and relaxed movements, all sorts of contrasting movements.

After that, we worked in pairs. One person would make a movement and the other person would make a movement in response. It was incredible to me how intense and direct the communication could be with a partner who had previously been a total stranger!

Sometimes, everyone in the group would be moving. Leadership would pass from one person to another, not by any previous decision, but by "natural authority." Someone might make a sudden movement that would catch the attention of others in the group, or change the tempo, and others would naturally follow.

Barbara Mettler emphasized the importance of allowing a moment of stillness before beginning a dance, and a moment of stillness at the end of the dance. She built on contrasts of movement and nonmovement, fast and slow, tension and relaxation, and on music as the sound that comes from movement such as stamping one's foot or clapping one's hands or using an instrument such as a drum as part of a dance, or adding color to movement in space by waving a scarf.

Barbara wanted us to overcome the idea that you have to study for years before you can dance. Dance is movement: you can do it now. She used the formula, "freedom, awareness and control": first you make a movement, then you pay attention to what you are doing, and then you decide how you want that movement to be when you repeat it. She had developed her teaching techniques over a period of many years, but was always open to rethinking her approach.

For me, Barbara Mettler was more than a dancer. I felt she was an exemplar of intellectual openness and honesty. Her kind of creativity was a way of life, and I loved it. It didn't matter to me whether I experienced that creativity through music or dance or some other medium, but I wanted that experience as an essential part of my life.

Discovering Childhood

My parents prided themselves on treating children as people, but mine was not a child-oriented home. When Mother and Father were writing books, I had to stand quietly at the door until recognized so that I would not interrupt their train of thought. Mother used to say that I knew what was "not me" but I did not know what was "me."

After I met Staughton, I dropped out of Radcliffe. I had reached a point where I felt that I was renting myself out to whatever a professor put on a reading list. Writing was such a struggle for me that most of every page was crossed out. (As I write on the computer, no one can see my constant revisions!) I needed to find out who I was and what I wanted to know before I returned to college.

For a while I taught handicrafts to children in an after-school program at a settlement house. After that, I got a job as a secretary at the Nursery Training School of Boston where I also took a course in child psychology. My assignments were to read ten books (the teacher let me report on one chapter out of each of ten books), and write up our observations of children on ten topics. For example, we observed the large muscle activity of two children one week, and the small muscle activity the next week.

One assignment was to observe an emotion. I decided to ask the question, What makes a little child laugh? I saw a child take some sand and spread it on the slide and laugh. During rest time the window shade was blowing and banging against the window frame and some of the children giggled. While the teacher was reading a story, a couple of little boys on the fringes were laughing with each other. The sudden, the unexpected, the out-of-bounds, is funny. Through those experiences, I discovered children!

I read about developmental levels and learned that children typically go through growth cycles that become apparent in periods of stable and unstable behavior. I was also taught that a professional does not describe any child as a "brat." The professional looks at the developmental level or emotional needs of the individual. (This attitude proved very helpful in later years, particularly in working with draft resisters and prisoners.)

I decided to become a full-time student at the Nursery Training School. We were student teachers every morning in various preschool and day care centers. In the afternoon we had classes in children's literature, music for children, and other subjects, introducing us to materials and resources. Most of our instructors had taught children for many years and, as they approached retirement, were teachers of teachers. It was a rare problem they themselves had not faced. They were not teaching out of textbooks. They were teaching out of their own experience.

I took a course in which the teacher talked about "preliminary scientific experiences." For instance, children may watch the direction in which the water swirls when a toilet is flushed. They try to catch marbles that inevitably roll down a marble shoot. I noticed that a little boy observing the sun and clouds would say (unlike adults) "sun's out" when the sun was hidden by clouds (as if a light switch had been turned off). I was fascinated.

The course that intrigued me the most was one in curriculum planning for kindergarten, because the emphasis was on "readiness for learning." Rather than push children to learn more and more academic skills at a younger and younger age, we were advised to let children mature to the point where learning is easy, and to let them learn by providing them with a variety of materials and centers of learning. When they are ready and interested they will learn.

The concept of readiness for learning seemed to fit perfectly with the exploration of movement that I was doing with Barbara Mettler. As a nursery school teacher in later years, I taught a music program for four-year-olds and incorporated much of what I had learned from Barbara Mettler. But it was at the Nursery Training School that I discovered a childhood I never had.

There were two more major influences on my education as a preschool teacher. One was learning about Adlerian psychology from Rudolph Dreikurs. In 1952, we moved to Chicago and I enrolled at Roosevelt College where I majored in early childhood education. I took a course in psychology in which I was introduced to writings by Rudolph Dreikurs. He analyzed what was going on in the "family constellation." He believed that family values are established in areas where the parents are the same or are in agreement, and sibling rivalry is expressed by being different in ways that the parents differ. Do not assume that the child who acts out is the source of the problem, he warned, it may be someone else or some other dynamic within the family that is the cause. He spoke of the teeter-totter twins: when one gets attention by being good, the other one gets attention by being bad. A person who feels insecure may conceal his insecurity by coming on as if he is super competent, and he may put other people down so that he does not feel he is less worthy than they are. (The reader is asked to forgive use of the words "his," "he" and "himself" to refer to an individual who may be either female or male.) Dr. Dreikurs instructed that if a misbehaving child is temporarily removed from the social group, it is necessary for the child himself to come to the point when he decides that he is ready to reenter the social group as a responsible participant.

It was through Dr. Dreikurs that I first had the experience of engaging in sociodrama wherein people act out a problem situation and, at the moment of crisis, exchange roles. Later on, when our daughter Barbara was four years old, she would ask me to play with her: "I'll be the mommy, and you be the little girl." OK, I thought, I'll act the way she does when she drives me to my wits' end and I'll see what she does as the mommy. "Oh, that's all right, honey," she would say, or some other affectionate words. The reaction she was wanting from me was love!

Dr. Dreikurs had another idea that has become part of my way of thinking. Instead of dealing out punishments unrelated to the child's behavior, you lead a child to understand that there are natural consequences of his actions: if he throws food, an appropriately related punishment is you don't give him more food that he can throw; but no bedtime story that night is not a punishment appropriately related to the offense. So I think in terms of natural consequences all the time. If you don't give plants enough water and light, they will die. If you don't put your dirty clothes in the laundry, you won't have clean clothes when you need them. If you are inconsiderate and rude to other people, they probably won't like you. If you cheat and tell lies, people won't trust you. If you don't do what you say you will do, people won't count on you. If you treat people like adversaries, they are more likely to act that way. If you bomb civilian populations, you escalate hostilities.

The other major influence in my education as a teacher was the concept of the superior-immature individual that I learned while working at the Gesell Institute for Child Development. Children who are very gifted in some areas may seem to be lagging in other developmental areas. For example, a seven-year-old whose IQ is that of a ten-year-old may have hand skills of a four-year-old. The same can be true emotionally: the brightest kids may do the most inappropriate things socially. Getting one's life organized is a particularly slow and difficult task for the superior-immature person and some, it seems, never do get it together.

I brought these perspectives into our marriage. But it took decades for me to figure out who I was, to have a sense of my own values and how to live by them.

STORY STREET, *STAUGHTON LYND*

Story Street was an inconspicuous street in Cambridge, Massachusetts, a short distance west of Harvard Square and near the old Brattle Theater. Alice and I met in an apartment on Story Street about July 8, 1950.

I had dropped out of Harvard in November 1948 and returned early in 1950. I did not want to live in one of the "houses" along the banks of the Charles River where most sophomore, junior, and senior Harvard students have rooms. Instead I rented an apartment on Story Street with Nicholas "Nick" Cunningham, a cello player and doctor-to-be, and Anatole "Tolly" Holt.

The three of us must have signed the lease in a hurry. The apartment was on the top floor. Its leading feature was a screened porch, from which one could look out over the Cambridge rooftops toward the Charles River. But there was no sink—dishes were washed in the bathtub—and no stove. Instead we used a hot plate, on which I cooked the evening Alice visited.

A Conversation and a Meal

Nick Cunningham had noticed Alice at rehearsals of the Harvard Glee Club and Radcliffe Choral Society. Half a year after the loss of her friend Bobbie and still grieving, Alice had resolved to accept social invitations she would otherwise have declined. Nick asked Alice to come to dinner at the Story Street apartment, and afterwards go to a Shakespeare play at the Brattle. She agreed.

Before supper Alice, petite and beautiful, sat on the screened porch with the three male residents and sought to make conversation. Searching for a topic to discuss she asked, "Has anyone read a book called *The Decline and Fall of British Capitalism*?" The book had been assigned in a course. But I, still full of thoughts about Trotsky and Rosa Luxemburg, inferred more than that in the question.

For her part Alice was struck by the way I savored a recent experience in the Harvard Yard. I had encountered three persons, an older man, a girl, and a boy, walking across the grass. All were barefoot and the man had a flute. I had a momentary impulse, so I said that evening, to join these Pied Pipers on their journey.

These are exchanges that linger in our memories. But I sometimes claim that what made the difference was the meal: hamburgers, green peas, and "Story Street dessert." The dessert was half cantaloupes, on top of which were large scoops of vanilla ice cream, on top of which were very big blueberries. Alice had never seen anything like it!

A Walk and a Letter

When Alice entered Radcliffe College, the college for women that was part of Harvard University, Radcliffe students lived, ate, and studied separately from Harvard students. Freshman and sophomore classes were conducted separately for men and women. A professor would lecture to males at Harvard, then repeat the same lecture at Radcliffe. Radcliffe students were not allowed to use Harvard libraries: they could fill out a slip and request that a specific book be brought to the Radcliffe library, which took several days. While Alice was still at Radcliffe, the Widener research library was opened to women but not the undergraduate library.

Harvard summer school was not subject to the same restrictions. Women as well as men could use the Harvard undergraduate library. Although they were housed separately, men and women could eat meals together at the Harvard cafeteria. Alice figured out when I usually went to lunch and she would show up at the same time. For my part, one day I went into Lamont Library on my way to lunch and saw Alice, her hair unbraided and nearly down to her waist, coming down the stairs!

A few weeks after we first met, I was alone in the Story Street apartment on an endless Sunday afternoon. I telephoned Matthews Hall, the dormitory used by women attending summer school. Alice was not in. (She was practicing piano on the other side of the Yard.) I left a message.

Alice returned the call later that afternoon. I proposed that we meet after supper and have coffee at the Oxford Grill, a restaurant just off the Square. Alice accepted. As we both remember, Alice wore a light blue dress with scallops around the neckline of the bodice.

The Oxford Grill was noisy and smoky. Alice suggested a walk. The riverside was all that the restaurant was not: quiet, wholly natural. Moreover there was a full moon that night. When we reached a point where it seemed right to turn and start back, Alice exclaimed, "Look at the moon!" I responded, "You look at the moon and I'll look at you."

In early August, it was only about a month since we had first met and only a few days after our walk along the bank of the Charles River. On the steps of Widener Library, I gave her the following letter.

Dear Alice,
   Other people don't feel about letters quite as I do; there's the school which says, everything goes wrong if you put it on paper, & the school which believes in "good" letters . . . while I think a letter to me is partly a diary, partly a prayer, I mean something with its own existence, justifying its pompousness only by being humbly offered to another person.
   What is difficult, is to prevent words from standing in front of, & blotting out, the pictures one's mind remembers & anticipates.
   I should like to have you hear, so faintly that you're not sure you didn't only think it, & so casually, that it's like rain, which bends a leaf without breaking it, & in the end makes the leaf grow, or like the sea which isn't heard until it's missed—like a dream that one knows really happened—that I love you, with much quiet happiness.
   Staughton

Fresh Pond

The Korean War had begun shortly before the dinner at Story Street. Leaving the country had crossed my mind, and even after that impulse faded there was tension in the air. Whatever hope for lasting peace had existed during World War II seemed long ago. Whatever expectation had been encouraged by the founding conference of the United Nations (attended by Alice's older sister, Cushing) now seemed unrealistic.

Alice remembers sitting under trees in the Harvard Yard during the early weeks of our togetherness and establishing, one at a time, our common ideas.

We often walked to Fresh Pond. Fresh Pond, today, lies forlornly in the middle of suburban sprawl, surrounded by a metal fence. In 1950 the pond was surrounded by woods. One evening in particular, we sat on a bench at the pond's edge and felt enveloped by a sense of peace. When in our later years people ask us to explain the secret of our long marriage, each of us spontaneously begins by thinking of that evening at Fresh Pond.

Husband and wife, in our experience, need to share something more fundamental than words and something more lasting than good times together. They need to share an inner togetherness, an intuitive compatibility. This is what we experienced quietly together beside the shore of Fresh Pond.

Aged twenty-one and almost twenty-one at the time we married, Alice and I were very young and very inexperienced. My head was full of new ideas but I had little conception of how to make them a reality. Recalling Alice and myself as we went forth together into married life reminds me of words my mother used to quote from Milton's *Paradise Lost*. For Adam and Eve, the poet said,

> The World was all before them, where to choose
> Their place of rest, and Providence their guide:
> They hand in hand with wandering steps and slow,
> Through Eden took their solitary way.

NOTES

1. Helen Merrell Lynd, with the collaboration of Staughton Lynd, *Possibilities* (Youngstown, OH: Ink Well Press, [1981]), 38. This book was based on interviews conducted for the Columbia University Oral History Project by Mrs. Walter Gellhorn and Dr. Elfie Stock (Raymond).
2. Robert S. Lynd and Helen Merrell Lynd, *Middletown: A Study in American Culture* (New York: Harcourt, Brace and Company, 1929), 8.

3. See "Father and Son: Intellectual Work Outside the University," in Staughton Lynd, *Living Inside Our Hope: A Steadfast Radical's Thoughts on Rebuilding the Movement* (Ithaca, NY: Cornell University Press, 1997).

4. Robert Lynd, *You Can Do It Better Democratically: A Comment on the Operation of Politics and Government as They Affect the Lives of Most People* (Detroit, MI: UAW-CIO Education Department, 1979).

5. H. M. Lynd, *Possibilities*, 36.

6. H. M. Lynd, *Possibilities*, 37.

7. H. M. Lynd, *Possibilities*, 38.

8. H. M. Lynd, *Possibilities*, 38.

9. H. M. Lynd, *Possibilities*, 38.

10. H. M. Lynd, *Possibilities*, 35.

11. R. S. Lynd and H. M. Lynd, *Middletown*, 8.

12. R. S. Lynd and H. M. Lynd, *Middletown*, 9.

13. R. S. Lynd and H. M. Lynd, *Middletown*, 479.

14. Robert S. Lynd and Helen Merrell Lynd, *Middletown in Transition: A Study in Cultural Conflicts* (New York: Harcourt, Brace and Company, 1937), 165 n.

15. R. S. Lynd and H. M. Lynd, *Middletown in Transition*, 425.

16. R. S. Lynd and H. M. Lynd, *Middletown in Transition*, 465.

17. R. S. Lynd and H. M. Lynd, *Middletown in Transition*, 464.

18. H. M. Lynd, *Possibilities*, 22–23.

19. Helen Merrell Lynd, *On Shame and the Search for Identity* (New York: Harcourt, Brace and Company, 1958).

20. When I was growing up, I was told that "Metacomet" was an Indian chief who had lived on the property that carried his name. Years later, Staughton learned that Metacomet was the name of the seventeenth-century Native American leader whom the Puritans called "King Philip." During what came to be known as King Philip's War, Metacomet was killed. His head was cut off and displayed on a pole by the English settlers.

Community

MACEDONIA

The Macedonia Cooperative Community was an "intentional" or Utopian community where we spent the years from November 1954 to September 1957. Instead of continuing in graduate school, or taking the first steps in professional careers, for the time being we immersed ourselves in what amounted to a prolonged spiritual retreat. Macedonia showed us that human beings can live together in a manner fundamentally different from the practices of a dog-eat-dog society.

We encountered at Macedonia a group of people who had conscientiously objected to participation in World War II and were now trying to create a positive way of life expressive of their pacifism. All had been raised as Christians, but were earnestly attempting to recognize other faiths. Gandhi's life, and the work of those who came after him in India, were especially honored.

We too came to Macedonia by way of an encounter with the United States military. Staughton decided to apply for unarmed service as a medic within the military (a classification known as 1-A-O). It seemed to him unjust for him to perform civilian public service (pursuant to a 1-O classification) while other young men his age were being killed. To our surprise, his New York City draft board approved his 1-A-O application.

Just after finishing basic training, however, Staughton received an Undesirable Discharge from the United States Army because of his political views. Apparently Senator Joseph McCarthy had discovered an officer at Fort Dix who belonged to the Communist Party. The Army hastened to rid itself of several dozen soldiers who, on the basis of information known

This is a picture of the cabin in which we lived when we moved to the Macedonia Co-operative Community in northeast Georgia in November 1954. We were forty-five min-utes drive, through creeks and over dirt roads much of the way, to the nearest phone. The cabin had electricity and an outhouse but no running water. The floor was tar paper laid over the earth. We had a wood-burning stove and a stone chimney for warmth in winter. When our first child was born in September 1955, we brought her home to this cabin.

to the Army at the time they were inducted, might be discovered by the Senator and portrayed to the world as security risks.

The Adjutant General's allegations against Staughton began:[1] "Derogatory information has been received in this office which reveals ..." One of the allegations was that "you ... [h]ave a mother, Helen, who ... [w]as described as a hyper-modern educator who follows the Communist Party line." Another allegation indicated that Staughton's college essays showed a Marxist influence. It seems that some of his teachers were among the government's informants. There was no way to confront the accusers.

Staughton was discharged in May 1954, almost coincidentally with sur-render of the French army at Dienbienphu, Vietnam. In August we made a two-week visit to the Macedonia Cooperative Community near Clarkesville, Georgia. We returned to Chicago, gave up Alice's job and Staughton's scholarship and arrived at Macedonia on November 1, 1954.

Consensus

The community owned close to a thousand hilly acres. Pine trees grew in a red clay soil. The sky was a piercing blue. Winter nights could be below freezing. Staughton would get up at 5 a.m. for morning milking. He would go for the cows with a wool hat pulled down over one ear to keep warm, but pulled up over the other ear to hear the cow bells. As the cows ambled toward the barn the sun came up over the black rim of the mountains. Everything one could see—hills, pastures, houses, cows—was part of a way of life we were creating together.

The first thing we noticed at Macedonia was how people listened to each other. There might be a meeting in someone's living room. In winter, a fire would be burning. Someone spoke. Then a pause, with the only sound the pop and sizzle of the burning wood. Another observation. Another pause, with little noises as logs burned through and resettled themselves. The speaking was, as Quakers say, "out of the silence."

Decisions were by consensus, not voting. Consensus decision-making, as practiced at Macedonia, or later, in the southern civil rights movement or the Workers' Solidarity Club of Youngstown, is a means of finding truth and of building community. It presumes that no human being is likely to see all aspects of a situation. Each of us is endowed with a conscience, and we need to use this conscience, to listen and be guided by it, to keep our hearts open. At Macedonia we felt that any member of the group might perceive something that the rest of us were missing. We treasured a particular member who often said at the end of a long meeting, "There's something off. Something just doesn't ring true." Whereupon, no matter how few the hours before morning milking, the discussion continued.

Our Students for a Democratic Society (SDS) friend, Richie Rothstein, has said that poor people need a right to vote because consensus decision-making favors big talkers. But he was thinking of projects in which the organizers come from the middle class. We suspect that consensus is the habitual mode of proceeding of poor people all over the world.

Another criticism of consensus heard in the late 1960s was that it was too slow and cumbersome in times of crisis, that decisions would have to be made in a more military, topdown way in truly revolutionary situations. But in the southern civil rights movement, decisions were made by consensus precisely because of the danger: no one wished to press or force another to a conclusion that, when acted on, might cost another's life.

Direct Speaking

We human beings have a talent for destroying the projects we set in motion.

The New Testament speaks of clearing up differences with a brother before going to the altar (Matthew 5:23). At Macedonia, where we were living together, not just going to church, we thought it equally important to straighten things out with someone before a business meeting or on the way to work together at the cow barn. Otherwise, misunderstandings or personal antagonisms could get in the way of intelligent decision-making and lead to unfortunate results. Gossip was forbidden. If something said or done by another person disturbed you, you had to get up the courage—and humility—to speak to that person directly, and not say behind someone's back what you would not say to the person face-to-face.

Group after group with which we've worked has broken up because the people in it couldn't get along together. This includes at least three local trade unions, where rank-and-file movements were elected to office only to split and destroy themselves. It also includes the student movements of the 1960s. Some people say that government repression destroyed the Student Nonviolent Coordinating Committee (SNCC) and SDS. We think repression played a part, but far more important was the sectarian madness that led erstwhile comrades first to demonize antagonists, as in calling policemen "pigs," and then to speak of "icing" and "offing" one another.

The consensus decision-making and direct speaking we did at Macedonia also characterized the early feminist movement in which circles of women slowly developed confidence in themselves and trust in each other.

A Common Purse

At Macedonia, we shared all things. We were poor, but not as poor as neighbors whose children walked to school barefoot in winter. The Macedonia property was owned by the community and when persons became full members they gave everything they owned to the community. Near the kitchen door of the community center was a nail set in a block of wood. Anyone who needed something wrote out what was wanted on a piece of paper and stuck it on the nail. The next person who made a trip to town in one of the communal vehicles purchased the items listed on the slips.

Sharing the struggle for livelihood among several families, rather than each person or couple shouldering the burden alone, lifted a great load of anxiety. There were also economies unavailable to a single household. For instance, the community bought large sacks of the shreds left over when biscuits of shredded wheat were made, sacks of wheat germ, and large cartons of raisins from which families could take food for breakfasts.

In our little community, where economic activity was small-scale and locally managed, common ownership did not stifle initiative. Quite the contrary. The principal source of income was a woodworking shop that made children's play equipment. Successful new products often came into being when parents invented Christmas gifts for their own children. The enterprise just beginning when we were at Macedonia has since grown into a flourishing, multimillion-dollar business called Community Playthings.

The Spirit

We often ended our meetings at Macedonia by standing in a circle on a high pasture, holding hands in the dark, and singing, "Spirit of the Living God, fall afresh on us."

What did we mean by the "spirit"? The community's creed was that there was an essentially similar experience common to all the great religions. We said that different persons might use quite different words to describe this common religious experience. Alice, for example, years later expressed her belief this way:

> During the time of the Old Testament the Jews didn't have a Bible. They learned by their experience and shared their learning with their young. Jesus was a Jew, but he rejected "an eye for an eye and a tooth for a tooth." We too, in our time, are continually confronted with new situations. We can look back to our religious roots, but we also have to listen to that which may be revealed anew in this moment, or learned through Buddhism or other religious traditions.

In dialogue with Christian friends we argued that there was Scriptural authority for such an experiential approach. Saying "Lord, Lord" does not assure salvation, for the righteous will be known by their fruits, not by their words (Matthew 7:20–21). The unbeliever who does good deeds—the Good Samaritan—is preferred to the church member who passes by on the other side (Luke 10:30–37).

At Macedonia, Staughton fashioned his own combination of Christian ethics and Buddhist metaphysics. His fourteen years in the Ethical Culture schools had been entirely about ethics. He never heard the word "God" and was not exposed to the New Testament.

When the Lynds moved to Chicago in the fall of 1952, Staughton did some research for a scholar named Helen Mims. He came across a "mystery play" produced in the city of York, England during the Middle Ages. As he struggled with the difficult text Staughton slowly perceived an astounding message. The dead, the "sheep" and the "goats," were brought before the throne of God to be judged. Whether they went to heaven or hell depended on whether during life on earth they had fed the hungry, clothed the naked, visited those in prison, or tended the sick. As to the sheep:

> For I was an hungred, and ye gave me meat: I was thirsty, and ye gave me
>   drink: I was a stranger, and ye took me in:
> Naked, and ye clothed me: I was sick, and ye visited me: I was in prison,
>   and ye came unto me. (Matthew 25:35–36)

Conversely, the goats would go to hell because they had not performed these works of mercy to God himself.

Both the sheep and the goats protest. We never saw you before in our lives, they exclaim! Oh yes you have, God responds: "Inasmuch as ye have done it unto one of the least of these my brethren, *ye have done it unto me.*" (Matthew 25:40 [emphasis added]; and, to the same effect, Matthew 25:45).

It took Staughton some time to conclude that these words were not created in York, England, during the Middle Ages, but derived from the Gospel of Matthew. Those verses came to mean more and more to him, first at Macedonia, and still more afterwards.

Staughton found in this passage a standard of ethics that he affirms with all his mind and heart, and has tried to practice. But it is otherwise for us both with respect to Christian metaphysics. The virgin birth and the resurrection of the flesh seemed to us then and seem to us now unworthy of belief by a rational mind.

Here again, the time at Macedonia was helpful. Seekers of all descriptions visited our little community. Among them were two young men from the west coast who wore black turtle neck shirts and told stories about the laughing Buddha and the teachings of Alan Watts.

Staughton made his way to the Atlanta library and borrowed the works of Professor Daisetz Suzuki. Therein was Zen Buddhism, story after story of how enlightenment came to this or that person when it was least expected and in paradoxical manner.

So it was with Staughton. One morning he was driving the cows out to pasture after milking. Cows and milkman proceeded single file, first the cows and then the milkman, on a trail by the side of a stream. Staughton walked along thinking heavy thoughts about Dr. Suzuki. Suddenly, instinctively, he stopped in his tracks. There was a newborn calf lying in the trail! Staughton was not a spectator to reality, assessing it with the help of a learned professor. He was inside reality, a part of it, along with the calf and all else in the created world.

When the Planer Fell

About six months after we moved to Macedonia, in the spring of 1955, a beneficiary in the north offered to give the community a heavy-duty planer for our growing woodworking shop. But he asked that someone from the community drive to Michigan to get the planer.

So Dick drove a flatbed truck to Michigan. He returned with the planer very late one night and went to bed, having (as he supposed) left strict instructions that no one was to try to unload it. Early the next morning, while Dick was still sleeping, Ivan ran a heavy chain from the planer over a beam, and drove the truck out from under the planer. The chain broke and the planer fell onto the shop floor, sustaining a major crack.

When Staughton became aware of these events, he appointed himself Chicken Little and ran around our rather spacious layout of homes and other buildings asking, "Did you hear? The planer fell!" His assumption was that the community might come to an end because of this catastrophe.

Gradually he became aware of something unexpected. Nobody else seemed quite as concerned as he. It even appeared that the community was continuing its preparations to celebrate Easter. Finally it was explained to him: "Staughton, we have experienced fire, jaundice, and the departure of valued members. This is a serious setback but by no means the end of our life together. Easter represents new life and new hope, just as it did yesterday."

Sadly, the Macedonian way of celebrating Christmas (enacting the birth of Jesus in our cow barn) or Easter (watching daybreak together from one of the high pastures) came to seem insufficient to our colleagues. Without exception they were from Christian, often fundamentalist backgrounds. As the community grew, serious problems multiplied. Our friends more and more wished to affirm a belief in a personal God to whom they could pray with the confidence that He existed and who could offer guidance and help. We could not make that leap with them.

AFTER MACEDONIA

In September 1957 the full members of Macedonia dissolved the community and merged it with the Society of Brothers or (in German) Bruderhof. Despite the lifetime commitment that we had made, we agreed to free one another from that commitment so that each member might be true to the spirit as best he or she could perceive it. The two of us decided to try life at the Bruderhof before making a final decision.

So one evening late that month Staughton drove the Macedonia truck up the winding carriage road to the Woodcrest Bruderhof, near New Paltz, New York, with the first emigrants from Georgia. Bruderhof children, who had been hiding in the woods along the road for hours, waiting for the truck, sprang out and sang: "Lift your hidden faces, ye who wept and prayed. . . ."

Life at the Woodcrest community was full. This was perhaps especially so for Staughton, who was asked to teach seventh and eighth grades. The class considered the social history of humankind, beginning with hunters and going on to herders. While studying the hunting stage of history, the children got a bearskin from a freezer in the nearby town and made bearskin hats. Years later, on a visit to the community, a young woman who had been Staughton's student came into a room where the Lynds were having breakfast, holding in her arms a baby on whose head rested the bearskin hat that her mother had made!

When the class moved on to the pastoral stage of history, Annie, who came from a Hutterite community out west, showed everyone else how to make wooden spindles. Then, after obtaining a mass of greasy sheep wool from somewhere, she showed the group how to wash the wool and how to "drop" the spindle so as to spin a thread, how to dye the thread, and eventually, how to weave it into a small rug-like fabric. Staughton still has a small rug, made of red and white and black wool, on our bedroom bureau.

But in the case of the Lynds, the inner change that was hoped for at Woodcrest didn't happen. We watched as our Macedonian comrades, with whom we had expected to spend the rest of our lives, one after another confessed to an experience of Jesus. The atmosphere was that of a religious revival. Staughton wondered whether he might just stay on as a happy teacher, without taking part in community gatherings. The answer was, no, and so in November 1957 we left.

Poems

The separation from intentional community was one of our most profound experiences. Alice considers it the most difficult period of her life. Thereafter, despite moments of deep fellowship in civil rights, antiwar, labor, and prison work, we would function in the cold outside world as a couple, a two-person community. Instead of dealing with the "slings and arrows of outrageous fortune" as one family among many, who together faced whatever life might bring, henceforth we were on our own.

Perhaps poetry, even poems of varying quality, can say it better than prose. Here are two poems by Staughton. The first was written in the fullness of life at Macedonia.

Deep-rooted in love
The wet pasture grass, thistle- and clover-matted
The grass stalks at the hill's edge
With the wind mated
And gifts around:
The boy face down on his pillow
Where we sang him to sleep
The baby loudly sucking
Deep-rooted in love.

Deep-rooted in love
The night wind tearing at the leaves
Trees stripped free of their bark
Laid open to the heart, where the grain shows
Its growth rings:
The years of little increase, the rich years
There to be seen
Deep-rooted in love.

Deep-rooted in love
The quiet places of the heart
Alive again
Astonished at the beauty
And joy held in the hand
Deep-rooted in love.

The next poem was written at the Bruderhof and posted by Staughton on a bulletin board near the door into the dining room in the fall of 1957.

The year is dying.
The aged one is ruddy,
Happy in his going,
But I watch with fear
The rain wash clean
The piles of bloody leaves around his bed.

We were led thus far by many solemn signs:
A blaze, a scuffed leaf
Told of foregoers;
Where the trail ended,
We found a dried-up stream
A hint of sky on up the slope.
What we came to was a death.
We did not reach the sun,
But came in time to see him die
Sinking blood-red
Behind the naked trees.

At this death
And through the winterdark
We need a light.
There are many wanderers in the wood
And in fear we may do each other harm.
We see no path ahead:
For us the journey is over
And the waiting begun.

Lord, see thy petitioner:
Wooden arms,
Heavy earthen feet,
Face red with shame;
Scarecrow world, poor man
Waiting for spring.

And Then

Alice was pregnant with our second child. Staughton went to New York City and asked Dorothy Day whether we might join her at the hospitality house of the Catholic Worker. She said that it was not a good place for small children. She recommended that we move to a community in Glen Gardner, New Jersey. Dave and Betty Dellinger were the central figures there.

It was a hard winter. We lived in a converted chicken coop. There was very little money and our diet was skimpy. The community nominally supported itself by printing, but apart from the monthly magazine *Liberation* there was very little work. And the communal spirit that had been the heart and soul of the shared life at Macedonia seemed to us lacking. Alice felt despair lurking in the dark woods. The winter seemed like a twilight zone with the sun not far above the horizon and the shadows long even at noon. She longed for the bright sun, the blue sky, the evergreen trees, and the red clay of Georgia. She dreamed of fire under the ground burning the pastures.

Two-year-old Barbara, our first child, missed community just as we did. As the truck drove north from Macedonia to Woodcrest, she had asked, "Where my house gone?" and worried whether the cows in the high meadow would go into the house.

Alice concluded that she wanted to return to the Woodcrest Bruderhof. Having actually shared the life of the Bruderhof for two months the previous fall, Staughton was even more resistant than he had been at Macedonia.

So we made a decision that each of us should follow his or her best light, even though this would cause us to be physically separated for an undetermined length of time. Our parents and friends opposed this decision. The Bruderhof had been known to sanction the separation of couples when one spouse was drawn to "the life," and the other not. Those who loved us thought that the decision to separate might break up our marriage.

Alice and Barbara returned to Woodcrest in March 1958, and in May 1958 our baby son, Lee, was born. Staughton moved to New York City where he was employed as a community worker by the University Settlement House on the Lower East Side.

It was a strange time. Alice struggled to be a part of the religious life at Woodcrest. Staughton had certain memorable experiences: the editorial meetings of *Liberation* magazine, where Dave Dellinger, A. J. Muste, and Bayard Rustin told of their most recent adventures; participation in creating an "alternative plan" for development of the Cooper Square neighborhood, just south of historic Cooper Union; hearing Pete Seeger sing a song entitled "We Shall Overcome." Inwardly Staughton determined to find a movement that sang that song. But these political happenings took place in the context of a personal life that was, for the moment, hollow and adrift.

In September 1958, when visiting together at Woodcrest, we two made an even more apparently outrageous decision. Alice said she wished to ask for "the novitiate," a stage of provisional membership previous to becoming a lifetime Bruderhof member. Staughton encouraged her to do so, and then hitchhiked across the United States to visit his best friend, Lee Hosford, for whom our Lee was named. Lee Hosford was in San Quentin prison.

Many years later Alice had further insight into her desire to be at Woodcrest. One day she heard Staughton singing some Bruderhof songs. Alice was reminded of a song by an early member of the Bruderhof, Philip Britts, and the calendar of Britts's songs and poems that a Bruderhof woman made for her birthday in 1958. She realized that Philip Britts's song, calling on people to "withhold no more" and to "come to a city on a hill" was very much a part of her consciousness then. It finally occurred to her that this corresponded to Staughton's desire for society to change and to be better. She thought that was why she asked for the novitiate at Woodcrest in September 1958: to find out whether the Bruderhof was a better way of living. She had not been turning in a different direction from Staughton. She was looking for what he wanted, too.

Neither of us remembers much about what happened in the months after our conversation in September 1958. Almost as if forgetting the trauma of an automobile accident, we recall outcomes more than the inwardness of events. In December the Woodcrest community asked Alice and our two small children to leave. Ramón Sender, who was present at the meeting, tells us that the spiritual leader of the community used the words: "We will not split this marriage." "Will not," of course, might mean "should not" but also might signify, "that marriage is unbreakable." In 2005, we asked our Macedonian colleagues who were still alive and at Woodcrest if they remembered the meeting or the decision. They did not.

Barbara and Lee came to live with Staughton a block from Staughton's parents. Alice went first to a Quaker mental hospital near Philadelphia, then to the home of a family in that city. In college, when she learned that her best friend had committed suicide, she felt she had to continue living for both of them. Even that feeling fell away. She recalls not wanting the spring to come, as if it would mock her.

Alice read some passages in a book about "the dark night of the soul." On subway trains, she saw ads by a Catholic organization. She knew that Betty Dellinger had become a Catholic and Alice wished she too could believe. The only thing Alice knew to be true was that she was a wife and a mother. That starting point became clear.

We were both helped by a Quaker and Jungian therapist, Martha Jaeger, for whom we later named our third child. Martha Jaeger said that if you had a cut, your obligation was to keep it clean. Life itself could be trusted to take care of the healing.

After a few months, Alice returned to Staughton and our children in New York City. As so often in our hard times, she got a job as a secretary. One of Staughton's fellow dischargees from the Army had brought a class action, and the courts ruled that the entire group must be given honorable discharges. Staughton received G.I. benefits and was able to go back to graduate school, this time in history.

Healing

During the period between the end of 1958, when Alice left the Bruderhof, and August 1961 when we moved south again and settled at Spelman College, we began to pick up the pieces and to heal. A change in emotional atmosphere can be seen in Staughton's poetry.

Deep-rooted in love: New Year's Eve, 1957

The earth that held the roots is broken now,
The flowers were broken by the plow.
And seeds go wandering in the air.
The new-born calf, the firelight and the frost
Have nowhere left to go
And linger there.

Nothing is lost:
The visionary sap has left the leaves

And run back to the roots
To find the food it needs;
Hands, earth, blood, books
Are waiting to be blessed
With life, and made again
Into a miracle.

And so I take my rest,
And listen for the rain
The silence of the growing grass
The thunder of the gods.

Healing required stability. The next poem is set in Central Park of New York City, but its last lines recall evenings in New Hampshire where Staughton's family spent summers when he was a boy.

Summer 1959

Here, on this asphalt and cement,
Summer will cast, like shells of seeds, its days,
And hide no muffled terror in the haze
But crown a childhood with a green content.
Now, like a falling leaf, the heart
Circles in summer spirals to its ground,
And what was lost forever, now is found,
What was cut off, becomes again a part.
Stroking the rough bark with its hot embrace
The sun draws out the marrow flowering from the bone,
Burns through all skins and shelters with its grace
Lifts up the heart, and leads it home.
And I remember why all evening long
The leaves hung still
And fireflies held up candles for the whitethroat's song.

Healing also required a renewed willingness to go forth, to make oneself vulnerable to pain and loss, as flowers do each springtime. The following poem borrowed from warfare in the period of the American Revolution which Staughton was then studying.

Spring 1960

Now is the advent of a raw and early Spring,
Which, lest the warmth come in too glad and sure,
Tries how much more can frozen earth endure,
Lets Winter's darkness go, but not yet Winter's sting.
As the mud loosens, frozen axles turn,
Armies go forth again to dare and die,

March courts engagements that November spurned,
The ranks press forward, though they know not where or why.
What does it matter if the sap is blind?
If ten shoots die for every happy flower?
If all that's green and growing serves a power
Which will cast this Spring, too, behind?
What does it matter
When against the shield of frozen sod
Spring sends its arméd legions of forget-me-nots?

Return (by Alice)

We returned twice to Macedonia. Once was soon after we moved to Atlanta in 1961. The new woodshop and dairy were in disrepair. A patch of four-leaf clovers was still there.

In February 1991, we spent a vacation at the Jubilee Partners community in Comer, Georgia. Folks there wanted to go and see where the Macedonia community had been. We went by bus. What used to be a forty-five-minute drive from the town nearest to Macedonia, along dirt roads, over precarious wooden bridges, fording streams, was now on a paved road. I sobbed deeply.

I carried someone's baby in my arms as we walked over the fields from one familiar place to another. One of the homes had burned to the ground. Another home, where we used to have community meetings and where one could look up at the beautiful knotted pine, was being used as a cow barn. The log cabin in which we lived when Barbara was a baby had a paved road right behind it and a sign beside the door saying "Daniel Boone's cabin." The four-leaf clover patch was gone.

We went to an area where I recalled that daffodils grew wild in the woods. They were blooming. We dug some up and took them back to Jubilee Partners. We planted most of them in the cemetery where Georgia's indigent death row prisoners are buried and where we have asked that our ashes be buried when the time comes.

I returned to where the bus was parked before others did. I sat on a bank beside the road. I watched as families wound their way along a path below. And I thought, What if we had stayed here? What kind of a life would it have been? What have we done that we would have missed? I did not regret the many twists and turns our lives had taken since we left. It was more of a life than staying in that protected community. We carried the heart of Macedonia within us. Finally, I was able to let go of Macedonia!

A Dream (by Staughton)

Much earlier, in the early 1960s, I experienced something similar. While we were at Macedonia, a family's picnic fire in the woods had gotten out of control and neighbors from miles around had assembled to help us fight a serious conflagration. I dreamed that, along with others, I was fighting a forest fire. The work was arduous. It appeared to go on forever. Then came a moment when, suddenly, it seemed that we could rest from our labors. Why, I wondered? The pause continued. Why were we able to stop our frantic shoveling and digging?

All at once I realized: it was raining.

We were not contending for the Good in the universe all by ourselves. Great natural forces were also at work, helping us. We were not alone.

STARFISH, *ALICE LYND*

One summer when Barbara and Lee were little, we took them to visit Staughton's parents in Maine. The children found two starfish and kept them in a bucket of water. After several days, the starfish were languishing. I told the children we would have to take the starfish back to the ocean and let them go. We went out onto a pier and dumped the starfish back into the water below.

The two starfish landed on their backs. I watched. Gradually, one of them managed, little-by-little, to muster the strength to turn itself over. And then, to my utter amazement, the first starfish wedged its tentacles under the second starfish until it also turned over! If starfish can do that for one another, what about human beings?

NOTE

1. Subject: Allegations, To: Private Staughton C. Lynd, US 55 435 330, 2131st ASU, Medical Replacement Training Center, Camp Pickett, Virginia, 18 February 1954.

On the twentieth anniversary of the atomic bombing of Hiroshima and Nagasaki, several hundred persons assembled in Washington, D.C., to register opposition to the rapidly escalating Vietnam War. On Monday, August 9, 1965, "Nagasaki Day," we attempted to walk from the Washington Monument, along the mall, and up the grassy slope to the steps of the Capitol. There we hoped to declare peace with the people of Vietnam. The three men shown in the photograph—from left to right, David Dellinger, Staughton, and Bob Moses—led the way. As we proceeded, counterdemonstrators threw red paint on us. What you see on our shirts is paint, not blood.

The Sixties

COOPER SQUARE, *STAUGHTON LYND*

All beginnings are difficult, says a Chinese proverb. Certainly my first steps in what Alice and I later called "accompaniment" were halting and uncertain.

When Alice decided to return to the Bruderhof, I opted for a job that would bring me into contact with poor people in New York City. A man named Charles Cook had been my seventh grade teacher. In 1958 he was "head worker" at the University Settlement House on New York City's Lower East Side. Mr. Cook hired me to be a "community worker."

University Settlement, begun in 1886, is the oldest settlement house in the United States. The settlement house movement started in Great Britain. Middle-class individuals would move to a slum neighborhood and live there, offering services, instruction, and supportive advocacy to neighborhood residents. In the United States, one of the earliest and certainly the most famous settlement house was Hull House in Chicago, founded by Jane Addams, where Alice lived when I was in the army.

Charles Bunstein Stover, the founder of University Settlement House, was a divinity student who discovered that his true calling was public service. Living at the settlement house, he successfully lobbied for city ownership of the new subway system. He helped to create the first playgrounds on the Lower East Side and was eventually named as Manhattan Parks Commissioner. Charles Stover fought for improved sanitation and street cleaning, organized public exhibits of art from major museums, and advocated for the rights of workers.[1] In later years, Mr. Stover turned his attention to the University Settlement's camp in Beacon, New York, where

I worked as a counselor in the summer of 1958 and where I first heard the song "We Shall Overcome," sung by Pete Seeger.

I had no training or experience in community organization. At no point during the time that I spent on the job did I live in the neighborhood. That I was able to contribute anything was thanks to two years (1951–1953) previously spent at the Harvard School of Design and the University of Chicago studying city and regional planning.

A woman named Frances Goldin, who would become a close friend, ran a tenants' clinic at the settlement house. Through Frances, I became aware that city planner Robert Moses wanted to tear down twelve city blocks from Delancey Street to East 9th Street and from Second Avenue to the Bowery, and start anew. Because it included Cooper Union, where Lincoln had spoken before the Civil War, the neighborhood was known as "Cooper Square."

Cooper Square was a low-income area. Almost half the tenants were living on less than $60 per week and almost half had been living in Cooper Square for fifteen years or more. On one sample block about a third of the site tenants spoke Spanish. Only 7 percent of the site tenants could have afforded the gentrified housing proposed by the city: the re-mainder were to be "relocated," that is, scattered to the four winds and lost from public view.[2]

Mr. Cook favored the Cooper Square project because it would expose low-income families to middle-class life styles. Frances Goldin and I op-posed Moses's plan. Through Frances, I met a number of Italian immi-grants who had lived in the area for many years, as well as Puerto Ricans who had moved in more recently. One of the newer Puerto Rican resi-dents was Radames Tirado. I recall a meeting I helped to organize of ten-ants in the building where Mr. Tirado lived. The purpose of the meeting was to present grievances to their landlord. "Be reasonable," the landlord said at one point. "Mister," replied Radames Tirado. "You are standing on my foot. Get off my foot and then I can be reasonable."

The Cooper Square site tenants agreed that their housing needed phys-ical improvement. They objected to being displaced, and they wanted to find a way to stay in the neighborhood while it was being renewed, and afterwards. They also opposed tearing down buildings of significance to the community like the Church of All Nations.

I went down to City Hall seeking the help of professional city planners. I found two men willing to assist residents in finding a way to preserve and rehabilitate the area.[3] The plan, as developed by Walter Thabit and Alan Shapiro in collaboration with site tenants, rejected bulldozing. In-stead it proposed to preserve those buildings that could be readily reno-vated, enabling people to stay in their homes.

As I used to explain it, instead of a single mega-site we imagined a collection of mini-sites. On those blocks where population was least dense, such as a parking lot or a warehouse, we might create new housing into which neighbors could move while their own mini-site was being rebuilt. In this way the physical renovation desired by all could happen without ejecting the people or destroying needed neighborhood institutions.

The most remarkable happening was not the creation of the Alternate Plan, but the fact that people fought for it for over thirty years and won! In June 1993, I got a letter from David McReynolds, whom I had first known as office manager for *Liberation* magazine and later as organizer for the War Resisters League.

It turned out that David had lived on East 4th Street, within the Cooper Square neighborhood, since the late 1950s. McReynolds wrote that the original Alternate Plan would have caused him to relocate because he "made too much for the low income apartments." There were violent arguments among the multiethnic site tenants about the justice of the plan. Eventually it was agreed that 15 or 20 buildings on the site would be repaired with city funds "and then placed into a Mutual Housing Association, in which the tenants have a voice and responsibilities. Rents would go up to about $350 a month, which is still far below market." David concluded: "People *are able to make up their own minds. The poor are competent*" (his emphasis).

As to David's own residence, "They decided they could reconstruct the building in two stages—starting with the back half, after which those who had been moved out would move back in, and they would rip out the front half and finish the work." During renovation, David was asked to move just down the hall from Apartment 11 to Apartment 13 in the same building. After moving back, "I have a wonderful studio apartment, clean paint, level floors, new stove and refrigerator, and most of all, a real bathroom," replacing "the small bathtub in the kitchen" with which he had lived for thirty years. In the past, the toaster had always blown the fuse, and if David planned to vacuum he first unplugged the refrigerator. Now he has new wiring.[4]

Achievement of the Cooper Square Alternate Plan was crowned by the opening of the Houston Street Center, in cooperation with the Chinatown YMCA acting on behalf of the newest immigrants to the neighborhood. The Center, it was said, would provide not only the traditional free or low cost athletic programs but also "program and office space to longtime residents and local non-profits."[5]

What the Alternate Plan accomplished was remarkable. Of 1,422 housing units built or renovated throughout Cooper Square, 888 or 64 percent were low-income. This was the highest rate of low-income housing on any urban renewal site in the United States. The new housing included the country's first homeless co-ops. Over time, "nearly 400 apartments were renovated with full modern conveniences for low-income residents."[6]

The essential components of the Cooper Square Alternate Plan were two: a step-by-step plan of development that preserved important existing elements, especially people; and a strong public role. These were precisely the features of the "worker-community ownership" that, in the late 1970s and 1980s, many of us would advocate in Youngstown and Pittsburgh as an approach to saving existing steel mills. (See the chapter below called "We Become Lawyers.")

WE SHALL OVERCOME, *STAUGHTON LYND*

Looking back, there were signposts on the way to civil rights work in the south.

When the Lynds were living in Chicago in 1952–1954, a coworker of Gandhi named Ashadevi Aryanayakam spoke at the University of Chicago. The audience was very small and I had the opportunity to tell her that Alice and I were wondering about going to live in an ashram in India. She said that she thought Gandhi would wish us, instead, to find a way to help the "untouchables" of our own country.

In 1955–1956, while we were living in northeast Georgia at the Macedonia Cooperative Community, the bus boycott began in Montgomery, Alabama. A member of our group visited Montgomery to ask how we could provide support. It was suggested that Macedonia offer rest and relaxation to hard-pressed participants in the boycott effort. Mrs. Aurelia Browder and her young daughter arrived soon after.

When it came time for Mrs. Browder to return to Montgomery, I drove her there. We reached her home in the late afternoon. Unthinking of how it might seem to others for a white man to spend the night at the house of an African-American woman, I took it for granted that I would stay at Mrs. Browder's before starting back to Georgia. As my expectation became clear to her, she seemed to draw herself together and said words to the effect, "Yes, I think that is what we should do." And we did. We talked into the evening beside a low fire in Mrs. Browder's living room.

A third signpost presented itself in the summer of 1960. I was halfway through graduate courses in history at Columbia University, and within a few months would need to find a teaching job. The Lynds—Alice, myself, and our two children at that time, Barbara and Lee—went for a picnic in Central Park with an African-American kindergarten classmate of Barbara's and his mother, Mary Murphy. Ms. Murphy told me, "You should teach at a Negro college [as they were then known]. They are always looking for teachers with degrees."

My Master's essay had won a prize and my teachers at Columbia had plans for me at one or another Ivy League university. I told them I was interested only in Negro colleges and asked them to write letters of reference to institutions they had never heard of in the deep south. At the American Historical Association meeting in New York City that December, I attended the Columbia University "smoker" in search of a job offer. About midnight there came across the floor in my direction a tall, skinny, dark-haired man, a few years older than myself, with such an offer in hand. It was Howard Zinn, chairperson of social sciences at a college for African-American women in Atlanta. Late in August 1961, the Lynds arrived at Spelman College.

Atlanta

I taught history at Spelman until June 1964. It was a time of endless discoveries. Late one evening I was reading blue books. A particular examination struck me as well above average in content but extraordinary—off the charts—in the way it was written. I stepped around the corner to the Zinns's apartment (both they and we lived on the Spelman campus) and asked Howard if he had a student named Alice Walker. "Yes!" he exclaimed. "And she has just written an incredible essay on Tolstoy and Dostoevsky!" Howard and I consider ourselves the codiscoverers of the future author of *The Color Purple*.

Other stories linger in the mind about the years at Spelman. In the middle of one night there came a call from an acquaintance. He said that Morris Eisenstein, who taught social work at Atlanta University, his wife Fannie, and two of their daughters aged about eight and twelve, had been arrested. Morris and Fannie were being held at the City Jail. The girls, however, were at an institution for juvenile offenders on the edge of town. Could I please get them out?

As I later learned, the Eisenstein family had been driving downtown the day before. In those years there was almost continuous picketing of segregated downtown enterprises such as department stores. The girls gave their parents a hard time. In the manner of youth everywhere in the 1960s, they said that their parents talked a good game but when would they walk their talk and put their bodies where their mouths were? Finally Morris exclaimed, "All right, all right. Once around the block." He parked, the Eisensteins joined a picket line, and they were all arrested.

When I arrived at the youth facility I was allowed to talk with the girls, who seemed to be all right, but was told that they would be released only to their parents. So I journeyed to the City Jail.

At the jail, the men were on one floor, the women on the floor above. I talked first with Morris. He said, "I am not leaving here until everyone leaves. I think the girls will understand. Moreover, I think the authorities are bluffing. But go see what Fannie thinks." I took the elevator up one floor. Careful to present the situation in neutral terms, and without disclosing what Morris had said, I questioned Fannie. She responded, "I am not leaving here until everyone leaves. I think the girls will understand. Moreover, I think the authorities are bluffing."

I returned to the juvenile facility. Sure enough, the authorities were bluffing. They released the girls, who stayed at our home until their parents got out of jail at the end of the week.

Another memory concerns the Cuban missile crisis in the fall of 1962. In the spring of 1961, the United States had sponsored an invasion of Cuba by Cuban exiles at the Bay of Pigs. In response, the Soviet Union stationed missile launchers in Cuba with the capability of reaching targets in the United States. U.S. intelligence operations detected the presence of the missiles. The two countries came very, very close to a nuclear war.

As tension mounted, the Mayor of Atlanta wired President Kennedy that Atlantans stood behind him "as one man" in threatening military action. That could not be permitted to pass. The United States and the Soviet Union appeared to have good reason to fear aggression from each other, but nuclear war would have been an unspeakable catastrophe. So the office staff of the Student Nonviolent Coordinating Committee (SNCC), together with sympathizers at Atlanta University, put up a picket line in downtown Atlanta opposing military action against the Soviet Union or Cuba.

I picketed next to a white English teacher named Esta Seaton. The caption under a photograph that appeared in the next day's newspaper identified us as Mr. and Mrs. Lynd. At the time Alice was teaching in a day care center. The director was a former military officer. He questioned Alice. She explained that it was not she in the photograph, that she had intended to be there but, because of the cold, had taken our daughter Barbara (who attended the day care center) home on the bus. However, Alice added, "If I could have been there, I would have." She was forced out of her job.

As that picket line was coming to an end, I was introduced to a young black man named John O'Neal. It was explained to me that he had dropped out of Southern Illinois University in Cairo, Illinois, to work full-time with SNCC. He would be getting his field assignment at SNCC headquarters a few blocks from the Spelman College campus. Could he stay with the Lynds overnight? Of course I said, yes. (John's first words to me were, "Where can I go to the bathroom?" Since downtown Atlanta was still segregated, I proposed that we return to Spelman as quickly as possible.)

SNCC being SNCC, by which I mean, the Movement being the Movement, it took John something like a week to get his assignment and in the interim we got to know him well. A year later, in the fall of 1963, it was John who called from Mississippi to ask me if I would coordinate the "Freedom Schools" in the 1964 Mississippi Summer Project. Thus I came to be offered the task that turned out to be my major contribution to the southern civil rights movement.

SNCC had begun to organize in Mississippi in 1961. Older African-Americans, who were often veterans of World War II and the Korean War, advised SNCC staff workers like Bob Moses that they wanted help in obtaining the right to vote. The vote, with its promise of full citizenship, was a higher priority for them than access to segregated lunch counters and other public facilities.

SNCC's initial efforts to help black Mississippians to obtain the vote were not successful. Very few African-Americans succeeded in registering during the years 1961, 1962, and 1963. Indeed in McComb, Mississippi, a hotbed of racism in the southwestern part of the state, organizers like Moses were jailed and protesting students were expelled from school. But it was a local resident named Herbert Lee, and later, a witness to Lee's murder named Lewis Allen, who were killed.

In 1962 and 1963, SNCC relocated its efforts to the Mississippi Delta in northwest Mississippi. Here SNCC staff workers discovered magnificent local organizers such as Fannie Lou Hamer. Mrs. Hamer was dispossessed, arrested, and brutally beaten in her efforts to obtain Freedom Now. She had a majestic voice with which she led Freedom Songs including her favorite, "This Little Light of Mine."

The 1964 Summer Project was an attempt to find a new voter registration strategy. It was suggested that if white students from the north came to Mississippi in large numbers to help with voter registration, Mississippi segregationists might find it difficult to jail, beat, and kill these well-connected volunteers. There was a downside to the idea that was well understood. African-Americans in Mississippi, although not yet successful in obtaining the vote, were beginning to find the confidence to speak up in public and to engage in direct action. If fast-speaking students from the north were to flood the state, would that not prove inhibiting for black residents who might consider their abilities inferior? After prolonged indecision, and only by a slim margin, SNCC decided to take the risk and support the Summer Project.

The Freedom Schools, which I coordinated, were a secondary part of the Summer Project. Segregated public schools for black children in Mississippi were abysmal. And so Charlie Cobb, a SNCC staff person, suggested

..........ry summer programs for African-American teenagers in which young people could for a few weeks experience some of the education they had been denied, especially African-American history. Although the ideas of Brazilian educator Paolo Freire were not yet well known, the Freedom Schools sought to create what Freire later called a "pedagogy of the oppressed": education that would be based on experience, in which the student would help to define and create what he or she needed to know, as opposed to a pedagogy in which a preconceived curriculum was imbedded in the student's mind as a liquid might be poured into an empty vessel.

Even in those times, it seemed a little odd that a white man would co-ordinate a program for black teenagers. So I turned to Harold Bardonille, an African-American veteran of the Orangeburg, South Carolina sit-ins, with whom I often played tennis. I asked him if he would like to be co-coordinator of Freedom Schools. Harold said he would take a bus to Mississippi and check out the scene. When he returned, he said we were all out of our minds. "People are going to get killed there this summer," he correctly predicted.

Freedom Summer

Just before the Summer Project was to begin, there was a two-day meeting of SNCC staff at Atlanta University. I attended only on the second day. The meeting was a somber one. People talked about the likelihood that there would indeed be deaths.

At the end of the meeting, we stood in a circle, held hands, and sang "We Shall Overcome." We sang all the verses that we knew or could make up. Then something I had not experienced before, and would never experience again, occurred. We hummed the tune, over and over, while John Lewis, then SNCC chairperson (and later U.S. Congressman from Georgia), spoke over the humming. He told about the time three years before when Freedom Riders sought to integrate interstate bus travel by riding buses into the deep south, black and white together. When the buses reached Alabama there was terrible violence. The organizations sponsoring the Freedom Ride decided to call it off. They thought that the point had been made and that to press on into Mississippi would be too dangerous.

John Lewis was then a student in Nashville, as were James Bevel, Diane Nash, and Bernard Lafayette. John and his friends felt that the ride should be continued into Mississippi, as originally planned. They took a bus to Birmingham where they were promptly arrested by Police Chief Bull Connor and driven to the Alabama-Tennessee state line. There they were left by the side of the road, in Klan country, in the middle of the night.

"We didn't know what to do," John said as we hummed. Any strategy that had existed was in shambles. The would-be Freedom Riders had no transportation and no money. If they somehow returned to Alabama, they would presumably again be arrested. "The only thing we knew," John said, "was that we should start back toward Birmingham."

At the orientation session for Freedom Summer volunteers at Oxford, Ohio, voter registration workers came the first week. Freedom School teachers arrived on Saturday for the second week of orientation. I drove the Lynds's Rambler from Atlanta together with three African-American students—Barbara Walker, Barbara Simon, and Gwen Robinson—who were summer volunteers like myself. The trunk was packed with copies of the Freedom School curriculum. Alice and I had reproduced it from purple ditto masters on the hectograph in our apartment at the Spelman College campus.

On Monday morning we learned that James Chaney, Andrew Goodman, and Mickey Schwerner were missing. The next few days were filled with long-distance telephone calls from Oxford, Ohio, to Movement offices in Mississippi and to government offices in Washington, D.C., and by volunteers to their parents. The question hung in the air: If, as was assumed, the three young men were dead, would other student volunteers go to Mississippi or would they go home?

One evening we all came together and Bob Moses, director of the Summer Project, spoke to the group. As he spoke, he often looked at his feet. He talked about a book that I had never read or heard about:

> He said that being a leader was like being Frodo in the Lord of the Rings trilogy. . . . A leader became attracted to power in the same way that Frodo, in the end, found it hard to give up the Ring of Power. Nevertheless, Bob went on, speaking very quietly and slowly with long pauses between the words, he felt that we should continue the Summer Project.[7]

He ended by saying that if we decided to go to Mississippi, the one thing he could promise was that he would be going with us.

Soon after arriving in Mississippi, I found myself in a pickup truck driving from Holly Springs in northern Mississippi to Memphis with SNCC staff member Ivanhoe Donaldson. Dusk fell. We were completely lost. It was only a few days after the disappearance of the three young men, and sitting in the passenger seat, I became more and more tense. Ivanhoe finally turned to me and said, "Staughton, where's your sense of adventure?"

The Freedom Schools

The Freedom Schools were improvised summer high schools that usually met in church basements. They were hugely successful.

Depending on how you counted Freedom Schools in Hattiesburg, which had a system of Freedom Schools, over forty schools were created. In the nature of a wholly voluntary program, attendance is also somewhat incalculable. A figure often cited is two thousand students, all African-American and almost all teenagers.

At Oxford, the main business of the week was forming school staffs. I designated certain individuals, often persons with some teaching experience, as "principals." Thus, for example, Liz Fusco became Freedom School coordinator in Ruleville and Wally Roberts in nearby Shaw.

That week also helped to define my own role. Tom Wahman asked me if he could be assigned to Jackson since his wife was to be part of the cast of Martin Duberman's *In White America* and the play would be rehearsed in Jackson before going "on the road." We arranged that he would report to Summer Project headquarters in Jackson every day, sit at a Freedom Schools desk, and answer the phone. This understanding freed me to spend the summer driving around Mississippi, visiting the schools.

The Freedom Schools were necessarily decentralized. A Freedom School teacher (usually Caucasian) would get out of a car or off a bus in the community to which he or she (usually she) had been assigned. There would be a courageous black family, previously located by SNCC staff, prepared to give the teacher food and lodging. A great deal of that summer's learning took place in the homes of those African-American hosts. How were hosts and guests to address one another? Would the adults of the host household sit at meals with their lodgers?

Although a site for the Freedom School had usually also been decided in advance, there could be last-minute problems, as in Philadelphia, where the church was burned to the ground, or Carthage, where the white community challenged the lease of the property on which the building designated for a school was located.

When teachers and students came together for classes, improvisation was the order of the day. The Freedom School curriculum, laboriously prepared in advance, functioned as a backup or security blanket when a school ran out of its own ideas. Completely unanticipated classes in French and typing were reportedly popular. Also widespread were the writing of poems and newspapers, and the performance of plays.

One of my trips was prompted by serious conflict among white and black volunteers. On another occasion, at the request of the school coordinator, I traveled to a place where the Freedom School was having difficulty getting started. The solution turned out to be to do voter registration work each afternoon. That made historical material about the years after the Civil War when Mississippi had black state representatives seem suddenly relevant.

I arrived in McComb, in southwestern Mississippi, just after the so-called Freedom House where civil rights workers were housed had been bombed. We sat on the grass on the lawn outside the damaged structure in the dark. We sang "I'm on My Way to the Freedom Land" and Bob Moses suggested the verse, "If you can't go, let your children go."

At least once I made a trip to schools all over the state—Gulfport, Holly Springs—with a young man named Andy Rust who showed movies. And I made sure to arrive in Holly Springs in time to see a play they had prepared there.

I was stopped twice by the police. Once was leaving Jackson, on the way to McComb. The officers contented themselves with commenting on the color of my pants. The second time was driving the wrong way down a one-way street in Meridian with a Spelman student beside me in the front seat. Again we were not detained.

Sandra Adickes was a professional teacher from New York City who, together with the late Norma Becker, arranged for many members of the American Federation of Teachers to be Freedom School teachers, and herself taught in Hattiesburg. According to Sandra it was I who suggested a "Freedom School convention." I have only a visual memory of a meeting in Jackson to which I had invited the coordinators of the Freedom Schools. It was at that meeting that we made the decision to have a convention. The idea was that each school would send two or three delegates to a gathering where they would discuss their collective future.

They came together in Meridian at the end of the first week in August. That week the statewide Freedom Democratic Party had held its convention in Jackson and the bodies of the three young men murdered in nearby Philadelphia were found. On Friday, Movement people made their way in a convoy of cars from Jackson to Meridian, stopping on the way for an informal memorial service in Philadelphia. James, Andrew, and Mickey had been killed when the Mt. Zion Church in Philadelphia, intended (after a long discussion by the deacons) for use as a Freedom School, was burned to the ground, and the three young men had driven to Philadelphia to look for another site for the school. The service in Philadelphia was at the site of the burned church.

In my mind's eye the ground on which we stood sloped toward a corner of the church lot where, under trees, Bob Moses stood and spoke. He emphasized that the bodies of the young men were discovered almost simultaneously with Congressional passage of a resolution concerning the so-called Tonkin Bay incident. This was the event at least partially fabricated by the Johnson administration to justify future escalation of the Vietnam War. I was unaware of it until Bob spoke about it. There was a connection between these two events, Bob said. Dark-skinned people were being killed both in Mississippi and Vietnam.[8]

It was dangerous for the young African-American delegates to the Freedom School convention to travel around Mississippi by themselves. They did it. I have another picture in my mind of that Friday evening, as dignified young black men, dressed in dark suits, walked silently along the Meridian sidewalks to a second, more formal memorial occasion for the three who had died. This was the gathering at which Dave Dennis made the angry remarks memorialized in the documentary series, *Eyes on the Prize*.

The Freedom School convention met in a large, ramshackle building on the outskirts of Meridian, which I believe had once been a seminary.

At the convention there were many workshops, which reported to the delegates as a body and offered resolutions for approval. The resolutions thus approved were collected in a mimeographed document, "1964 Platform of the Mississippi Freedom School Convention."[9] The sophistication and degree of detail in these resolutions is remarkable. They concerned Public Accommodations, Housing, Education, Health, Foreign Affairs, Federal Aid, Job Discrimination, the Plantation System, Civil Liberties, Law Enforcement, City Improvements, Voting, and Direct Action.

Apartheid in South Africa was condemned but it was felt that a resolution on Cuba would be too controversial. In a major decision, the group concluded that it would not be possible to turn the Freedom Schools into a permanent alternative school system, so they would have to return to their segregated and grossly underfunded public schools.

What was the legacy of the Freedom Schools? I am convinced that the vigorous Mississippi version of the preschool Headstart program met in the same church basements, and recruited teachers from the same group of brave African-American women who had opened up their homes to volunteer teachers in the summer of 1964. Professor Dittmer of Tougaloo College near Jackson has stated that he could always tell which of his students had been in the Freedom Schools: they thought for themselves, they asked questions. And I shall never forget returning to Jackson that Sunday evening, side by side with Bob Moses in a back seat. He had spoken briefly at the Freedom School convention, characteristically confining himself to asking questions. He said little on the way back to the state capital but his face was aglow.

A Forgotten Disagreement[10]

After the discovery of the bodies early in August 1964 came the national Democratic Party Convention in Atlantic City later that month.

The voter registration part of the Summer Project was an effort to send Mississippi Freedom Democratic Party (MFDP) delegates to the Democratic Party Convention in the hope that they might be seated in place of the so-called regular delegates from the all-white Mississippi Democratic Party.

I first heard of the idea of going to Atlantic City from Jack Minnis, SNCC research director, late in 1963. Jack and I collaborated that winter in publishing one of the first critiques of the official, single-shooter version of President Kennedy's assassination.

I ran into Jack on a red brick sidewalk between the Spelman College campus and the SNCC office. He had apparently just come from a discussion of going to Atlantic City. He was excited about it. He imagined Dr. King addressing the delegates. It is crystal clear to me in memory that Jack Minnis did not expect the MFDP delegates to be seated, and that he thought of going to Atlantic City not as a strategy, but as a magnificent tactic.

Yet a strategy was implicit in the tactic. In the spring of 1964, Bob Moses and legendary SNCC adviser Ella Baker went to the national convention of the United Automobile Workers (UAW) and arranged for UAW attorney Joseph Rauh to represent the MFDP at Atlantic City. It must have seemed a logical move at the time. Rauh was an influential Democrat. The National Lawyers Guild attorneys who were doing the day-to-day legal work in Mississippi were *persona non grata* to many persons in the national Democratic Party because the Guild was alleged to be influenced by Communists. No one imagined that a conflict could arise between the UAW, which had contributed heavily to the 1963 March for Jobs and Freedom, and the MFDP. As late as August 6, a summer volunteer wrote home "from the floor of the State Convention of the Mississippi Freedom Democratic Party":

> Attorney Joseph Rauh . . . addressed the group. Mr. Rauh is also Walter Reuther's attorney and his appearance indicated the support of Mr. Reuther who is, of course, one of the powers of the Democratic Party.[11]

But just as there had been controversy within SNCC as to whether to invite hundreds of white volunteers to Mississippi, so there was a less-well-known controversy within SNCC as to whether the Atlantic City strategy was a good idea. On the eve of the 1964 Summer Project, SNCC staff had expressed their deep uneasiness with the idea of seeking to be seated at Atlantic City. The following are extracts from the minutes of the SNCC staff meeting on June 9–11, 1964.[12]

Ruby Doris Smith opened a discussion on goals with the words: "We could begin with discussion of whether we're working to make basic changes within existing political and economic structure. . . . What would the seating of the delegation mean besides having Negroes in the National Democratic Party?" Here were some of the responses as noted at the time:

IVANHOE DONALDSON. Disagrees with just making more Democrats and more Republicans. Perhaps the way is to create a parallel structure. . . . Our problem is that our programs don't change . . . basic factors of exploitation. Perhaps it's better to create a third stream. . . . [W]hat is the point of working within the Democratic Party? It is not a radical tool.

CHARLIE COBB. Feels there would be negligible value in merely being part of the Democratic Party structure. . . . There is a danger of Negroes being manipulated by the national parties. . . . It is bad if you make people part of a decadent structure.

JOHN LEWIS. He is not sure that we can get what we want within "liberal politics." . . . The basic things we want to achieve are equality for Negro and white, liberate the poor white as well as the Negro.

JIM FORMAN. We should agitate for dignity. . . . Dignity is an umbrella concept. E.g., a man without a job has no dignity.

JIM JONES. SNCC's program is limited to desegregating facilities and voter registration.

LAWRENCE GUYOT. If our goal is just voter registration then we should stop. We have to organize around something.

The day after the conference ended I wrote a letter to Howard Zinn. I wrote in part: "We have just finished an extremely moving staff meeting, which I was permitted to attend because of my involvement in the Summer Project." Continuing, I said:

I tend to feel (as I said at the SNCC conference) that it is a mistake to emphasize only a) the vote, and b) protection, without at the same time sketching out some sort of vision and program as to what sorts of measures will ultimately solve the problem. Several staff members said this week: I'm ready to die, but I need a program worth dying for. I know Ruby Doris feels this way. I don't think either the vote or Federal protection is worth dying for unless one can see beyond them by just what steps the society will be changed. I said this in substance to Bob, Cortland, and Tim Jenkins in March and their response was: You want us to have an ideology. But this week I heard my own question asked in substance by several field workers. Thus, I think that both for the movement's effectiveness and for its morale there really must be more thinking as to program. Bob said this week he had never supposed that anything more than limited goals could be achieved. But there is a question as to how many people will continue to risk their lives for limited goals; and there is also a question as to whether, in fact, those limited goals can be achieved within present American society except in the context of more fundamental changes.[13]

Ten days later, we all learned that three young men who had risked their lives for the limited goals of the Summer Project had in all probability been murdered. It became much more difficult to continue the discussion begun at the SNCC staff meeting in June. On the one hand, nationwide support for actually seating the MFDP delegates at the Democratic Party Convention increased dramatically. On the other hand, a feeling grew that only if the delegates were seated would the sacrifice of Chaney, Goodman, and Schwerner have been worthwhile.

During June and July 1964, the MFDP, in order to distinguish itself from the Mississippi regulars, felt obliged to emphasize its fidelity to President Johnson and to the program of the national, as distinct from the state, Democratic Party. Organizing materials prepared by Donna Richards, Casey Hayden, and other SNCC folk for MFDP precinct and county meetings accordingly called for a "loyalty pledge" to the national party.[14]

This was the latent or suspended state of dialogue within SNCC when, at Atlantic City, President Lyndon Johnson and UAW president Walter Reuther teamed up to prevent the MFDP delegates from being seated. Nelson Lichtenstein in his biography of Reuther, and Taylor Branch in his biography of Dr. King, tell essentially the same story.[15]

At Johnson's request, Reuther broke off negotiations with General Motors and flew to Atlantic City by chartered plane. Arriving at 3 a.m. Reuther went into session with Hubert Humphrey and Walter Mondale. They agreed that the MFDP would be required to accept a so-called compromise: the Mississippi regulars would continue to be the official delegation and the MFDP would have two "at large" delegates named by the president, who, so Humphrey made clear, would not include "that illiterate woman," Mrs. Hamer.

The next day exhausted MFDP delegates instructed their attorney, Joseph Rauh, to hold out for at least the same number of seats allotted to the regulars. However, Reuther told Rauh: "Here's the decision. I am telling you to take this deal." If Rauh did not do what he was told, Reuther added, he would terminate Rauh's employment with the UAW.

The same kind of strong arm tactics were used with Dr. King. Reuther told him: "Your funding is on the line. The kind of money you got from us in Birmingham is there again for Mississippi, but you've got to help us and we've got to help Johnson."

Rauh yielded to the pressure and the so-called compromise was accepted by the Convention Credentials Committee. But MFDP delegates and SNCC staff members almost unanimously voted against the proposed compromise. No MFDP delegates were seated at the Convention.

At a conference in Waveland, Mississippi, in November 1964, SNCC tried to digest the summer's experiences. Most accounts have emphasized the tension between black staff and white volunteers, exacerbated by the fact that so many volunteers stayed on in Mississippi; or the conflict between Jim Forman's desire to make SNCC into a Marxist-Leninist vanguard party and the aspiration of others that SNCC continue as a decentralized network in which those who did the work made the decisions.

I suggest a third explanation for the difficulty experienced by SNCC folks in finding a way forward. Bayard Rustin and others were encouraging SNCC to look to its "coalition partners" for allies in confronting the economic and social structures that underpin racism in the United States. But precisely those allies—the national Democratic Party, and the allegedly most progressive trade union leader in the country—had just finished compromising the hopes of MFDP delegates at Atlantic City. Here is how Bob Moses put it at the Waveland conference:[16]

> Let's sum up the box we're in:
>   1) Labor unions are political organizations, now within the Establishment.
>   2) When labor is organized, it can only discuss a narrow aspect of the problem: wages. Reuther sat in the meeting with King, Humphrey and others to urge the FDP to accept the compromise, talking anti-Goldwater, keep morality out of politics, etc. . . .

A Few More Memories

One morning that summer I woke up early in the room I had rented near the Summer Project headquarters. I went over to the office. Someone was already there. It was Jim Forman, national chairperson of SNCC. He was sweeping the floor. He is the only person in a similar position of authority whom I have ever encountered performing such a task. Alice and I attempt to act likewise.

When I left Mississippi in mid-August I drove first to New York City, carrying the three MFDP candidates for Congress—Annie Devine, Victoria Gray, and Fannie Lou Hamer—to a meeting at Carnegie Hall. Then I drove further north to New Haven. In June 1963, Spelman College had abruptly discharged Howard Zinn. Thereafter we no longer felt welcome there and so, when Yale offered me a job for a second time during the winter of 1963–1964, I said Yes. I might have been able to go to Tougaloo College in Mississippi, and almost certainly could have joined the faculty at Morris Brown College in Atlanta, but our two children insisted, "No further south!" (The Morris Brown campus was a few blocks south of Spelman.) I thought that for the sake of our family as a whole a move was imperative. I underestimated the degree to which my heart remained in the south with the civil rights movement. My body arrived at Yale but my spirit never got there.

Ten years later I was a student at the University of Chicago Law School. I read the Supreme Court decision in which the high court held that the First Amendment protected a high-school student in Iowa by the name of

Tinker who wore a black arm band to protest the Vietnam War. In its decision, the Supreme Court repeatedly cited a decision by a federal court of appeals in the south. I looked up the case.

It turned out that on the first day of school in the fall of 1964, African-American students in Philadelphia, Mississippi, came to school wearing buttons that said "SNCC" and "One Man, One Vote." Like Ms. Tinker in Iowa, they were sent home. On appeal, the federal court held that wearing the buttons was constitutionally protected. Because of the action of these black students in Mississippi—the single most courageous action I remember from Freedom Summer—a white student in the north was later protected in protesting a war against people of color on the other side of the world.

A TRIP TO HANOI, *STAUGHTON LYND*

I became notorious, and lost my teaching job at Yale, after I made an unauthorized trip to Hanoi in December 1965–January 1966. I went at Christmastime so as not to miss any of my scheduled Yale classes. I traveled with Herbert Aptheker, author of the well-regarded book *American Negro Slave Revolts* but also a member of the U.S. Communist Party, and with Tom Hayden, one of the founders of Students for a Democratic Society (SDS).[17]

The Year of Wrath

The Catholic requiem speaks of "dies irae," a day of wrath, when the dead will come before the throne of God to be judged.

Nineteen sixty-five was truly a year of wrath. In February, SNCC folks asked me to come to Selma, Alabama, to discuss the possibility of starting Freedom Schools there. As I flew back to New Haven I read in the *New York Times* that South Vietnamese insurgents had attacked U.S. forces near the town of Pleiku, and that President Johnson—he who had run for the presidency as a peace candidate—had ordered the bombing of North Vietnam in response. I can recall an almost visceral moment of enlightenment when I said to myself, "Oh, so that's what I am now supposed to be doing: resisting what is happening in Vietnam."

Then came the nighttime killing of Jimmy Johnson, a young African-American, near Selma, Alabama, and the decision of civil rights activists to march from Selma to Montgomery in protest. Meantime a tiny stream of protest about Vietnam was carrying me toward a waterfall. There was a meeting at Yale when a handful of professors publicly condemned the war. No doubt because I was a Yale professor, albeit in my first year there and one of several young historians seeking tenure, I was asked to chair a meeting against the war at Carnegie Hall. I remember Senator Gruening from Alaska speaking on that occasion.

Then SDS decided to hold a march against the war in Washington, D.C. I was asked to chair that, too. Paul Potter, the youthful president of SDS, was to deliver the keynote speech, but the mimeographed copies of his remarks had been left in the SNCC office elsewhere in Washington. So Rennie Davis of SDS and I hurried to the SNCC office. It was locked. We jimmied the window, slithered inside, and with our arms full of papers hastened toward the rally.

When we arrived the rally had already begun! No matter; remember, we believed in participatory democracy. I ran to the platform, and when it was my turn, said my say. I believe I focused on an incident in which a Vietnamese named Nguyen van Troi was executed at the United States Marine base in Danang. Potter's speech was indeed memorable: he called on protesters to "name the system" that was producing the holocaust of Vietnam.

That evening a variety of activists assembled at the Institute for Policy Studies near DuPont Circle. It became clear that SDS, despite what we all considered an enormously successful rally attended by approximately twenty-five thousand persons, did not wish to be distracted from its efforts to change the "system" so as to prevent what Paul Booth called "the seventh war from now." (Count them: Lebanon, Grenada, Panama, Nicaragua, Haiti, Gulf War I , Afghanistan, and Number Eight, Gulf War II.)

What was to be done? I was acutely concerned that by the time students came back to college campuses in the fall, so many U.S. servicemen would be in Vietnam that protest within the United States might not be permitted. In subsequent conversations, some members of various pacifist networks—the War Resisters League, the Committee for Nonviolent Action, the editors of *Liberation* magazine—decided to convene an "Assembly of Unrepresented People" on the twentieth anniversary of the atomic bombing of Hiroshima and Nagasaki. Our intention was to reach the steps of the Capitol and there to "declare peace" with the people of Vietnam.

After one of the planning meetings in Washington, I went out to the Pentagon with a handful of protesters. As we began to picket we were surrounded by a larger number of Military Police. They seemed to think that we were out of our minds. Summoning all possible dignity, I said, "You don't understand. We are just the first of thousands," as indeed we were. Then I caught a train back to New Haven, and hastened to dinner at the home of the chairperson of the Yale History Department, all the time wondering whether my blue pants were too dusty to be presentable.

The assembly was in its own way another success. As Bob Moses, David Dellinger, and I led protesters from the Washington Monument toward the Capitol steps, counterdemonstrators threw red paint on us (that was the end of those blue pants). At the foot of the lawn sloping up toward the Capitol several lines of police officers were waiting. I recall wondering, "How do you make your way nonviolently through a line of policemen?" I tried, and was arrested. As the paddy wagon drove away I saw through the window that the remaining protesters had seated themselves in a circle, and Dave Dellinger, his back to the officers, appeared to be leading a seminar. I learned later that they were reading aloud "A Declaration of Conscience Against the War in Vietnam."

Norman Morrison

Whatever we might do, the dreadful war continued to escalate.

Earlier that summer of 1965 I was part of a meeting at the Pentagon between a number of antiwar activists and Secretary of Defense Robert McNamara. As in so much else my memory is largely visual. I see McNamara at the head of the table, his hair slicked back. The rest of us sat around the table. I do not remember what we said, which was apparently ineffectual.

However, another participant in that encounter was the poet Paul Goodman. After that meeting, he wrote a poem in which he quotes me.[18] According to Paul, I asked the Secretary of Defense, If I were to pour gasoline over my seven-year-old son, could he strike the match? McNamara said nothing. I then asked, Goodman says, How then can you order your soldiers to burn little yellow children?

Paul Goodman seems to think that Norman Morrison was present at this meeting. I am certain that he was not. But Norman, a Quaker in his early thirties, was thinking along similar lines. Late on an early November afternoon, he went to a terrace at the Pentagon, placed his infant daughter Emily to one side, poured kerosene over himself, and set himself on fire.

What Norman did was to act out for McNamara what my words had so much more weakly sought to convey: this is what it means for one human being to set fire to another and burn him or her to death.

We now know for sure that Norman Morrison's action deeply affected Secretary McNamara. Stationing himself within sight of McNamara's office window—and was this by mere happenstance?—Norman, as his body smoked and burned, caught the Secretary's attention. "Years later McNamara was barely able to talk about what had happened," writes one biographer.[19] And apparently it was in these months of late 1965 that the

Secretary of Defense began deeply to doubt the wisdom of the war he later called a terrible mistake.

Norman's immolation energized antiwar activists as well. Brian Willson describes how the librarian at the Air Force base in Vietnam where Brian was stationed noticed the unusual assortment of books that Willson was checking out of the library, and invited him to dinner. Brian writes that after the meal the family sang songs, "one of which . . . they translated into English specially for me." The song was about Norman's death. Brian Willson suddenly realized that this was the same Norman Morrison who like himself had graduated from Chautauqua High School, and was "the first Eagle Scout I ever knew." Overcome, Brian Willson broke into tears.[20] Eighteen years later he would sit down on the track of a railroad train carrying munitions to a port for shipment to anti-insurgent government forces in Central America, resulting in the loss of both his legs.

Most consequentially, Norman Morrison's sacrifice was a transforming experience for many, many Vietnamese. As I will explain, I had the opportunity to be in Hanoi less than two months after Norman's death. At a factory we saw a poster captioned, "The flames of Morrison will never die." The members of a village we visited sent their "best wishes to Mrs. Anne Morrison." The Vietnamese attorney general compared the event to an old story in which "unity comes from shared suffering."[21]

Simply, Norman's death caused Vietnamese to believe that there was at least one person in the United States who understood what they were experiencing.

If Not Me, Then Who?

I was seeking my own way to escalate protest against the war. In September, I got a telephone call from Herbert Aptheker. He asked me to meet him at his office on Union Square in New York City. I remember the square, surrounded by trees that had not yet lost their leaves.

Herbert said that the "North Vietnamese Peace Committee," whatever that might be, had invited him to visit North Vietnam with two non-Communist leaders of the antiwar movement. He invited me, and asked me to invite a second person.

I first asked Bob Moses, with whom I had been arrested at the Assembly of Unrepresented People. He canvassed others in SNCC. Bob reported that SNCC organizers were refusing induction, and SNCC was preparing to make a public statement in support of draft resistance (a year before SDS took a similar step). Likewise, Julian Bond was in the midst of his campaign for election to the Georgia legislature that would result in that body refusing to seat him until overruled by the United States Supreme Court. A trip to Hanoi was felt to be unwise under these circumstances.

Accordingly I prepared to go alone with Herbert. Then early in December, Tom Hayden visited us in New Haven. Our children (Barbara and Lee), Tom and I went sledding on a hill in the outskirts of town. When the two children went down the slope by themselves, Tom and I stood waiting for them at the top of the hill, and I said to him, "Hey Tom, how'd you like to go to Hanoi?" Since I had to travel during the midwinter holiday in order not to miss a class at Yale, we would be leaving in two or three weeks.

Tom, too, checked with his network of fellow organizers. He said, Yes.

Leaving was difficult. Our son Lee, then seven years old, put his arms around my knees to keep me from going. Lee says that he remembers this. He went to a camp between Christmas and New Year's Eve, and also recalls that, unusually for him, he got into a number of fights with other children. Alice remembers, however, that when Staughton was in Hanoi there was an "invisible community" of support for her. The most unlikely people, it seemed, understood what she might need and came to her assistance.

Two conversations during that trip stand out in memory. The first was an interview in Moscow with Dang Quanh Minh, the National Liberation Front (NLF) representative in the Soviet Union. Minh was slight and very frail. Because our group knew no French, we had to speak through an interpreter. After my return, I reported on "perhaps the most impressive interview of our whole trip" in a talk to the Yale community as follows:

> This 56-year-old man, [a] member of the NLF central committee, was first imprisoned in 1930. During the Japanese occupation of Vietnam he was again imprisoned for five years. As he spoke harsh thoughts to us in a musical, almost inaudible voice, one had the sense of having penetrated through a fog of bureaucratic arrangements and travel plans to the very mind of the Vietnamese revolution.[22]

Somehow, despite the language barrier, Minh grasped my assumption that if the United States were fully to unleash its military technology, Vietnam would be destroyed. He looked at me and said: "No, Professor, you're wrong. We are going to win." He continued, as I recall his words: "This can happen in one of two ways. The first, which we would much prefer, is for you to withdraw your troops from my country now. But let me assure you that if you send more soldiers to Vietnam, for every soldier who lands there one more Vietnamese will come to the National Liberation Front." Ten years later, when the United States finally left Vietnam, Minh's prediction appeared uncannily accurate.

The second conversation was in a factory in Hanoi that manufactures agricultural implements. There was excitement among the workers when I pointed to a picture of a demonstration in Berkeley on October 16, 1965, which showed me speaking from the back of a pickup truck. After touring the plant, our hosts and we withdrew to a small room near the entrance. There was a table covered with a white tablecloth and dishes of hard candy. As the manager launched into his remarks, I concluded that this was Welcoming Speech No. 101, bent my head toward the table, and fiddled with the candy. "We like Americans because of their practical minds," the manager said through an interpreter. "We like Americans because of the first Declaration [of Independence] by Lincoln." I began to smirk to myself about the manager's ignorance until I remembered that he knew more about the history of my country, even if he wrongly connected the dots, than I knew about the history of Vietnam.

The interpreter's voice continued. "The word American means something beautiful to us, but it is difficult to say since the intervention." There was a long pause. I continued to play with the candy. Frustrated, I finally looked up. The manager was weeping. I think that any lingering notions about Orientals who do not show feelings in public vanished from my mind at that moment.

Academic Consequences

Alice and I had no idea what the consequences of the trip would be. The government took away my passport but I was eventually able to get it back through legal action. I was not indicted or imprisoned. However, I was denied tenure at Yale and blacklisted by other universities.

I have mixed feelings about revisiting that patch of history. On the one hand, I am thankful not to have spent the past forty years as a history professor at Yale. I am even thankful that at five Chicago-area colleges where the history department offered me a job, the administration said no because of my antiwar activities. I have never stopped writing history. But because I was pushed from the academic nest, and became a lawyer, I have had an opportunity to come to know rank-and-file workers and death-sentenced prisoners that I never could have had as a university professor.

On the other hand, I have a deep need to clarify the record, if that is possible. After Alice and I moved to Chicago, a committee of graduate students in history at Yale came to our house to ask me about what had happened. I told them I was convinced that the denial of tenure was politically motivated but I could not prove it. Now, thanks to the research of a young scholar named Carl Mirra, and especially thanks to John Blum's recently published memoir,[23] I believe a case can be made that meets any test for objective historical inquiry.

If what were at stake were only my personal situation, I would keep my peace and move on. But academic repression, all too evident in the 1960s, is once again with us. And in assessing individual cases both then and now the myth lingers that Ivy League institutions do not behave in the crass manner of public institutions, or of private universities in other parts of the United States. A columnist in the *Yale Daily News* asked in September 1967 whether "the narrow-mindedness displayed by the Illinois Board of State Colleges and Universities—so easily dismissed as midwestern provincialism—does not find its counterpart here under the guise of a smoothly-run establishment." Then and now, I share this question. And it is an important question to answer as we seek to understand the repression periodically visited on the community of historians.

A Pattern of Proof

I was for almost twenty years a Legal Services lawyer specializing in employment law. I litigated dozens of discharge cases. Let me restate the known facts about the denial of tenure in my case in the context of the pattern of proof with which I am familiar.

One begins with a so-called *prima facie* (on its face) case. The burden is on the employee to make this initial showing. The employer then has an opportunity to articulate a nondiscriminatory reason for its action. Finally, the employee must seek to demonstrate that the reason given by the employer is, in fact, a pretext.

In my case, I took the position that what I did when I was not fulfilling my duties at Yale was my own business. Some of the time the Yale administration appeared to agree, but at other times, under intense pressure from alumni, the University displayed obvious political motivation. In a public statement shortly after my return from Hanoi, Yale president Kingman Brewster said that I had given "aid and comfort to a government engaged in hostilities with American forces." The words "aid and comfort to the enemy" appear in the law of treason, which carries the death penalty. Although a decision as to whether I would receive tenure would not be made until 1968, President Brewster's statement made a *prima facie* case that my application for tenure would be decided on nonacademic grounds.

Once the discharged employee makes a *prima facie* case, the employer has an opportunity to rebut. Throughout 1966 the University articulated a nondiscriminatory rationale for why Staughton Lynd might not receive tenure. In the department chairman's one-on-one conversations with me, in his subsequent statements to the campus press, and in the private conversation of at least one senior History department professor, the offered rebuttal was that a financial crisis made the likelihood of promotion for all assistant professors in the History department "minuscule."

Publication of the chairman's memoirs has shredded that rationale. John Blum ceased to be chairman of the Yale History department at the end of June 1967. In his autobiography, Blum reveals that "just after" he left the chairmanship, and well before the History department denied me tenure, the financial crisis was resolved.

Yale also had a backup rationale for denying me tenure: my scholarship was not good enough. Of course this is a matter that my peers, not I, must speak to in the end. I think that rationale is not credible. What I am told is now the standard one-volume history of the American Revolution singles out for special mention in its bibliographical essay three of the articles in my *Class Conflict, Slavery, and the United States Constitution*, published before the History department denied me tenure. Another of the articles in *Class Conflict*, which I believe was my best piece of work, was an essay entitled "The Compromise of 1787" in which I adduced evidence that the drafting of the Northwest Ordinance in New York City and the drafting of the United States Constitution in Philadelphia were parts of a single process of legislative compromise between sections divided by the presence or absence of slavery. Another of my books that the History department reviewed in making its tenure decision is entitled *Intellectual Origins of American Radicalism*. In their 1968 letter eventually denying me tenure, the Yale historians said that this book "considerably weakened the case for your promotion." Yet on the back cover, a distinguished historian named David Donald stated: "this is a major work in American intellectual history [which] will abundantly satisfy any serious student of American thought." And *Intellectual Origins* was republished by Harvard University Press in 1982.

I believe that we must set aside money and scholarly deficiency as persuasive rationales for Yale's action. In the language of employment law, these were pretexts. Surely, the real reason I was not offered tenure was that my politics were unacceptable. It was acceptable for Yale faculty and alumni to manage the Bay of Pigs invasion for the CIA (Richard Bissell), repeatedly to advocate the invasion of North Vietnam (Walt Rostow), and to plan an unprovoked invasion of Iraq (Paul Wolfowitz). But it was unacceptable for me to be arrested on the steps of the Capitol in a symbolic effort to declare peace with the people of Vietnam, or to make an unauthorized trip to Hanoi with a member of the American Communist Party and a founder of SDS.

DRAFT COUNSELING, *ALICE LYND*

In the spring of 1965, a friend visited us who had met several Vietnamese women at a gathering in Asia sponsored by the Women's International League for Peace and Freedom. Our friend said that Vietnamese women would go out at night and talk with South Vietnamese soldiers, trying to persuade them to side with the villagers rather than fight.

I felt challenged by this. Under the Selective Service law in force at that time, young men were being drafted to fight in Vietnam and resistance in the United States was growing. I was not going to sit in at a draft board and get arrested. What could I do, consistent with being a mother of two children, and a teacher of young children?

On August 6–9, 1965, various antiwar activists rallied on the mall in Washington, D.C., in an "Assembly of Unrepresented People" to declare peace with the people of Vietnam. In effect, we were saying, our government may be at war with you, but we are not!

Between August 6 and August 9, there were workshops, small groups on the mall. I went first to a workshop on the House Un-American Activities Committee. When that ended, I looked around for another one. I saw a tent sponsored by the Central Committee for Conscientious Objectors (CCCO). I went in, and heard a man saying they needed more draft counselors. When that workshop was over, I asked the man whether I could become a draft counselor. "Well, I guess you could if you could get anyone to come to you," he said. "There is one woman who does it."

We were living five blocks from Yale University at that time, and students were frequently in and out of our apartment. I put up a little sign, provided by CCCO, with my name on it saying that draft counseling was available here.

As a counselor, before I became a lawyer, I could not give legal advice. I asked questions. Have you thought about this? Have you considered that? The typical draft resister had gone to church when he was a child and he believed what he had been taught, but he did not see the church doing what was preached.

One evening in the fall of 1966, a group of Yale divinity students came to our home to discuss whether they (the men, that is) should give up their privileged exemption from the draft. One student said she knew a man who went to prison for refusing to register for the draft. She thought he regretted it. I knew that same man and I wondered, "What would he say?"

After the students left that evening, I suggested to Staughton that his next book should be about what various conscientious objectors had done and how they felt about it. "Why me?" Staughton replied. "I'll help you do it!"

I went to a conference sponsored by Catholic Worker draft resisters in New York. Staughton and I went to a conference in Chicago where we heard David Mitchell put forth the "Nuremberg" defense that no one should be ordered to commit war crimes. I contacted lawyers who put me in touch with the "Fort Hood Three" who refused to deploy to Vietnam. I asked *New Left Notes* and other publications to print a notice that I was looking for people who would send me things they had written about why they would not fight. The editor of Beacon Press saw the notice and came to see me: he wanted to publish the book.

This was the year when our third child, Martha, was born. I worked under pressure to get the book finished so that it could be useful to men who, I thought, needed to know that others had tried some of the things they were considering, and as background for sorting out their own thoughts. *We Won't Go: Personal Accounts of War Objectors* was listed by the American Library Association as one of the best books for young adults in 1968. I later was told that it was most useful for resisters to give to their parents as a way of showing that they weren't the only ones who were doing such strange things.

We moved to Chicago in the summer of 1967. Draft calls were escalating and so was the "We Won't Go" movement of students on college campuses. Men and women in "The Resistance" organized "days of resistance" that included burning of draft cards and blocking of induction centers. The Chicago Area Draft Resisters group (CADRE) was made up mostly of nonviolent draft resisters who chose to go to prison rather than to cooperate with Selective Service.

To be recognized as a conscientious objector, a person had to show that he was "conscientiously opposed to participation in war in any form" based on "religious training and belief." Members of CADRE attempted to reach out to working-class draftees who were not opposed to war in any form, or who had reasons other than religious reasons for not wanting to be drafted. CADRE counselors offered draft counseling on a range of options including hardship, medical and psychological grounds. As counselors, they rigorously disapproved of "mind bending." After all, the counselee was going to have to live with the consequences so it had better be his decision!

We had an open house on Wednesday nights in our home where young people could come and talk with others who were trying to figure out what they thought and decide what they wanted to do. They challenged each other with questions of effectiveness, and whether nonviolence was a tactic or should be a way of life. One night our oldest child, Barbara, then thirteen, called me into her room and asked, "Ma, if grownups don't know what to do, what hope is there for us?"

In 1968, the CCCO opened a branch office in Chicago. I was hired to train draft counselors. We were advised to assume that everything we said was being bugged, but then go ahead and say what needed to be said. I would tell counselors not to write any notes that could hurt a counselee if seized. Those timely lessons have continued to be relevant.

I understood the importance of training, but I did not like being cut off from doing counseling. I felt as though my right hand was tied behind my back. After one year, I took a position as coordinator of draft counseling in the Chicago Regional Office of the American Friends Service Committee (AFSC).

I think my most successful innovation in training at the AFSC was an evening once a month that I called a "clinic" for draft counselors. I would arrange for an inexperienced counselor to bring a counselee, and I would invite an experienced counselor to counsel that counselee. Then the rest of us would ask the experienced counselor questions like, "Why did you ask that?" "What were you driving at then?" We would look at the regulations and in other ways demonstrate good counseling. We learned from each other new ways to ask sensitive questions and how to get at the heart of the matter.

I was known for knitting during such meetings. A friend observed, "The more involved she gets, the faster she knits!"

One of my responsibilities was to interview men who were about to refuse induction to make sure that everything that could have been done through administrative procedures had been done before referring the man to an attorney.

I got feedback from resisters after they went to court. They complained that lawyers had their own theories of how to challenge the draft. The resister who was going to prison wanted it to be for *his* reasons, not for some theory his lawyer wanted to try out.

When I was counseling, I believed, there were two experts in the room: I was an expert on the Selective Service regulations and what was required to support a particular kind of claim; the counselee was an expert on what he had experienced, what he thought, and what he was willing to do. We put our expertise together.

Staughton and I carried the "two experts" model forward into our legal work when we became lawyers. We learned from our clients. The local union president knew how the contract was actually interpreted. The local grievance man knew how the system was supposed to work and where we should look for evidence. A prisoner explained to me how to find my way through the maze of the Rules Infraction Board policies and procedures.

I loved draft counseling. I was meeting a person who was considering life-altering choices, bringing together what life meant to him, what his aspirations were for his future, what family pressures he was under, and what consequences he was willing to face. I felt awed and humbled by the depth of what these young men and their loved ones were telling me. In later years, I wondered whether I could ever find such meaningful work again.

WAR CRIMES AND THE END OF THE SIXTIES,
STAUGHTON LYND

At Spelman College in the early 1960s we hosted two guests from the Soviet Union. Sitting together with the Zinns and Lynds, they talked about Khrushchev's 1956 speech condemning the misdeeds of Stalin. The question arose, How should that misconduct be characterized? Our guests suggested the Russian word for "mistake." "No, no," I responded, thumbing through my Russian-English dictionary to find the Russian word for "sin."

In the spring of 1966 a young man came to our home in New Haven to invite me to join the War Crimes Tribunal then being organized by Lord Bertrand Russell. I was flattered, and initially assumed I would agree.

But as I talked with the young man I raised the question, "Wouldn't it be more persuasive if the Tribunal were open to evidence of war crimes by any side in the Vietnam conflict?" I made it clear that I believed the crimes of the insurgency would be as dust in the balance compared to the saturation bombing, the use of napalm and Agent Orange, the confinement of prisoners in "tiger cages," and the rest, carried on by the United States and its puppet government in Saigon.

To make my concern as specific as possible I asked, "Suppose it were proved that the National Liberation Front had tortured unarmed prisoners?" My interlocutor responded (as I remember his words), "Anything is justified that would drive the imperialist aggressor into the sea."

I wrote to Lord Russell. I put it to him that the definition of a "crime" is conduct that is wrong no matter by whom committed. He, or someone writing on his behalf, disagreed. So I declined to join the Tribunal.

Soon after my exchanges with Lord Russell in the spring of 1966, my friend and comrade David Dellinger returned from a trip to Hanoi. While in North Vietnam his hosts had brought up the Tribunal. They asked Dave if he thought Martin Luther King would participate. He said, "No." (In fact it would be another year until Dr. King came out publicly against the war.) "But," Dave added, "if Dr. King says no, then Staughton and I will do it."

Dave had every reason to say this. He and I had not disagreed about anything for many years. But in this case, I explained to him, I had a problem. I described my exchanges with the young man in New Haven and with Lord Russell. Dave said that he agreed with me, but he was anxious to publicize the use by the United States of horrible weapons like "cluster bombs" which exploded near the ground releasing countless tiny metal fragments. He would take part in the Tribunal.

It was a small difference, a difference in which each of us respected the other's decision. Yet it proved to be a parting of the ways. I was not at the Pentagon with Dave in the fall of 1967, when a protester put a flower in the rifle barrel of a soldier and said, "Join us." I was living in Chicago in the summer of 1968 when demonstrators confronted police on Michigan Avenue. I was arrested in a separate effort to establish the right to demonstrate adjacent to the amphitheater, where the national convention of the Democratic Party took place, but to do so nonviolently. I did not stand at Dave's side in his effort to dissuade other friends of mine from provoking violence.

Years later, Dave and I quietly discussed all this at his home in Vermont. I asked him how our separation had caused him to feel. He responded, "I felt abandoned."

Still later, I would ponder these differences again in reflection on the Nuremburg Tribunal after World War II. A fellow historian expressed the opinion that sometimes it is appropriate to have a court consider the misdeeds of only one side, "as at Nuremburg." I disagree strongly. The misconduct of Germans and Japanese during World War II was an abomination. But it was a miscarriage of justice for those who had just dropped the first atomic bombs on Hiroshima and Nagasaki to sit in judgment on those who initiated the Holocaust.

The late sixties was a time of choosing. Alice and I had moved to Chicago in part to find ways to be full-time participants in the Movement. The national headquarters of SDS was in Chicago, and it appeared that black organizers like Curtis Hayes from SNCC were in Chicago seeking to create an interracial movement of the poor.

But the Movement as we found it when we arrived in Chicago was changing rapidly. We moved there in June 1967, and that summer uprisings in Newark and Detroit made any kind of interracial movement seem distant indeed.

The culture of the Movement with regard to violence was also changing. The death of Che Guevara, books by Regis Debray and Frantz Fanon, filled the minds of young activists. I remember clearly a public meeting in Chicago when a member of the SDS national leadership spoke of "icing" and "offing," that is, killing, political opponents.

Likewise I clearly recall a morning in our Chicago living room when I made a personal decision. After returning from Hanoi I had been one of the most sought-after Movement speakers in the United States. In those days I felt an obligation to accept almost any invitation to speak against the war. It seemed to Alice that I would get off the bus or train from the airport and give my attention to our children, Barbara and Lee. The children apparently do not remember neglect by their father. Barbara, for example, recalls how I would lie on the floor between their rooms and read aloud at bedtime (while Alice answered the phone and told callers that Staughton was not available). To Alice it seemed that the Movement came first, the children came second, and she came third.

Up to this point Alice and I had carried into life outside community the assumption that the Movement, the cause, was one's highest commitment, and everything else must find its place afterwards. In the spring of 1966 we decided that in an effort to build a communal society one must begin with the community of family. If community could not be brought off with spouse and children, parents and grandchildren, how could one presume to try to create it in the larger society? Many Movement marriages failed to survive the sixties. Ours, in the end, put down new roots and flourished.

Now, in 1968 or 1969, I faced a second decision. The Black Panthers ritually referred to police officers as "pigs." How did I feel about that? There was an emerging consensus among SDS activists that serious revolutionaries should set aside past practice and create hierarchical, militarized fighting groups. But I had witnessed SNCC organizers confront equally serious and immediate dangers in the south. They had practiced consensus in the belief that no one should decide whether and how another person risked his or her life.

I knew, that morning, that if I spoke out publicly against calling policemen "pigs" or against the creation of a Marxist-Leninist vanguard party, I would rapidly fade into Movement obscurity. From being a name regularly quoted in the *National Guardian*, and a person repeatedly sought out as a speaker, I would once again be a mere single individual, trying to find my footing in the currents of a dramatically different movement.

As the particles of dust turned in the sunbeams that poured in through our living room windows, I decided to go on believing what I had always believed and not to hide it. I did publicly condemn calling police officers or prison guards "pigs." I opposed abandoning participatory democracy and creating a Marxist-Leninist vanguard party. I did not offer uncritical support to black revolutionary groups in the United States or to the governments of Cuba, the Soviet Union, China, or North Vietnam. I continued to advocate nonviolence.

My career as an academic historian was no longer open to me. But the possible alternatives for full-time Movement work available in the late 1960s and early 1970s seemed unacceptable. I found it embarrassing and shameful that the organizations created in the hopeful early years of the 1960s—first SNCC and then SDS—no longer existed ten years later.

It was a lonely and confusing time.

NOTES

1. University Settlement, *Houston Street Center Gala Opening Celebration, Jan. 25, 2006.*
2. Cooper Square Committee, *45th Anniversary Gala, 1959–2004*, 1.
3. University Settlement, *Gala Opening.*

4. David McReynolds to Staughton Lynd, June 28, 1993.

5. University Settlement, *Gala Opening.*

6. University Settlement, *Gala Opening.*

7. "Freedom Summer," in Staughton Lynd, *Living Inside Our Hope,* 32. A letter from a volunteer describing Moses's talk in a similar way will be found in *Letters from Mississippi,* edited by Elizabeth Sutherland Martinez (Brookline, MA: Zephyr Press, 2002), 36–37.

8. To my knowledge there is no tape recording or other contemporary record of what Bob Moses said. I base this account on what I remembered and wrote for publication within the next few years, in the Introduction to *Nonviolence in America,* ed. Staughton Lynd (Indianapolis, IN: Bobbs-Merrill, 1966), xliv, and in a preface to Bob Moses, "Mississippi, 1961–1962," *Liberation* (Jan. 1970), 7.

9. Lynd Papers, Kent State University, Box 6, Folder 3. I should like to thank Carl Mirra for unearthing this document.

10. The following pages are based on my presentation at the meeting of the Organization of American Historians in March 2003, in Memphis, Tennessee. The panel, entitled "Remembering SNCC and SDS," was held at the Lorain Motel where Dr. King was assassinated, which has since been converted into a museum.

11. Quoted in *Letters from Mississippi,* 251.

12. Staff meeting minutes, June 9–11, 1964, SNCC Papers, Roll 3, Frames 975–92. I wish to thank Wesley Hogan for making these minutes available to me.

13. Staughton Lynd to Howard Zinn, June 12, 1964. Carol Polsgrove found this letter in the Zinn Papers at the Wisconsin State Historical Society in the course of researching her book, *Divided Minds: Intellectuals And The Civil Rights Movement* (New York: W. W. Norton & Company, 2001), and quotes from it therein, 226–27. She kindly made it available to me.

14. Casey Hayden, "Fields of Blue," in *Deep In Our Hearts: Nine White Women in the Freedom Movement* (Athens, GA: University of Georgia Press, 2000), 357. I believe that such maneuvering took a toll. By the Waveland conference in November 1964, Casey felt "uninterested in electoral politics." *Deep In Our Hearts,* 367.

15. Taylor Branch, *Pillar of Fire: America in the King Years, 1963–1965* (New York: Simon & Schuster, 1998), 469–75, and Nelson Lichtenstein, *The Most Dangerous Man in America: Walter Reuther and the Fate of American Labor* (New York: Basic Books, 1995), 394–95.

16. Minutes, discussion of Nov. 9, 1964, SNCC Papers, Reel 11, Frames 935–59. Once again I have Wesley Hogan to thank for the opportunity to see these records.

17. A portion of this chapter was prepared for a panel on "The Historian in Time of Crisis" at the meeting of the American Historical Association in Atlanta, January 2007. I have also drawn on a talk that I gave in 2005 at a forum entitled "God and War at Yale," held in Battell Chapel in New Haven, and sponsored by Historians Against the War. Other participants included the Reverend William Sloan Coffin, David Mitchell, Michael Ferber, and a grandson of David Dellinger.

18. Paul Goodman's poem appears in his *Collected Poems,* ed. Taylor Stoehr (New York: Random House, 1973), 180–81. Thanks to Andrej Grubacic and Carl Mirra for retrieving this poem for me.

19. Deborah Shapley, *Promise and Power: The Life and Times of Robert McNamara* (Boston: Little, Brown and Company, 1993), 353–55.

20. S. Brian Willson, *On Third World Legs*, with an Introduction by Staughton Lynd (Chicago: Charles H. Kerr, 1992), 19–20.

21. Staughton Lynd and Thomas Hayden, *The Other Side* (New York: New American Library, 1966), 69–70 (the factory, where the manager said of Norman, "He sacrificed himself for justice, not for economic self-interest"); 74 (the village); 80 (the attorney general).

22. Promoting Enduring Peace, "Part of the Address of Professor Staughton Lynd of Yale University in Woolsey Hall, January 17, 1966." Extracts from our interview with Minh appear in Lynd and Hayden, *The Other Side*, 29–34.

23. The evidence as to all aspects of my nonpromotion at Yale is reviewed in Carl Mirra, "Radical Historians and the Liberal Establishment: Staughton Lynd's Life with History," *Left History*, vol. 11, no. 1 (Spring 2006), 69–101. John Morton Blum, chairman of the Yale History Department in 1966–1967, discusses my trip to Hanoi and its aftermath in *A Life with History* (Lawrence, KS: University Press of Kansas, 2004), 183–85. He states on page 185: "the decision to deny Lynd tenure had no basis in budgetary stringency."

Accompaniment

THE IDEA OF "ACCOMPANIMENT"

In the 1970s we found ourselves wondering how we could make a living and raise a family and still contribute to the movements for civil rights, peace, and a better world. We rejected many of the directions in which the Movement of the sixties had splintered.

In the course of the 1980s, we would encounter the term "accompaniment" during visits to Central America and in reading about liberation theology. For us, the idea of accompaniment is that there should be a relationship of equality between the professionally trained person who has a skill to contribute and the poor or exploited person who can offer the lessons of a different kind of experience. We began to use the word to describe how we wished to relate to workers and to people resisting U.S. imperialism in other parts of the world. Later we sought to approach prisoners in that same way.

We embraced the idea of "accompaniment" because it seemed to describe what we had already begun to experience in practice. In her work as a draft counselor (1965–1970), Alice had developed the concept of the "two experts," one the professional with expertise about law and regulations, the other the counselee with a different kind of expertise gained through his or her own life experience. Even before then, in helping to create the Cooper Square Alternative Plan in New York City (1959–1961), and as coordinator of Freedom Schools during Freedom Summer in Mississippi (summer 1964), Staughton was introduced to what we later understood as aspects of accompaniment.

Staughton and Alice in Guatemala, 1998.

It has been supposed by some that "accompaniment" requires uncritical deference to however the soldier, worker, peasant or prisoner may act at a given moment or whatever he or she represents to be true. We disagree.

Archbishop Oscar Romero of El Salvador stressed that "accompaniment" must not mean excusing misconduct by the poor. Romero's Fourth Pastoral Letter, written in August 1979, less than a year before his assassination, most fully describes his understanding of "following" or "companionship." He called on believers "to accompany Christians in their political options" but without disguising their own identities or beliefs. He made it perfectly clear that:

> [i]n the name of the preferential option for the poor there can never be justified the machismo, the alcoholism, the failure in family responsibility, the exploitation of one poor person by another, the antagonism among neighbors, and the so many other sins that [are] concurrent roots of this country's crisis and violence.[1]

Uncritical deference to another's version of the truth can be equally misguided. Our friend the late John Barbero, a former grievance chairman at LTV Steel's Brier Hill Works, told the following story. A member of John's union was fired for hiding out in the back of the mill during the night shift, drinking beer. Through every step of the grievance procedure the discharged worker maintained his innocence. As they were about to enter a hearing before an arbitrator, John turned to his fellow worker and said: "Now, one last time, you weren't hiding out in the back of the mill drinking warm beer?" The grievant replied: "That beer wasn't warm!"

During our years in Chicago before moving to Youngstown in 1976, other models were offered by persons who longed to change the world in fundamental ways just as we did. We encountered, considered, and rejected as options for ourselves, a number of such alternatives.

Symbolic Direct Action?

Friends of ours were involved in what was called the "ultra resistance." Inspired by Phil and Dan Berrigan, small groups would enter a Selective Service office and burn or pour blood over the files, do what they could to smash the nose cone of a missile, or otherwise seek to impede the war effort through direct action.

We ourselves engaged in a kind of symbolic direct action when for years we refused to pay taxes for war. We found that the Internal Revenue Service would seize the money from our bank account and add interest and penalties, so that we ended up paying more. Our protest had no effect whatever on the U.S. war effort. After we retired, when a colleague asked us why we did not seek money for our legal work, Alice responded, "because we would be paying more taxes to be used for bombing people in other countries."

To be sure, the distinction between symbolic and politically effective direct action is not always clear. An action initiated by one or a few persons may be taken up by a multitude, all doing the same thing. Individuals burning or returning their draft cards in the early 1960s became a "We Won't Go" movement within a few years. When in August 1965 a few hundred of us sought to declare peace with the people of Vietnam on the steps of the Capitol, it was symbolic. But the wide publicity the protest received helped to keep alive the possibility of protest until students returned to campuses in the fall.

What came to be our attitude was expressed when our younger daughter indicated that she wished to "protest apartheid and get arrested" at the South African embassy in Washington, D.C. Alice responded that she thought Martha should do what she felt the need to do by way of protest, which might indeed result in arrest, but without the preconceived intent to be arrested.

From the standpoint of "accompaniment," symbolic direct actions often do not communicate beyond the small circle of middle-class idealists who engage in them.

Alinsky-Style Organizing?

Staughton spent a couple of years as a community organizer. He was soaking in a hot bath after the dramatic events of the 1968 Democratic National Convention when the telephone rang. It was Saul Alinsky. Alinsky was starting a school for organizers to be called the Industrial Areas Foundation Training Institute. He asked Staughton to be one of four instructors. Staughton said yes. He thought the Movement needed all the help it could get in learning how to organize!

There followed a period of contradictory experiences. Staughton learned a great deal. He learned that before trying to impose his or her own agenda, an organizer is well advised to find out what ordinary people are thinking and feeling: to ask with regard to any issue, "Is it there?" He learned that the real leaders of a community are likely to be, not elected officials or persons who hold titles in organizations, but individuals to whom others turn when they have a problem. As Mr. Alinsky conceptualized the organizing process, such informal leaders should be gathered together in a temporary steering committee. Then the organizer can

observe which of these grassroots leaders emerge as best-suited to take responsibility in developing the organization.

Mr. Alinsky liked to say that an organizer needed "brains and guts."
Underneath this machismo was an attitude that Staughton has found end-
lessly helpful, namely, that no matter how Bad what may happen, something Good can be made out of it if the organizer doesn't panic. The key
is to maintain a certain cool, a certain inner poise. Then, even in the midst
of catastrophe, the rational mind can still examine all aspects of a situation to discern a creative way to turn any negative into a positive, and
move forward.

Nevertheless, there was (and is) a fundamental difference between the
organizing attempted by Students for a Democratic Society (SDS) and
Student Nonviolent Coordinating Committee (SNCC) in the early 1960s
and the organizing promoted by Saul Alinsky and those he trained. Alinsky borrowed his style of organizing from labor organizers in the 1930s.
He thought that human beings are motivated by money, sex, and the desire for power. Such human beings included Alinsky's colleagues. One
day at the organizing school Staughton was asked if he had forgotten
something. It turned out that he had not collected his paycheck!

Alice had her own criticisms of the organizing she was seeing. The goal
was to build an organization that would have power. "An organization to
do what?" she would ask. "Power for what purpose?" The underlying assumption was that you had to build on people's self-interest. At a national
conference of Jobs and Justice years later, Alice encountered the same
mindset when she suggested as an issue abolition of the death penalty.
"No, we can't bring up an issue like that," she was told, "it would be too
divisive." And when churches in the Youngstown, Ohio area were being
recruited by Alinsky-oriented organizers to form an urban/suburban al-
liance, that was a parting of the ways for Alice. The organizers assumed
that people should be attracted by self-interest (on the part of inner-city
residents) and guilt (experienced by suburbanites).

But Alice also learned some lessons that were valuable in other contexts.
Think through what needs to be discussed before the meeting. Make
phone calls to be sure people know when and where to meet, ask whether
they have transportation, and perhaps begin to sound them out and get
them thinking about the issues. Bring appropriate literature or documents.

Health and Safety Paraprofessionals?

One evening Marcus Raskin, a founder of the Institute for Policy Studies and a defendant in the trial of Dr. Benjamin Spock (the famous baby
doctor) and other persons who promoted the return of draft cards,

showed up on our doorstep in South Chicago. He was wearing a bearskin coat that seemed bigger than he was.

Marcus had an idea. The Occupational Safety and Health Act (OSHA) had just been enacted. Marcus wanted young paraprofessionals to assist local unions in dealing with health and safety problems in the steel industry in the Chicago area. He asked us to organize such an interdisciplinary team. We said yes and did our best to recruit knowledgeable and enthusiastic, but uncredentialed, associates.

Fundamentally the idea was a failure. Once again, we learned much along the way. We discovered that noise could have an impact on the entire person, not merely cause hearing loss; that chemicals used in combination could be especially toxic; that the most dangerous place in a steel mill was on top of a coke oven. However, the basic problem was that the members of our team did not have expertise in industrial hygiene or professional licensing in physiology or law. Any lawyer who was willing to work with us knew nothing about industrial hygiene or environmental law, and the lawyers who did have some expertise did not have time for us.

Becoming a Steelworker?

A final alternative that Staughton briefly considered was going to work in a steel mill. It was a time when voices on the Left were pushing the idea that only the working class could make fundamental social change, and members of many Marxist-Leninist groups were getting jobs in steel mills and automobile plants. There they sometimes encountered older workers who had similarly decided to become "colonizers," as they were then called, in the 1930s and 1940s.

A young friend of ours was working in U.S. Steel's Gary Works. Staughton ran the idea past him. Steve shook his head, chuckling. "Staughton," he finally explained, "you could be there for twenty years and people would still say to each other: Let's see what the Professor thinks."

In the end, it came to seem to Staughton that he could best be a long-distance runner for social change if he did not pretend to be a worker, but found a way to use and not to hide all those years of higher education and to be the Smart Cookie that he was apparently fated to remain.

Our Path

Finding none of these alternatives satisfactory, we developed our own practice of "accompaniment." First in doing oral history, then in becoming lawyers, we made our own path.

DOING ORAL HISTORY TOGETHER

Starting in the late 1960s, we began to do oral history together.[2] The process began before the first of our oral histories were published and still continues.

An early exposure to actually doing oral history came during our years in Atlanta. Staughton arrived at Spelman College having made an unconventional career choice but with a head full of conventional ideas about doing history. He asked his friend Howard Zinn what scholarly papers Howard was preparing for which scholarly panels. Howard looked at him as if Staughton were speaking a foreign language. Howard Zinn was one of two adult advisers to SNCC, along with Ella Baker. The history he was thinking about writing had to do with civil rights struggles in Albany, Georgia, and across the south.

Howard and Roslyn Zinn lived just around the corner from us on the Spelman campus. One day Staughton entered their apartment and found Howard taping interviews with two young SNCC staff members who had just been released from jail. It was a moment of enlightenment. As a teacher, Staughton had already been using Botkin's book of Works Progress Administration (WPA) interviews with former slaves, and a record on which W. E. B. DuBois narrated his life journey. Suddenly it seemed possible actually to do oral history oneself.

First Steps

When Staughton had been writing his Master's essay on Dutchess County, New York, in the American Revolution, Alice typed most of it. While he was in Mississippi in the summer of 1964, Alice compared our typescript with documents in the Yale library for the first edition of *Nonviolence in America*, edited by Staughton alone.

During 1966–1967, along with having our third child and a difficult move from New Haven to Chicago, Staughton watched oral history being done in our home as Alice collected the personal accounts for her book, *We Won't Go*.

In a related effort, Staughton and Michael Ferber invited local draft resistance groups to send them their old newsletters and leaflets, and asked eight or nine groups to make tape recordings.[3] Staughton recalls a group interview with the Boston Draft Resistance Group. An old-fashioned reel-to-reel tape recorder sat in the center of the floor. As topics emerged, members encouraged each other to remember. "That was early in the morning, wasn't it?" "Wasn't so-and-so there that day?" Another such session, with David Harris and Dennis Sweeney of the California draft resistance group, took place in our Chicago living room. *The Resistance*, a history of the draft resistance movement against the Vietnam War, was published by Beacon Press in 1971.

Rank and File

Thereafter we began to do oral history together, and as the list of our publications indicates, have published three such collections.

We deplore the practice whereby some oral historians ask an interviewee, often semiliterate, to sign a written contract giving up all "property" rights in the conversation to the interviewer. We have never done this. We have assured each interviewee that, if we decided to use an interview, we would submit to him or her an edited transcript of the tape-recorded session for the interviewee's corrections and approval.

One group of interviews in *Rank and File* were tape recorded at a series of three occasions organized together with our friend, Charles McCollester, and offered to the public in East Chicago, Indiana, under the title, "Labor History from the Viewpoint of the Rank and File." On these occasions, organizers of unions in the 1930s were talking to a younger generation facing labor struggles of their own. Their accounts appear in *Rank and File* in a section captioned "Your Dog Don't Bark No More." The words are those of African-American steelworker Jesse Reese, summarizing what he perceived as the deterioration of CIO unionism during his time in the mill.

George Patterson, picket line captain at the Memorial Day Massacre of May 1937, drew a connection to the seven men indicted by the federal government after the demonstrations during the 1968 Democratic Convention in Chicago:

> We were charged with exactly the same thing these seven fellows [the Chicago Seven] were charged with: conspiracy to commit an illegal act. Every time you put on a demonstration, always take for granted that this is what's going to happen. I haven't seen it change from the Haymarket days, to the Memorial Day, to the 1968 National Democratic Convention, when the police are faced with a plain group of citizens and are stirred up by the newspapers and foolish propaganda. . . . My heart bled the night of the Democratic Convention.
>
> You know these things happen, and you'll have to be prepared to face them. . . .[4]

John Sargent was the first president of Local 1010, United Steelworkers of America, an eighteen thousand member local union at Inland Steel. To the consternation of traditional labor historians, John steadfastly maintained that in the late 1930s:

[w]ithout a contract we secured for ourselves agreements on wages and working conditions that we do not have today. . . . [A]s a result of the enthusiasm of the people you had a series of strikes, wildcats, shut-downs, slow-downs, anything working people could think of to secure for themselves what they decided they had to have. If their wages were low there was no contract to prevent them from striking, and they struck for better wages.[5]

Another group of narratives in *Rank and File* grew out of meeting Vicky Starr (who, to safeguard her job at the University of Chicago, asked us to identify her as "Stella Nowicki," a name she used when she worked in the stockyards). Vicky and her husband came to see us because they were interested in an alternative school for their children, as were we. Somehow our interest in interviews with rank-and-file activists surfaced. Vicky directed us to Katherine Hyndman ("Christine Ellis" in the book) and Sylvia Woods. Sylvia described the local union she became part of during World War II:

We never had [dues] check-off. We didn't want it. We said if you have a closed shop and check-off, everybody sits on their butts and they don't worry about organizing and they don't care what happens.[6]

(Alice later recalled Sylvia Woods's comment when she was assisting Visiting Nurses. Since all the nurses wanted the union, they took up a collection when they needed money, and they didn't need a closed shop or dues checkoff.)

Vicky, Katherine, and Sylvia became the stars of the documentary movie *Union Maids*. Another memorable experience was sitting together with the three when we all saw, for the first time, a rough cut of the film. When Sylvia saw footage of a laundry in the 1930s she cried out, "That's just how it was!"[7]

There are many other narratives that affected us as well as the audiences for whom the words were spoken. It was because of Ed Mann, John Barbero, and their caucus "The Rank and File Team," whom we were just beginning to get to know when *Rank and File* appeared, that we moved to the Youngstown area in 1976.[8]

We found it difficult to accept the advice of our editor at Beacon Press that *Rank and File* should take the form of a collection of relatively brief accounts. John W. Anderson, Katherine Hyndman (Christine Ellis), and George Sullivan provided us with book-length materials that we carefully edited and reviewed with each of them. Kate Hyndman had written her life story while in jail expecting deportation under the McCarran Act.

George Sullivan grew up in a part of southern Illinois where there were no African-Americans. He was taught to fear black people.[9] George transcended his racism when the military was integrated while he was in the air force:

> The first real association I had [with black people] was in England. I transferred to a new base. I got there in the middle of the day. They told me what barracks I was assigned to. . . . I walked in and I didn't see a white face. It was a barracks full of black people.
>
> I knew, of course, that the sergeant had made an error. . . . I went to the headquarters and told him he'd made a mistake. "No, we've been having some problems about not integrating enough. As new white guys come on the base they're going to be put in there. You just happen to be the first." . . .

The first couple of days I didn't talk to any of them.

Then:

> I was a meat-cutter and I got a bit careless. I cut three or four of my fingers. I had them all bandaged up. I had just been promoted to sergeant but I still wore my corporal stripes. I was sitting out in front of the barracks and the sergeant came by and said, "Sullivan, aren't you a member of the first class?" "Yes." He said, "Well, get your stripes on." "I can't sew with one hand," I said. . . . "I don't care. You'll have stripes on your uniform by tomorrow or we'll just take the stripes away from you."
>
> I was sitting there by myself just wondering what to do. One of the guys in the barracks who'd heard it, he came out and said, "Have you already got your stripes?" I said, "Yeah, I bought them already." He said, "Well, if you go get them I'll sew them on for you." So that was the first thing that really broke the ice. He sat and sewed those stripes on my uniform while we got to know each other.[10]

Guerrilla History and Accompaniment

Oral history is necessarily different from history written only on the basis of documents stored in libraries. It was a kind of "history from the bottom up" for Staughton, as a graduate student, to write about the special experience of farm tenants and artisans during the American Revolution. But in doing oral history there is an inevitable interaction with the viewpoint and motivation of the person interviewed. Oral history went beyond academic history and became a version of "accompaniment": a journey together with another person whose background and experience are very different, and a sharing of insights as between equals.

One learns in doing oral history that ordinary people are driven to try to comprehend what has happened to them and what options they may have in the future. Thus they are obliged to do history, with or without the help of professional historians. That is why some of the best oral history we have done, especially in *Rank and File*, simply transcribed an occasion like that three-part forum in East Chicago when an older generation of activists passed on the lessons of their experience to the young.

It will be obvious to any reader that we learned a great deal from those whom we interviewed. We learned about the particular circumstances of their lives, but we also became wiser about the meaning of the history in which they took part. Staughton has described such learning from persons ordinarily viewed as the mere objects of historical research as "guerrilla history." As we said in the introduction to *Rank and File*:

> Rank-and-file groups tend to be isolated from one another. Individuals trying to transform their work situations (among whom we include ourselves) are also isolated in a deeper sense. Family, church, school, army and workplace combine to make us distrust our own feelings and to be fearful that the dream of solidarity and human dignity is, after all, only a dream.

We said that our book "stands at the side of anyone doing such dreaming." We expressed the hope that the book would offer readers "encouragement to work in their own lives for the release of the human spirit."[11]

WE BECOME LAWYERS

By 1973, Staughton had not been able to get a full-time teaching job for six years. Alice had recently returned to work after two years of disability. She did not have the physical stamina to work with young children any more. Funding for her job and all similar jobs related to child care had been cut by the Nixon administration.

Alice had done well as a draft counselor, putting to use her ability to work with rules and regulations. Staughton could deal better with abstract ideas. We wanted to work together and we thought we had complementary abilities. We decided to go into law.

Staughton at Law School

We knew that it would be much easier for Staughton than for Alice to get through law school. But getting into law school was another matter!

Staughton had taken part in a major sit-in at the University of Chicago not long before he applied for admission to the university law school. In the hope of facilitating a negotiated settlement, it was suggested that one person from the occupation forces and one person from the university faculty might hold a conversation over campus radio. Staughton and Professor Harry Kalven of the law faculty were designated as the representatives. As Staughton remembers it, they became so interested in talking with each other that they forgot to be suitably adverse!

Staughton received a very high score on the Law School Admission Test and applied to the University of Chicago Law School. But, having participated in the sit-in, Staughton was asked by the dean to sign a statement saying he would not engage in civil disobedience on campus. He refused. Why study the First Amendment if he could not exercise it? If he violated university rules, he could be disciplined, but he would not sign anything relinquishing his First Amendment rights in advance, he told them. They warned him that he might not be admitted to the bar but they let him enter law school. We were led to believe that one professor refused to teach that year in protest, but Staughton had that same professor as a teacher during his second year.

Staughton would quietly sit in the back of the classroom. Occasionally a professor would bait him. The topic of contracts that offend the conscience arose. "Ah, Mr. Lynd," said the professor, calling on Staughton from among dozens of students. The dialogue continued for something like half an hour. Staughton did his best to defend the idea that contract law assumes equal bargaining power on the part of the contracting parties, and that workers in their dealings with employers, tenants seeking help from their landlords, or consumers complaining about a manufacturer's products, lack such power. Hence contracts between such parties may have the form of an agreement between equals but in reality are contracts in which the stronger party imposes its terms on the weaker.

Staughton also had the privilege of studying with Harry Kalven. Professor Kalven was an expert in two things: the First Amendment, and the way in which the law grows from one specific case to the next. In his book, *A Worthy Tradition*, published after his death, Professor Kalven combined these two interests, showing how First Amendment law did not manifest itself as the application of unchanging principles but grew from case to case.

One day, at the close of a large lecture class, Professor Kalven asked to see Staughton. He told Staughton that a summer job was available at a public interest law firm in downtown Chicago. Awkwardly, Staughton explained that he intended to work for a "personal injury" firm in Hammond, Indiana. It seemed to Staughton important to be in an office where ordinary people came through the door, seeking help, rather than in a firm located high in a skyscraper, where lawyers devised legal theories and then sought plaintiffs to litigate them.

When Professor Kalven died suddenly in Staughton's second year at law school, his son Jamie asked Staughton's help in preparing for publication Professor Kalven's unfinished manuscript on the First Amendment. Staughton later wrote a comment for the law review on Professor Kalven's favorite First Amendment case, *Brandenburg v. Ohio*.

Staughton did nothing connected with law school after three in the afternoon. Thereafter he was picking up children from school, playing baseball with our son, or heating meals that Alice had prepared over the weekend.

Alice Becomes a Paralegal

Meanwhile, Alice got a job as a secretary in a law-related office. This was the one time in her life when it was important to her to dress well. Why? Because it was the only way she knew to maintain her dignity and self-respect. The job itself, sorting and organizing files about which she knew nothing, was boring and humiliating.

There were law students working in that office. One young man came up to Alice and said, "Why don't you become a paralegal?" Paralegal training was just beginning in the Chicago area. Alice found out about a program at a junior college sixty miles west of Chicago. She signed up for testing. There was a major snowstorm that January evening. For five hours, Staughton drove through the snow, arriving at 9:00 p.m. after the test had concluded. Nevertheless, Alice was permitted to take the test, and soon began her paralegal training. That night is permanently fixed in our memories as Staughton relentlessly battled with the elements, determined to do whatever he could to support Alice.

It was an excellent course, taught by a practicing attorney, on how to do legal research and how to write a short summary of the relevant facts and holdings of published cases. How do you decide what is relevant? Some detail is critically relevant in one context and totally irrelevant in another. How do you use factual differences to "distinguish" the result in one case from what should be the result in another?

During the summer of 1974, Alice went full-time to a new paralegal program at Roosevelt University. Alice remembers being told, don't assume being a paralegal will be a glamorous job: you'll be in a little booth dealing with forms. "Not me," Alice muttered to herself.

For several months, Alice worked for the State of Illinois looking up records to find out why unemployment compensation claims had been denied. She would carefully figure out all of the earnings in each of the relevant periods of time, to determine what the basis was for denying the claim, or to add wages that had not previously been part of the calculation. The problem was, there were only certain paragraphs that had been approved to explain the problem. If none of the paragraphs explained the problem, her supervisor would pick one of the approved paragraphs— not what Alice had actually found based upon the records. Alice would have been furious if she had received such a response and knew it was wrong!

Upon completion of the paralegal program, Alice applied for a job with lawyers who had defended draft refusers. Alice had a lovely little office where she was assigned to go through a hundred leases, all in tiny print, to find out what the deviations were from the standard lease agreement in connection with the sale of a shopping center. This was not what she had in mind doing! Her other work was keeping track of every date when any lawyer in the firm had to appear in court and every deadline for any document to be submitted.

While photocopying a legal notice, Alice saw on the back of the paper an advertisement for a secretary/paralegal to manage the office for a workers' compensation attorney. She thought, Well that job is probably filled, or it's too far away, or. . . . But she could not get that advertisement out of her head. Within a few days, she had a new job. She learned every detail connected with the administration and costs of running a small law firm. We thought that experience would help us in the future if we needed to set up our own law office.

The Private Practice of Law

Staughton graduated from law school in 1976. Through contacts with steelworkers in Youngstown, Ohio, we were able to get jobs at the leading law firm representing unions in Youngstown, Staughton as a lawyer, and Alice as a paralegal.

Alice was hired to assist with workers' compensation cases but very soon a lawyer took her to a filing cabinet that contained Social Security Disability cases. He told her to look at the cases, see what needed to be done and do it. That was all the orientation she had.

After a year, Alice was called into a meeting with the partners who looked at how much money she had generated for the firm and how much it had cost to hire her. Her employment was continued. But Alice took this as a warning that money, not high quality work, was most important to the firm.

Staughton ran into trouble because the clients of the firm were unions but he was determined to help rank-and-file workers. On one occasion the head of the firm asked Staughton on the telephone to prepare a brief for the United States Supreme Court on behalf of a union that failed to file a meritorious grievance for a member. Without thinking, Staughton responded, "I'd drop dead first!"

Sometime later Staughton completed a little book entitled *Labor Law for the Rank and Filer*, published by two west coast longshoremen who ran Singlejack Books. We debated whether we should give the book to the head of the firm or wait until someone else did so. We invited the boss and his wife to dinner and presented the little book to them. Staughton was fired before eleven o'clock the next morning.

After Staughton was fired, Alice continued her job for nearly a year with the attitude that she was working for the clients, not for the firm. One day when our daughter, Martha, was sick, Alice stayed home. (That was one of the benefits of working for a man who believed a mother's first obligation was to her children.) Alice phoned Staughton, who by then was working for Northeast Ohio Legal Services. She asked him to go to her office and bring home incoming mail that she needed to complete a brief. Staughton was seen by business agents of the local Teamsters union, a major client of the law firm, as he walked in and left with the mail. If Staughton could do that, thought these men, how could the union's files be kept confidential? So Alice's job was abolished.

Alice next worked as a paralegal on Social Security disability cases for another private attorney. She recalls being told by one of the partners, "If you can see that there is not much money in a case, don't put much time into it." Alice remembers her response but not whether she said it out loud: "If you ask me to take a case, I will do what the case requires." But she also knew that she had to generate enough income to cover the costs of overpayment cases that were time-consuming and offered no prospect of income for the attorney.

The *U.S. Steel* Case

Staughton's biggest case as a Legal Services attorney was *Local 1330 v. U.S. Steel*, in which he sought to prevent the closing of U.S. Steel's Youngstown-area mills.[12] He had been out of law school only three and a half years when, at Thanksgiving 1979, this crisis came upon the local community.

The people themselves helped to create a legal strategy. One evening soon after moving to Ohio, Staughton visited our friend John Barbero, a steelworker who lived near us in Niles. John showed Staughton a newspaper article in which Arizona politician Stewart Udall drew a contrast between "greenfield" and "brownfield" development. "Greenfield" development was what Robert Moses had proposed in Cooper Square. You destroyed or walked away from an existing situation, and built something completely new from the ground up. This was also what U.S. Steel wanted to do with its steel mills. According to plans developed in the late 1970s, U.S. Steel would abandon its existing facilities in Youngstown and build an entirely new, state-of-the-art complex on the shore of Lake Erie in Conneaut, Ohio. The new mill would have polluted Lake Erie, destroyed a stopover refuge for migrating birds, and endangered the vineyards that lined the shore of the lake from Conneaut to Buffalo.

"Brownfield" development, in contrast, was industrial renovation in the spirit of the Cooper Square Alternative Plan. You began with your existing assets. There were skilled workers, generations of whom had graduated from high school, perhaps spent a few years in military service, and then, with the help of an uncle, a father or a brother, gone to work in the mill. There was an "infrastructure" in the form of access roads and rail spurs. The question was how to preserve these existing assets while replacing the outdated steelmaking technology of the mills.

Steelworkers knew they had been promised that if they could make the mills profitable, U.S. Steel would keep them open. They relied on that promise. According to *Restatement of Contracts 2nd* section 90, when one party makes a promise and the other party relies on it, an enforceable contract comes into being. Even though the management prerogatives clause of the Basic Steel Contract gave U.S. Steel the right to close its mills unilaterally, we argued that because of the additional contract formed by promise-and-reliance, U.S. Steel was legally obligated to keep the mills open as long as they were profitable.

The facts that mattered most were stories steelworkers spoke into Staughton's tape recorder. For example, there was the worker who in reliance on promises he had heard made by David Roderick, chairman of the board of U.S. Steel, purchased a house. On his way home he stopped at one of the area's many railroad crossings. He turned on his car radio and heard that U.S. Steel had just announced the closing of the mill! The young attorney who first represented the company made the mistake of asking for a "more particular" statement of facts. We used the opportunity to present stories like this one.

Shortly before trial, Staughton "deposed" (questioned in the presence of a court reporter) William Kirwan, the company superintendent in the Mahoning Valley. He revealed that he had created and printed on glossy paper a plan for "brownfield" development of U.S. Steel mills in the Youngstown area. There were two major facilities. The Ohio Works, across the river from downtown Youngstown, made molten steel in open hearth furnaces. The steel was then cooled and transported by railroad car to the McDonald Mills, seven miles up river, where it was reheated and rolled into finished coils. Kirwan's idea was to build new electric furnaces adjacent to the McDonald finishing mills. When the new furnaces were ready to operate, steelmaking would be transferred from the Ohio Works to the McDonald Mills without "missing a beat" or disappointing a customer. The cover of Mr. Kirwan's glossy brochure displayed a red light and a green light. At the same moment, Mr. Kirwan explained to me, he would press the red light at the Ohio Works, stopping production there, and press the green light putting into operation the new electric furnaces at the McDonald Mills.

Mr. Kirwan had presented his idea to higher-ups in U.S. Steel's Eastern Division in early 1979. "I want to take this opportunity to sow a seed," he told a budget meeting:

> The seed I want to sow is a "Greenfield" plant on a "Brownfield" site complete with customers. . . . The plant can be built independent of interference with present production and, when complete, you can push the Stop button on one and the Start button on the other. . . .

All that was required, Kirwan had concluded, was some positive thinking and "one helluva lot less dollars than a Conneaut would require to retain a million tons of profitable participation for United States Steel." When Staughton repeated these words to Mr. Kirwan at trial, the Youngstown courtroom broke into cheers.[13]

Mr. Kirwan's plan seemed to provide precisely the concrete alternative that workers and community groups had been seeking. Kirwan, an experienced steel man, had given us the same thing that two city planners provided at Cooper Square: the expertise needed to legitimize a people's vision of the future.

During the trial, Staughton could hardly wait to question board chairman David Roderick about Mr. Kirwan's plan. Why, he finally asked Mr. Roderick, did you not implement the Kirwan plan? Roderick said he had never heard of it! William Roesch, chief executive officer, said the same thing.[14] In other words, the brochure painstakingly developed by the company's own employees with hands-on knowledge of our local steel mills had never made it through the layers of corporate bureaucracy to reach the ultimate decision-makers.

Each day of trial in March 1980, Staughton and other lawyers met with steelworkers and their supporters in a church across the street from the court house. Plans were made to ring the church bells of Youngstown should we win.

We lost. But our friend and colleague Jules Lobel has done us the honor to include the U.S. Steel case as one of a series of cases that he considers "prophetic." A prophetic case, Jules argues, proclaims a principle—in this instance, an industry's responsibility to the community where it is located—that history and later legal decisions vindicate in the end.[15]

Alice at Law School

By 1982, we had not yet found a way to work together in the law. Alice quit her job at a private law firm and went to work as a volunteer with Staughton at Legal Services.

Alice wrote a brief for one of Staughton's cases. Staughton wanted Alice to sign it. "I can't," she said, "a paralegal can't sign with the attorney."

Staughton immediately began to inquire whether Ohio or Pennsylvania were states where a paralegal could take the bar exam and be admitted to the bar without going to law school. The answer was no. It was springtime and law students had already been accepted for the coming year.

One evening in early June, we went to Pittsburgh to meet with some students and law school faculty about using eminent domain to contest mill closings there. On the way, we stopped at the University of Pittsburgh School of Law. Alice asked for an application form and was told it was too late. But she saw a table with information about the Law School Admission Test and there were application forms for the law school as well. She picked up both. The deadline to apply for the Law School Admission Test had passed. That evening, one of the students told Alice that it was possible to "walk in" on the night of the test and take the test if there was enough room. Alice walked in and took the test in Youngstown a few days later. She also applied to several law schools.

On her birthday in mid-July, Alice received the results of the Law School Admission Test. She had done poorly. That seemed to be the end of any hope of going to law school. We continued to go to meetings with law students and faculty in Pittsburgh during the summer. But late in August, at the end of a Thursday afternoon, the phone rang in Alice's office. "This is the University of Pittsburgh School of Law. We would like to offer you a place in the first year class. Can you be here tomorrow morning for orientation?" It turned out that one of the professors at our meetings in Pittsburgh was on the Admissions Committee. When the committee was considering who to accept to fill last-minute vacancies, he had said, "If we offer Mrs. Lynd a place, I know she will come." Alice was placed in a special program for older and/or disadvantaged students.

We rented a minuscule one-room apartment about a mile from the law school. Staughton drove to work in Youngstown and back each day during the week, and Alice took the bus to Youngstown on Friday afternoons. Each semester, we decided which of Alice's courses would be of most interest to Staughton, such as constitutional law, civil rights law, and international law. In the evening, Alice would read aloud to Staughton as he dozed on the bed (but, Alice claims, grasped more than she did).

There was no course on occupational safety and health. However, in a course on environmental law Alice was introduced to the concept of "cost/benefit" analysis. She was troubled to learn that courts actually approve of chemical exposure and pollution standards based on the assumption that a certain percentage of people will be harmed, but it would cost too much to protect everybody. The vulnerable are dispensable.

Preparing for exams at the end of her second year, Alice's right hand became inflamed. The inflammation progressed to both hands over the summer. She could not write. She could not type. She could not slice bread or even a tomato. She returned for her third year at law school with a small tape recorder and a variety of small, colored, self-adhesive dots. Alice had an elaborate color code: as she read cases, she used one color for the facts, another color for the holding, and so on. During class, if the professor made three points referring to a particular case, Alice would put three paper clips on the page in the textbook. After class, she would force herself to recall the three points and then speak into the tape recorder, summarizing what she needed to remember about that case. At exam time, she and Staughton were assigned a room where Alice dictated and Staughton typed her exams. Alice did better in her third year than ever before and graduated with honors.

Operating Engineers

Alice went to law school with the expectation that she would work with Staughton at Legal Services and that she would concentrate on a few specific areas such as employment discrimination, health and safety, and pension law.

While she was still in law school, Alice and Staughton began to work together on a case involving racial discrimination against African-American "operating engineers." It was a first opportunity to combine their different skills in the new medium that they had chosen, the law.

When Staughton was in law school (1973–1976) the University of Chicago did not offer a course in employment discrimination. A decade later, Alice was able to take a course in that subject. We considered Title VII of the Civil Rights Act of 1964, which prohibits employment discrimination, a major tool that we expected to use in our work together. And so on many weekday evenings, after Staughton returned from his long commute to work at the Legal Services office in Youngstown, Alice would read aloud from her huge green paperback textbook on employment discrimination.

One day three black men walked into the Legal Services office. Since their problem concerned employment they were directed to Staughton. They said that they were operating engineers, the workers who drive the huge earthmoving machines needed to dig foundations or build roads.

David Morgan, Early Cooper, and Joe West complained of discrimination by both the union and the employers. Union members were assigned to work by a union functionary known as a dispatcher. The contractor would call the union hall, specifying the type of machinery on which proficiency was required for a particular job. The dispatcher would go down the list of union members and supposedly assign the work to the next man qualified to operate that kind of machine. When he had been sent out to a job, the man would go to the bottom of the list.

David, Early, and Joe said that African-American union members were dispatched to work of brief duration that required only elementary skills. Moreover, during lunch breaks at the job site, experienced white operators would give younger Caucasians the opportunity to drive more complex machines under the guidance of the older worker. African-Americans were rarely provided such "seat time," were thus denied the opportunity to develop their skills, and hence tended to receive repetitive job assignments to the simplest (and poorest-paying) jobs.

Staughton filed a class action with David, Early, and Joe as named representative plaintiffs. The Youngstown local union of Operating Engineers and the Builders Association were named as defendants.

The first challenge was to make a *prima facie* case of discrimination. We decided to use as a microcosm the people who had been in apprenticeship classes jointly operated by the Operating Engineers union and the Builders Association. This had two advantages: the number of apprentices who had passed through the program in a defined number of years was manageable, and defendants considered the apprenticeship program as the strongest evidence of their efforts to overcome racism.

While still a student, Alice took the statistical data provided by defendants about their apprenticeship program and analyzed them. A pattern emerged. So long as minorities were in the apprenticeship program, the work to which they were assigned was more or less equivalent to the work assignments of Caucasians. Once minorities completed the program, however, their hours of employment decreased dramatically when compared to the hours worked by nonminorities.

We presented this evidence to the court. The judge approved a consent decree that required defendants to provide reports from the pension fund jointly administered by the union and the employers. These reports set forth the number of hours worked by each member of the union during each month.

By this time, Alice had finished law school and took on the responsibility of extracting relevant information from the reports and attending a monthly meeting with representatives of the union and the Builders Association. Later, in the supermax prison litigation, we used this experience as a model. Rather than ask for a court-appointed "monitor," we requested production of documents and monthly meetings at which Alice would play the same role that she had in the operating engineers class action.

On the morning of one of the monthly meetings, a young black man called the office and told Alice that the dispatcher had skipped over him for a job that he was qualified to do. She asked him, "Will you go with me to the union hall this afternoon?" As he sat beside Alice at the meeting, she noticed the tattoo on his arm: "Born to Lose." This time, he did not lose. The facts as he reported them turned out to be correct and the dispatcher was fired!

When the lawsuit was filed, minorities worked approximately 4 percent of the total hours worked by union members. Six years later, that percentage had risen to approximately 12 percent, more or less corresponding to the percentage of minorities in the local union's total membership. Minorities were still not getting enough "seat time" to improve their skills. However, very much as in school desegregation cases, the judge took the position that the numbers showed the problem of discrimination to have been solved so that no further intervention by the courts was justified. The court terminated the litigation.

A couple of years later, Alice received a call from one of the minority operating engineers. Referring to the site where a new jail was being built in Youngstown, he said, "They're moving a lot of dirt down there and I don't see any black faces."

This time, we did not go back to court. We tried another strategy. An Ad Hoc Committee for Jobs and Justice, consisting of representatives of the Youngstown Area Urban League, the NAACP and other organizations, agitated the issue. Records were obtained and Alice found that the percentage of hours worked by minorities had reverted to what it was before the operating engineers class action.

The threat of direct action produced better results in a later encounter with Burger King. Throughout the Youngstown area, Burger King hired only a few African-Americans, and only to work "in the back." Our written protests produced no results. We then wrote Burger King and said that, regrettably, we would be calling for an area consumer boycott on Dr. King's birthday. Within twenty-four hours we had a written agreement with Burger King! Once again Alice would monitor compliance.

For both of us, the practice of law became a way of entering into the lives of other people whom we would otherwise never have known, and to provide services that were useful to them.

OUR UNION MAKES US STRONG

Varieties of Union Experience

The first of us to have personal experience with trade unions was not Staughton, but Alice. In the fall of 1952, when we moved to Chicago, we needed jobs. Staughton got a job as a stock boy at the Hyde Park Co-Op and Alice was hired as secretary of the Education Department at Roosevelt College.

Alice soon became active in the Roosevelt College Office Employees Union (RCOEU). She remembers one union meeting when there was a controversy over the union's wage demand. The officers were recommending an across-the-board wage increase of ten cents an hour except for employees at the lowest level who would get only a nickel. Alice was not on the lowest level, but she protested: "A loaf of bread costs as much for someone on Level 1 as it does for me." A vote was taken and her position lost. However, in later years as an employee at Northeast Ohio Legal Services, Alice advocated an across-the-board raise of so much per hour rather than a percentage increase in salaries. "To those who have, more shall be given"—a spreading wage gap—always seemed wrong to her.

In May 1972, Alice was hired by the Chicago Regional Board of the Amalgamated Clothing Workers of America (ACWA). The membership of this union was 80 percent female and low-paid. The Amalgamated had determined that it could not bargain for wages high enough to cover child care and health care costs for its members. So it built a child care center, and a health care center for its members and retirees in the Chicago area. The federal Office of Economic Opportunity (OEO) was interested in promoting employer-based and union-based child care and the ACWA received a grant for one of ten demonstration projects. Alice became the Demonstration Project Coordinator for the Amalgamated Day Care and Health Center.

This job had many facets, one of which was to prepare written materials about the day care center. As an employee of the union, Alice was instructed as to what she could and could not say. She was told never to say anything negative about the union. She could not say, "we tried one thing and it didn't work so we tried another." No. She could only speak and write about the union's positive accomplishments.

When the grant came to an end, there was a job open in the union's Education Department. One of the men who worked in that department took Alice aside and said, "Alice, that is not the job for you! When you are out in the field and someone brings you a legitimate complaint, you have to defend the union, right or wrong."

At one point, the union called a local meeting to vote on a dues increase. At that meeting, a spokesman for the union told those in attendance, "all we want you to do is come to meetings, pay your dues, and we'll take care of the rest." The minutes of a meeting of the Chicago Regional Board were read. The Board recommended a dues increase. We voted to accept the minutes and people began to leave the meeting. Alice didn't understand. It turned out that approval of the minutes was regarded as a vote on the dues increase. She thinks that meeting lasted no more than ten minutes. She was disillusioned.

In later years, Alice was a lawyer for a group of retirees whose interests had not been protected by their union. One of the retirees said, "I always thought that if I paid my dues the union would take care of me!" Alice remembered the words of the Amalgamated representative: pay your dues and leave the rest to us. Union membership had become like an insurance policy, not something that brought people together—in the words of the National Labor Relations Act—for "mutual aid and protection."

The Workers' Solidarity Club

We moved to Youngstown in the summer of 1976. For the first year, Staughton tried to "fly under the radar": to present himself as a labor lawyer, not a notorious radical who had been to Hanoi in wartime. But in August 1977, a story about him appeared in the Youngstown *Vindicator*, with a picture of Dave Dellinger, Bob Moses, and Staughton, at the Assembly of Unrepresented People, covered with red paint thrown by prowar hecklers.

Jack Walsh had just been discharged for leading a wildcat strike at the Schwebel Baking Company. He saw the newspaper story, and the photograph, and jumped to the conclusion, "That's the lawyer for me!" Staughton represented Jack then and for years thereafter. Wherever he worked Jack tried to organize a union, acquiring the nickname "Union Jack." Jack would often say, "If you drove a pickup truck loaded with hundred dollar bills to Staughton's house, Staughton wouldn't get up off the couch!"

Early in the 1980s members of a Utility Workers local union approached us. The local owned a frame house on the south side of Youngstown that it used as local union headquarters. Would Staughton offer some classes there on labor law?

He did. The next fall the invitation was renewed, but this time, Staughton decided he would talk about more than how to file a grievance or a National Labor Relations Board (NLRB) charge. He would put on the table a question he intuited was felt by all: "What has gone wrong with the union movement? Why are we all brokenhearted lovers?"

The class Staughton recalls most clearly was a discussion of the Pope's encyclical "On Human Labor," which had just appeared. His Holiness said that there were two kinds of labor: labor for an external reward, and labor for the greater glory of God. All one long evening Bob Schindler, an electric lineman (and brother-in-law of Jack Walsh), maintained that when he went up on the utility pole he was working for the glory of God. (Bob later explained that when an elderly woman lost electric power due to a storm, after fixing the outside lines he made sure she had power inside the house, rather than leave her to wait over the weekend without power until some other technician could come.)

When the classes ended we decided that we did not want to stop meeting. We would reorganize as a club to which any rank-and-file worker with a problem could turn for help. The Utility Workers local had just been through a long strike during which it received very little support from the Mahoning Valley central labor union. We resolved to be a "parallel central labor union" where, on the second Wednesday evening of every month, a worker in trouble could get help in a hurry. Alice suggested the name, the Workers' Solidarity Club of Youngstown.

At several of the Club's early meetings participants gave long speeches, as they might have at a union meeting. Gradually we developed our own distinctive style. We had no bylaws and no officers. Whoever had something on his or her mind at the beginning of a meeting—a guest to introduce, or a problem to present—was asked to be chairperson for the evening. We had no dues but regularly passed a hat. Our decisions were not exactly by voting and not exactly by consensus: often Ed Mann[16] would ask, "Is anybody opposed?" Typically we ended the evening by standing in a circle, arms around each other's shoulders, singing the first and last verses of "Solidarity Forever!"

An important difference between the Club and almost any other organization we know had to do with the way it was decided to do things. We did not ask, "Does the Club approve support for the [so-and-so] strike?" Instead, someone would say, "I heard the [so-and-so] workers were on strike. I went by their picket line, and they need firewood. I'm going over first thing tomorrow morning. Would anyone like to come with me?"

Our first big challenge came in the fall of 1982 when the American Federation of State, County, and Municipal Employees (AFSCME) local union at Trumbull Memorial Hospital in Warren, Ohio, went on strike. As is the case with many strikes, there had been inadequate preparation, and the people on the picket line were mainly women whereas the local union leadership was male.

Ed Mann and Ken Porter visited the hospital picket line. A few nights later, several members of the Club met in our basement to discuss what could be done. Alice took notes. When someone said, "We should put out a leaflet," she read the notes she had taken and that became the text of the leaflet. It began this way: "Think before you cross a picket line! Think before you take your neighbor's job!"

The Club called for supporters of the strike to rally early every Wednesday afternoon at the hospital entrance. The rallies became larger and larger, drawing on different kinds of workers and unions throughout the area. Demonstrators chanted, "Warren is a union town! We won't let you tear it down!"

The hospital obtained an injunction, and in due course, a hearing was held at the nearby courthouse to determine whether Ed Mann and others should be charged with contempt. The courtroom was so crowded that strike supporters stood against both walls. The judge asked Ed, "Why didn't you obey the injunction?" Ed responded, "What injunction? No one ever read it to me." There was a silence as the judge surveyed the crowd in his courtroom, all of whom might vote in the next election for Common Pleas Court judges. "Well," he finally said, "unless the police can prove that you had notice of the injunction, I guess what I will do is give you a warning. You know about the injunction now. Don't let it happen again!"

There was, however, another happening before the strike was finally settled and the union survived. One Wednesday afternoon the crowd at the hospital entrance decided to march to nearby Country Club Lane, where several of the hospital trustees had their homes. A strike supporter wrote with her lipstick on the front door of one home. She was arrested and led to a nearby patrol car. The crowd sat down around the patrol car (just as in the Berkeley Free Speech Movement twenty years before)! More arrests followed. Finally strike supporters went back to the hospital where Ed Mann was arrested and dragged across East Market Street by two hel-meted officers. It would be four years before the Ohio Supreme Court dis-missed all charges against him.

Radicals talk a good deal about how to create "class solidarity" among workers. It was our observation that the Workers' Solidarity Club created class solidarity because of the fact there were many different kinds of workers in the circle. (We always put the chairs in a circle for our meet-ings.) A tow motor driver at the Delphi plant compared contract language with a steelworker. A nurse explained that when she went to work for the Service Employees as a union organizer and tried to form a union of or-ganizers, she was fired.

The sentiment of solidarity extended beyond Youngstown, and beyond the United States. When Pittston coal miners went on strike, a Youngstown delegation traveled to Camp Solidarity. The Lynds made several trips to Nicaragua (see the next chapter), and one year, Bob Schindler and Ed Mann's son Ned went with us. Ned, a sheet metal worker, helped to erect a vent over a particularly smoky furnace at Nicaragua's only steel mill. Bob spent a joyful week with a Nicaraguan utility crew on the streets of Managua. He spoke no Spanish, and they no English. They got on fine. On their last day together, work ended early and they got a head start on alcohol consumption at our *despedida* (good-bye party).

The next summer, Bob and a young fellow worker from Ohio Edison re-turned to Nicaragua. They went to the Bocay area in the far north, where Benjamin Linder had been killed by contras while installing a hydroelec-tric system. There they contributed what they could to finishing Linder's project.

Solidarity USA

Soon after Alice graduated from law school, LTV Steel, the conglomerate that had acquired Youngstown Sheet & Tube, Jones & Laughlin, and Republic Steel, declared bankruptcy and immediately cut off retiree medical benefits.[17] Delores Hrycyk (pronounced "her-is-sik"), wife of an LTV Steel retiree, worked as a receptionist in the office of an optometrist two floors below our Legal Services office. Ms. Hrycyk telephoned Youngstown-area radio stations and called a meeting of LTV Steel retirees to be held in the public square the next Saturday. A thousand people attended. Ms. Hrycyk invited those interested to attend a second meeting a few days later. On that occasion she asked, "What shall we call ourselves?" A man suggested from the floor that we resembled Polish Solidarity. All right, Delores responded, we'll call ourselves "Solidarity USA."

Staughton and Alice became lawyers for the retiree group, Solidarity USA.[18] Retirees have limited leverage in the world of labor because in most unions, including the union representing workers at LTV Steel (the United Steelworkers of America), retirees do not vote on provisions for their benefits in the collective bargaining agreement and do not vote for union officers. On one occasion we estimated that the collective bargaining agreement under consideration by LTV Steel and the Steelworkers union would provide $7 in benefits for every current worker, who still produced something of value to the company, for every $1 planned to be made available to retirees.

Solidarity USA sought to overcome this handicap by its physical presence. Elderly men and women took long chartered bus rides to city council meetings in Cleveland and Pittsburgh, and to the headquarters in those cities of LTV Steel, Blue Shield/Blue Cross, and the Steelworkers union; to Congressional hearings in Washington, D.C.; and to sessions of the bankruptcy court in New York City. Our standard *modus operandi* was not to ask for a meeting but to inform the targeted party that we would arrive on a certain day. If they met with us, we said politely, well and good; if not, they could anticipate a very large picket line. Our uniform experience was that, after our chartered buses from Youngstown, Cleveland, Pittsburgh, Aliquippa, and Canton arrived, we would be invited inside. If the invitation were limited to a designated number of people or to "your leaders" or "your lawyers," we would make it clear that we had a committee that included a number of retirees who would describe their own experiences. We were never refused.

Solidarity USA was effective. When LTV Steel emerged from bankruptcy, we calculated that the average retiree had regained most of the health benefits and pension payments that the company had tried to take away.

And, like the Workers' Solidarity Club, Solidarity USA did not limit its concerns to the problems of its own members. At one meeting the question arose, Should we be content to ask for health insurance only for retirees or should we demand single payer health insurance for all Americans? The latter position was endorsed by acclamation.

Very few lawyers had experience representing the workers or retirees who lost medical, life insurance, and pension benefits. Most lawyers who knew anything about such benefits worked for employers, or unions, or the plans themselves.

Gradually, in Solidarity USA, Alice found her voice as an advocate. At first, Alice was alarmed by one steelworker who would say, "It's time to bring out the baseball bats!" But she came to realize that this was not what others in the group wanted to do. Within a few years, she was working with employees and retirees of twelve different companies that failed to meet their contractual obligations to provide benefits. She loved to meet with a group of men and women and with their assistance piece together what the plans provided and what their situation was. Sometimes, in larger meetings, she would be able to call on one group of workers to answer questions from another group of workers who were just beginning to encounter problems that the earlier group had already confronted.

Workers Against Toxic Chemical Hazards (WATCH)

Ever since our introduction in Chicago to issues of health and safety, we had sought ways to pursue such problems more effectively.

There was one plant where the noise from a compressor was causing hearing loss. A couple of workers came to the office, Alice wrote down what they said and drafted an OSHA complaint. About forty workers signed it. An inspector came to the plant, tested the noise levels, and tested the men for hearing loss. The offending piece of machinery was soon enclosed in soundproofing. After that, we were told, "You could hear a pin drop."

A very important part of what we did as lawyers was to try to help clients who had become chemically poisoned by toxins at work. In a steel processing plant in nearby Warren, Ohio, the workers looked at old seniority lists and indicated to us the names of fellow employees who had died from some form of cancer. The men worked over vats of acid with no protective clothing and no exhaust system. Alice drafted a complaint to the National Institute of Occupational Safety and Health (NIOSH). NIOSH did not do anything because there was not a significant showing of a large number of men dying from the same kind of cancer. But as soon as the complaint was filed, the company began to clean up. The union steward told us he had been trying to get gloves and aprons for twenty-five years and now they got them. A ventilation system was installed over the vats.

One day four men, two black and two white, walked into the Legal Services office. They had been referred to Staughton by a representative to the state legislature. The four described themselves as "chemically disabled" workers for General Motors at its nearby Lordstown assembly complex. They said they had reacted to chemicals in the plant, and eventually developed sensitivity to a wide range of chemicals such as fumes from new carpets or cigarette smoke or perfume.

Staughton responded that he had heard about Black Lung among coal miners, and even Brown Lung among textile workers, but chemical poisoning among auto workers was something new. Did it really exist? One of the four men invited us to tour the Lordstown plant. "When you finish the tour, I'll be waiting for you at the stairs and take you upstairs to the paint booth," he said.

The paint booth turned out to be a rectangular-shaped space that could accommodate perhaps half a dozen workers. Automobile bodies moved through the area on an assembly line. The workers stood on both sides of the line, wearing flimsy white cotton masks, and sprayed paint not just onto cars but across the cars into each other's faces for ten hours a day. Excess paint dropped down into moving water at the base of the booth, and thence to a collecting tank on the floor below.

Another problem at Lordstown was that fumes from one part of the plant mixed with fumes from another part of the plant. Mixtures of chemicals can be more toxic than exposure to a single chemical, but testing and standards are for exposure to one chemical alone. Furthermore, toxic air that was expelled from the plant was being sucked back into the plant and recirculated.

With our help, the four men organized a group called Workers Against Toxic Chemical Hazards (WATCH). Alice recalled from the days we worked on occupational health and safety in Chicago that the United Automobile Workers (UAW) had published a pamphlet on how to do a "proportional mortality ratio" (PMR) study. Since the UAW represented the auto workers at Lordstown, we suggested they ask the union for a PMR study.

The local union officers were hostile. If Lordstown workers called attention to a problem there, Lordstown might not get the next model car. The plant might close and the jobs go to Mexico.

Staughton recalls returning to the Legal Services office with the four men to regroup. Since the company was creating the problem, and the union wouldn't help, what could we do? Again the men themselves suggested a next step. "What about the obituaries?" they asked. "Well, what about them?" Staughton responded. It turned out that these workers regularly followed the obituaries of former General Motors employees in the two local papers. The obituaries often did not provide the cause of death but nearly always reported the decedent's age. "They died so young!" Staughton was told.

He asked the men to go to the local libraries and photocopy obituaries for the past eighteen months. They did it. The next question was how to bring this information to public attention so as to pressure the company and the union into doing a PMR study. One of the men said, "What about a Lordstown Memorial, like the Vietnam Memorial in Washington?"

And that is what they, not we, did. They got large pieces of plywood and painted them white. Then they entered, in elegant black Gothic lettering, the names and ages at time of death of workers who had been employed at Lordstown. We called a press conference at an out-of-the-way location (because we could use it for free), at a bad time of day for the media (early afternoon).

All that morning calls came to Legal Services. "This is the Cleveland *Plain Dealer*," said a voice. (The *Plain Dealer* rarely sent a reporter to Youngstown.) "How do we find this press conference?"

Somehow workers at plants other than Lordstown, such as a group of women from Packard Electric, got the word and showed up for the event.

The plant manager and the president of the local union also came but soon left. It was not their show. Instead the occasion was chaired by GM worker Chuck Reighard. The most dramatic moment was when a woman in the audience told how her husband would come home from work and cough up terrible black phlegm. Then he died, she said. "What was his name?" Chuck asked. The woman called a name and Chuck said, "I worked next to him!" They fell into each other's arms.

The press conference and our demand for a PMR study were front-page news. The company and the union announced that they would do the study. They did. The study showed that deaths among former GM workers at Lordstown were significantly higher than in the general population, even though workers usually are healthier than the population from which they were drawn. For pancreatic cancer, the incidence among former Lordstown employees was as much as seven times higher than in the community.

Years later, when we were passing the Ford plant in Warren, Michigan, near Detroit that makes SUVs, the shop chairman pointed to the plant's high smoke stacks. "You did that," he told us. The stacks had been raised to prevent the problem of recirculating toxic air that we had identified at Lordstown.

When new carpet was put in our office, Alice's first thought was to warn our chemically sensitive clients not to come to the office. But within a couple of days, Alice began to realize that her eyes were burning even after she left work, and it was as if her entire breathing system had been burned raw. Thanks to our clients, she was able to recognize that she herself was becoming chemically sensitive. As she stood at the photocopy machine, she realized that she did not have to stand at an industrial machine in order to do her work.

For the last four years of employment, Alice worked at home and had to avoid direct contact with clients who smoked or wore perfume. She recalls telling the president of Solidarity USA that she would no longer be able to attend meetings because of the cigarette smoke. He, however, promptly announced, "There will be no more smoking at meetings." Cheers went up! Lots of the retirees were bothered by the smoke but no one had felt able to ask others to stop smoking.

Visiting Nurses Solidarity

Visiting Nurses Solidarity (VNS) was a coming together of women, all of whom contributed time and energy to improving their working conditions. VNS numbered at the outset twenty-two Registered and Licensed Practical Nurses (LPNs).[19]

When we first came in contact with the nurses employed by the Visiting Nurse Association (VNA) of Youngstown, they had gone through a great deal of struggle. They were already calling themselves the "Solidarity" group.

At one meeting, several alternative directions were discussed. One was seeking to meet with the VNA board of directors, either individually or collectively. A second was forming an independent union. Nurses who had previously belonged to unions in hospitals did not want the kind of union they had previously known. And they could not imagine ever going on strike because the whole point of their work was to take care of people who needed timely care.

Staughton suggested a "straw vote." When it came to a show of hands for forming an independent union, every nurse raised her hand. Weeks later, when the NLRB held an election, everyone voted and every ballot was for the union.

Soon after the union was organized, management decided to lay off three LPNs. Two were black, had many years of service with the agency, and had children to support.

The nurses discussed what should be done. Maybe they should propose to management that all the nurses would take rotating layoffs for two weeks at a time. After the first week, everyone could draw unemployment compensation for any additional weeks on layoff during the year.

But, the discussion continued, What if management said they would retain the high seniority LPNs and lay off the nurses with least seniority? The three nurses with least seniority were asked to go to another room and discuss whether they were willing to be put in such a vulnerable position. In a few minutes they returned, saying they would take the risk and declared their support for proposing rotating layoffs.

The agency accepted the proposal. Later, one of those black LPNs became a very effective president of this predominantly white union, and another became secretary.

During the early years, VNA hired first a lawyer and then a labor negotiator who were as obstructive as they could be. It became union policy to be sure that every member of the union had an opportunity to be present at collective bargaining, so everyone would know why progress was so slow and difficult.

A number of the nurses worked part-time because they had elderly parents or young children for whom they had responsibilities. Management wanted to take away medical insurance and other benefits for part-timers. We asked the full-timers at a VNS meeting how they felt. Were they willing to take less in their own paychecks, if necessary, to cover the cost of continuing medical insurance for part-timers? "Of course," answered one of the full-timers (an LPN whose job the union had saved), "they're only trying to divide us."

We hung tough on the issue of benefits for part-timers and we won. It made a big difference to the part-timers. They felt a part of the union and they contributed a great deal of work to it. Two part-timers later became copresidents of the union; they worked on alternate days. Another part-timer was very sharp in putting her finger on problems that needed to be corrected and suggesting contract language.

Our approach was to put into our negotiating demands everything we wanted, and not put in anything we didn't want just so we could bargain it away. We knew we wouldn't get everything we wanted. But sometimes management liked an item we suggested and we didn't have to give up anything to get it. For example, the home health aides wanted a tote bag with the VNA logo on it to carry their supplies when they made home visits. They won that with no discussion. We didn't press for a union shop with dues checkoff. We didn't need it.

From time to time, as happens in many workplaces, management would offer a job to a member of the union. It came as somewhat of a surprise to Alice when the union president took a job with management. Alice began to think over what the union president knew that she would carry with her into her management position. Alice recalled one phone call in particular in which the union president was complaining about management and saying, "They lie!" Alice responded, "That doesn't mean that we lie." Alice hoped the union president would take with her the confidence that, when the union said something, management could count on it.

Gradually, lawyers were phased out of the negotiating process. The nurses—and by this time, home health aides also—did everything themselves: drawing up bargaining demands, negotiating, whatever had to be done.

We learned a great deal from working with VNS. We saw solidarity being acted out. Alice has a fundamental disagreement with a male union organizer with whom she has discussed solidarity and power. She saw the solidarity of VNS save jobs by sharing the layoffs, and save part-time benefits by being willing to share the economic pie. She totally rejects the message from a male voice that "solidarity may give the union power, but power is the name of the game; power is the whole game."

Belonging to a union should not mean paying dues as if you were buying an insurance policy, and expecting to receive a certain package of benefits and protection in return. To us, union means taking care of one another by standing together the way we saw VNS do time and again.

Solidarity Unionism

The four major groups that we helped to organize in Youngstown—the Workers' Solidarity Club, Solidarity USA, WATCH, and VNS—no longer exist. They were experiments in an approach to labor organization that we came to call "solidarity unionism." Solidarity unionism has been more or less adopted by the Industrial Workers of the World (IWW) and very successfully implemented at Starbucks stores in New York City and elsewhere.

Disguise it as they may, mainstream trade unions do not trust their own members. Their reform proposals tend toward the creation of larger and larger union structures that can more easily be controlled from above. As we have sought to explicate in a series of publications,[20] even the most "progressive" unions now take it for granted that a collective bargaining agreement will include, first, a "management prerogatives" clause that permits the employer to shut down plants and relocate work unilaterally, and second, a "no-strike" clause that prevents union members from doing anything about these livelihood-destroying decisions. The result has been that during a generation stretching back to the 1970s unions have stood by passively while companies moved productive capacity to the southern United States or abroad. As Ed Mann and John Barbero used to say, unions have been able to do no more than negotiate "funeral arrangements": severance pay, Trade Readjustment Assistance benefits, and the like.

By contrast, in all the groups that we helped to form in the 1970s, 1980s, and 1990s, rank-and-file workers took the initiative and provided leadership from below.

Our positive experience with solidarity unionism is qualified by the fact that the organizations with which we worked did not prove permanent. Yet in contrast to a traditional unionism that endlessly repeats the same mistakes and has no answer at all to capital flight and "globalization," we think that solidarity unionism offers a signpost toward the future. Any group of workers can start with concrete, winnable demands and seek through collective direct action a change in their conditions of labor.[21] The desired form of organization should be a horizontal network with many centers of initiative. The organizer must work *with* people, not just for them: it is *their* lives that are at stake and they must have the last word in the decisions with which they will have to live.

NICARAGUA

In the mid-1980s, two things drew our attention to Nicaragua.

First, a fragment of evening television showed a Quaker woman—someone like ourselves—describing the project of a group calling itself Witness for Peace. They were going to Nicaragua in the hope of positioning themselves between struggling cooperatives and the "contras," based in Honduras, who were harassing these settlements by blowing up infrastructure and killing supporters of the Sandinista national government.

Second, we read an editorial, which reported that when the Sandinistas displaced the Somoza government in 1979, they freed captured soldiers except for persons believed to have committed specific crimes. Indeed, Tomás Borge, one of the founders of the FSLN (*Frente Sandinista de Liberación Nacionál*), had the opportunity to confront a man who had tortured him when he was in a Somocista prison. "This will be my revenge," Borge is supposed to have said. "I'm going to let you go."

We made five trips to Nicaragua, using our two- or three-week summer vacations. The last of these trips was in August 1990, when we spent several days in one of six cooperative settlements in northwest Nicaragua collectively known as El Bonete (pronounced "bow-neh-teh"). The blue mountains along the Honduran border could be seen on the horizon. Our friend Father Joe Mulligan drove us to El Bonete, and returned for us at the end of the week. There were about 110 families in El Bonete. We stayed in the home of Catholic nuns who were members of one of the cooperatives. There, Staughton concluded, he had finally come face to face with what liberation theology calls the "preferential option for the poor."

Alice

El Bonete was the poorest community we had ever seen. The cats and dogs looked like skeletons with skin and mangy fur. There was not enough food, not enough water. Soap, toilet paper, or a new toothbrush were unexpected luxuries.

My first impression of El Bonete was of children one would not want to touch. They had mucous oozing from their eyes and noses, and skin rashes on their faces and arms.

Before he left us, Father Joe announced that I could sew. I was taken to a home where there was an old treadle (not electric) sewing machine. I was asked to fix the machine. Much to my surprise, I did! Then I was asked to clean the machine. They brought me gasoline to do that. I recall three sewing projects. The first was basically to reassemble rags into a dress for a girl maybe ten or twelve years old. I fitted it on her.

I was told there was another sewing machine. It was in a house with more light and I preferred to work there. I asked for a chair to sit on at the machine. In this home of perhaps fifteen people, they were able to find only a child's wooden chair. My chin was at the level of the cloth as I operated the treadle with my feet.

Next, I was asked to take a dress with a pleated skirt and convert it into a maternity dress for a teen-age girl who was expecting her first baby. I took cloth from the pleats to make gussets under the arms, extending down the length of the dress. I folded the dress carefully and delivered it to the girl's home.

The most challenging project was to make a pair of pants for a two-year-old boy. For cloth, I was given one leg from a pair of women's slacks. The crease down the leg was stitched, and I had to make two legs for the child's pants with the crease running down the front of each, plus a belt, and the mother said she wanted pockets! She gave me a short zipper. I had no pattern. It was not easy to find something that fit the child to help me get the right size.

I needed a button to go at the top of the fly. One of the nuns went from door to door asking whether anyone had a spare button. Finally someone came up with an old U.S. military button.

When I finished the pants, I told the mother I would like to take a picture of her son wearing the pants. The mother insisted first that the boy be bathed (by pouring several bowls of water over him) and dressed in a white shirt that was so long it covered most of the pants.

In the course of these several days, I was not only touching the children. I was trying to enhance their appearance. It was a way to overcome my initial revulsion and to reach out to them.

Staughton

This is a slightly edited version of a diary that I wrote while we were in El Bonete.

Tuesday

It is so hot in El Bonete that outdoor work virtually stops between 10 a.m. and 4 p.m. That's why this is written at midday.

The nuns who have given us a place to stay belong to the Little Sisters of Jesus. It is a nonpastoral order that lives with the poor but does not attempt to give them religious instruction (which suits us just fine). At present two of the four sisters are here: a third is visiting her mother, and a fourth is at a ten-day retreat for persons who live in "difficult situations."

One of the sisters present is Nelly. She was born in Argentina. Her father was a doctor for workers building the state railroad. The family was middle-class but too poor for Nelly to go to the university. Nelly lived in Chile before coming to Nicaragua. She is fifty-three.

The other sister is Carmencita. She is Salvadoran and from a *campesino* family. The province in which she was born is very fertile, she says, but the land is in the hands of a few *patrons*. In 1980 the army forced her family to leave, along with the rest of the village. First the young men of draft age left under cover of a rainy night, then the little children, and finally older persons. Several members of her family have been killed. The rest are scattered in different countries. Carmencita chose a religious vocation when she was twenty-five, and is now forty-two. She expects to make her final, lifetime commitment this coming December. (But, some time after our return to the States, we learned from Father Joe that Carmencita had chosen not to take her final vows.)

The sisters' home is much like every other home in the settlement, with the addition of pots of flowers. Inside is a cleanliness and order that is partly the work of the sisters but also reflects an artistic instinct evident in this part of Nicaragua. In 1987 we visited the nearby settlement of El Ojoche (pronounced "oh-ho-cheh"), from which residents of El Bonete left to obtain land of their own. We were struck then by the red tile roofs, set on roughly hewn beams; the smooth white adobe walls; and the artistic design of the stoves, the drying racks for cups, and other household implements. El Ojoche reminded us of the Macedonia Cooperative Community where we lived from 1954 to 1957.

In El Bonete bamboo and concrete blocks have replaced the adobe, but the rest is the same. There is even a neat, clean outhouse, an immense relief in this nation of toilets (without seats) that don't flush.

A small *capilla* (chapel) is part of the house and adjoins one of the bedrooms. It is about ten by twelve feet. The altar is a tree stump with a vase of flowers on the floor before it. The concrete block of the wall next to the altar is in an open flowered pattern that admits air. Shoes are left at the door. Worshippers sit on planks resting on concrete blocks or on mats that cover most of the floor. On one wall hangs an orange fabric, with photographs of Archbishop Romero and of the six Jesuits killed in San Salvador in November 1989. On it Carmencita has embroidered Romero's famous words about grains of corn that must die so that there may be new growth, and two ears of corn, yellow and brown in their green sheaves.

In the adjoining cooperative, members of which arrived later, the homes are of wood. They will have concrete next year, Nelly says, and we saw stacks of concrete blocks beside many homes. Electric light came to the settlements recently. The next project is piped water. For now, water is hauled from wells each of which is perhaps half a mile away. Nelly gets up at 3:45 a.m. to draw water before it gets muddy. When I went with her this morning the first well was already dry. The second well, a mere hole in the ground, requires the drawer to pull up the bucket without scraping mud from the sides of the well (and without falling in). I wasn't very good at it. Installation of water pipes for pumped water requires digging trenches down one side of the streets. Each family has been assigned a certain length of ground to dig. This will be one of my tasks while we are here.

We've explored two shelves of paperbacks in our room. It is a working collection of liberation theology, for readers who need these ideas so as to persevere. The books include Dietrich Bonhoeffer, Eric Fromm (*The Art of Loving*), *The Communist Manifesto*, and the writings of Che Guevara, but consist mainly of works such as the homilies of Archbishop Romero, as well as three copies of that bible for pastoral workers in the campo, *Donde No Hay Doctor* (Where There Is No Doctor).

Wednesday

The Sandinista government, aided by funds from the Swiss government, assisted the residents of El Bonete in obtaining land, materials for building homes together with some technical assistance in constructing them, materials for digging two of the three wells, and the health center and five-room schoolhouse that stand on the hill overlooking the settlements. There are thought to have been only six votes against the Sandinistas in El Bonete.

In response to a question about the Sandinista Front, however, Carmencita told the following story. There was a stray cow from which the whole community drew milk while they waited for the owner to appear and claim her. A Sandinista security officer appropriated the cow for a friend. When Carmencita—who says what she thinks—expressed criticism, the officer spread stories about her in the community.

What about Sandinismo in general? we persisted. Carmencita replied that it was a very good thing "but we are all human beings." What about now, the Sandinistas having lost the national election? I think, said Carmencita, that there are many seeds which will need to seek new ways (literally *caminos*, or "paths") to grow.

Staughton continued the discussion with Nelly as they walked in quest of a liter of milk to the place where the cooperative keeps its herd of cows.

Our destination was the location where the families of the settlements lived when they first came from El Ojoche. It is near a river, and very lush, but the river floods and so the people had to move. The cattle are still kept there, the lactating cows and calves in one corral, the rest of the herd in another. (Alice heard volleys of shots last night. The rumor at the wells was that cattle were stolen.)

Near fields of tall green corn there were fields of rice and corn that had failed. One rice field had been tilled by fifteen women from all six cooperatives. It failed partly because of the terrible drought—only four small rains since last November—but also because a rice field should be plowed four times before planting, and the women had money to plow only twice. Nelly said it would have been wiser to do a smaller area but do it better.

We saw a man plowing with two oxen. His plough handle was a thing of beauty, a tapering piece of smooth hardwood with two large notches.

To say that El Bonete is a group of "cooperatives" explains little. What one has here is a constellation of arrangements as complex as any medieval manor. So far we think we have learned the following:

1. Each cooperative has title to its land. This was the reason for moving to El Bonete, in that those who came were landless where they lived before. Ownership is a source of great pride (and of conflict all over Nicaragua, as former owners try to reclaim their property). In El Ojoche, Carmencita says, a ceramics cooperative failed because the owner of the clay charged too high a price. The women of El Bonete have revived the project. Do you have to get clay from the same *dueño*? we asked. No, Carmencita flashed back, we have our own clay. "Here we are the bosses."

2. Preparation and seeding of the land are done in common. These and other collective tasks, like stringing barbed wire fence, are performed Wednesdays and Thursdays. Cultivation and harvesting on assigned plots are apparently individual responsibilities. Thus the household in which we live is responsible for two *manzanas* of land,

on which the sisters work in rotation during the peak periods of the agricultural cycle such as the month of September.

3. Anything that might be understood as capital—land, cattle, a tractor, three sewing machines, water pipe, barbed wire, axes, picks, and shovels—is obtained and owned by the group. Individuals own radios (common), wrist watches (rare), televisions (only one, purchased recently), hammocks, machetes, the stones on which corn is kneaded into tortillas. We see no cars and few trucks. A bus is said to come to El Bonete on occasion, although we have yet to see it. Yesterday Nelly got a ride with Father Joe to Chinandega, expecting to return with the cooperative's tractor, which was making a market run. She missed connections and had to walk the six miles from the highway, in the hot sun, carrying a heavy load of produce. Arriving exhausted in the late afternoon, she found that the beautiful bananas she had bought in town had turned to mush in the heat.

4. There is very little sale to the outside world, and so, very little cash income. One teacher left the school because she could not be paid. Because of the drought, El Bonete is selling off its animals for cash.

5. Despite all these elements of common life, Nelly and Carmencita are reported by Father Joe to believe that since the election the people of El Bonete have become more individualistic. A clue to what the sisters may have in mind is Carmencita's description of the effect on refugees from El Salvador of life in the refugee "concentration camps" in Honduras. It unified them, she says, interlacing the fingers of her two hands. Now as the refugees return to El Salvador they do everything together, according to Carmencita.

This brings us to Nelly's view of Sandinismo. As we ducked through barbed wire fences on our way back from the corral she said, as I understood her: "People in this area voted for the Front because it gave them so much. But nationally the Front lost touch with its base and that is why it lost the election. It did not understand the people's perception that the war had become perpetual, and the longing to end the draft."

It is appalling at El Bonete to see girls who could not be more than fourteen years old pregnant or holding their babies in their arms. We asked the sisters for their views on family planning.

Carmencita spoke first. She said that, of course, she had not had the experience of having children. Her opinion, she went on, was that in some cases having many children seemed to make their parents happy, but in other cases many children meant not enough food and not enough clothing. Many children also limit a woman's ability to take part in meetings and other community activities. Carmencita favors dialogue about family planning on a case-by-case basis. She said that some women in the community already practice it.

Nelly delivers babies when the midwife is not available. She expressed a concern that too many children deform a woman's body. She said that in her experience some contraceptive devices cause inflammation and infection. She favors the rhythm method as the most natural but also believes that it isn't sure and requires a discipline that *"no existe."* Thus the question is difficult.

We asked Carmencita whether she believed that *machismo* in Nicaragua had decreased in the ten years since the Revolution. She answered, No.

At supper we discussed violence and nonviolence. Carmencita described in detail the behavior of the Salvadoran army in her canton, and of the contras on the one occasion that they approached El Ojoche. The soldiers have no respect for old persons, for children, or for women, Carmencita said. Both in El Salvador and in El Ojoche the people did not attack in any way but this did not protect them, according to Carmencita. In El Salvador, Carmencita said, torture is the people's daily bread. She concluded in her straightforward way: "I think there is a right to defend oneself."

Thursday

The four of us sing a great deal. Some songs are primarily religious. Thus a song of this part of Nicaragua begins, "When a group of brothers approaches the altar, God's smile is there." In other songs the longing for a more just world is uppermost: "When the poor come to believe in the poor, we will be able to sing of freedom and we will build fraternity."

We have learned more about the history of the move from El Ojoche. One family there owned just over thirty *manzanas* (about fifty acres). Because the land was to be divided among ten children the owner was not really wealthy, but the people considered him *rico* (rich).

The sequence of events paralleled the evolution of Sandinista agrarian policy: First, people spontaneously put up houses on the thirty *manzanas*, arguing that they had no alternative. The Front supported them. This made the owner angry.

Second, the Front offered to find land for the owner in another location so that the people could have the thirty *manzanas* in El Ojoche. The owner refused to move.

Third, the people of El Ojoche, anxious to find a way to support themselves, at the suggestion of the Front formed cooperatives to bake bread, make ceramics and hammocks, and keep bees. (This was what was going on when we visited in 1987.)

Finally, the land at El Bonete became available after the owner moved to Miami. Under the Agrarian Law of the revolutionary government, abandoned land was subject to expropriation. Accordingly, the land was nationalized and offered to the people of El Ojoche and other communities on condition that they form cooperatives to own and operate it.

Carmencita thinks that the people who moved to El Bonete have an unusual unity because of their ceramics craft, passed on from mother to daughter in the home. Their large jugs with painted designs are considered *sucio* (dirty) by people from other communities because of the Indian origins of the craft.

Just before supper we visited Doña Petrona, a woman of about seventy who is the "mistress potter" of El Bonete. She was firing two large pots by the simple expedient of building a conical fire around them. The firing takes about two hours, we were told. Doña Petrona invited us to return tomorrow to see how the pots are made. Carmencita learned the craft from Doña Petrona in El Ojoche. But here they don't have the same kind of clay, so the pots they make cannot be as large.

Friday

At breakfast we exchanged little gifts with Nelly and Carmencita. Their present to us was a ceramic representation of the flight into Egypt, Matthew 2:13–21.

We are tying up loose ends. As promised, I visit the cooperative's ploughman and photograph him with his oxen. His name is Isaías (Isaiah). We visit Doña Petrona and observe the steps by which she makes her splendid pots.

Carmencita says she doesn't find this life so hard because she is a *campesina*. Watching her, tall and erect, carrying twenty liters of water on her head as do the women and children of El Bonete, one can believe it. It seems that the other sisters find the life harder. We remarked that Father Uriel Molina, who (like Nelly and Carmencita) critically supports the Front, believes that God has temporarily hidden (*escondió*) his face. No, Nelly smiles, I think God is here right now. Life is hard but good (*duro pero bueno*).

Alice and Staughton

We have never seen such poverty as in Nicaragua: the children who would beseech us to let them wash the car for a few cordovas, or to buy chewing gum when the car was stopped at a traffic light; people along the roads gathering every stick to use or sell as firewood; and Rosa salvaging from the waste basket a plastic bag Alice threw away, or asking Alice to let her use the water in which Alice had washed clothes with some powdered detergent she had brought from the States. Later, when we visited refugee camps in Palestine and Alice saw well-fed pets, she asked our friend Sam where they got enough food. He told us the butchers throw them scraps. There were no such scraps in Nicaragua!

We loved Nicaragua. We loved the sunsets over Managua. Ordinary people appeared to have extraordinary awareness of social and political issues, and in their own ways they were willingly making very great sacrifices. The government ministers and intellectuals we met seemed much like ourselves, doing their best to build a new and better society but not having much relevant experience to bring to so daunting and complex a task.

At the end of our fifth and last trip to Nicaragua, in August 1990, the Sandinistas were no longer in power and a government more acceptable to the United States was in office. The Nicaraguan revolution was over. We were not there to see the revelation of what came to be known as "the Piñata"—not candy falling on the ground when a child struck the object in which it was suspended, but computers, houses, and other spoils appropriated by the Sandinistas as they left their positions. We had tried to listen and not be taken in by the official lines. But we had not seen the seamy side of Nicaraguan politics. We wondered what disillusionment the mothers, wives, and sisters of the fallen must have felt. And it has made us hesitant to draw conclusions about what is going on in other parts of the world without living in those societies for a period of years.

PALESTINE

Staughton

During Gulf War I, we helped to organize a series of weekly meetings on conscientious objection and topics related to military counseling. We planned to repeat the series, and had reserved the space in the basement of the Cathedral in Youngstown, when the Gulf War ended. Someone suggested that we continue the weekly meetings but change the topics to the Holocaust, Palestine, Lebanon, Middle Eastern poetry, and other topics about which a few of us had a lot of personal knowledge and most of us knew nothing.

That year, Easter, Passover, and Ramadan fell at almost the same time. The idea presented itself of an occasion at the Arab-American Community Center in Youngstown devoted to the sharing of experiences. There would be no political speeches, attendees were instructed. It was a magical evening. Our friend and future colleague in prison lawsuits, Jules

Lobel, described a visit to Israel. During the day he collected accounts of civil rights violations in the West Bank. In the evenings he spent time with members of his father's family, who had lived in the area since the eighteenth century. Their political positions ranged from ardent support of a greater Israel from the Mediterranean Sea to the Jordan River, to opposition to service in an occupying army in the West Bank.

The two most moving accounts were by Sami Bahour and by a young man who grew up in the Ein El Hilweh refugee camp in southern Lebanon.

Sami Bahour came to the United States from Palestine in the 1950s. He had expected a life of ease. Instead he found himself working long hours in a bakery in Youngstown, Ohio. A friend suggested that he buy a carload of cheap products, drive to Mississippi, and sell the junk to African-American sharecroppers too frightened to say "No" to a man who might be white. He did so. Then one day something occurred to him. Mississippi was a good deal like Palestine, with one difference: here, he was one of the oppressors. Sami Bahour went back to Youngstown, eventually started a grocery business, and assisted African-American competitors to set up their own stores.

The young man whom we called "Mazin" was imprisoned by the Israelis along with all other males between the ages of sixteen and sixty in a part of Lebanon invaded by Israel in 1982. He spent many months in a concentration camp called Ansar. After the event at the Center, Alice and I were urged to collect oral histories of Palestinians. We tape recorded an interview with Mazin. At the end of the interview I asked him with fear and trembling what he made of his experience. To my astonishment he answered:

> When I lived in the [refugee camp], I never met a Jew, I never met an Israeli. The propaganda was that they were all killers. The first time they bombed the Camp, I was eleven years old. It was 1972. They destroyed a lot of houses. They killed a lot of my friends. What would you expect me to feel about Israelis? . . .
>
> When I went to prison, I met some Israelis. I changed my attitude. When we heard that [an Israeli guard] killed himself because he could not stand the situation and was very sympathetic with us, and when I met [another guard, he] was really a nice person! He was a human being! I started distinguishing between one person and another.[22]

After the culminating event at the Arab-American Community Center, Sam Bahour (son of Sami Bahour) invited us to go with him to Palestine. Sam was taking a group of high school students who had relatives there for a couple of weeks during the summer of 1991. We went. And, after we completed the first draft of the book of oral histories that was later published as *Homeland*, we went again with Sam in the summer of 1992.

Alice

The following images from those two trips have profoundly influenced how I think about the Middle East, "terrorism," and United States foreign policy.

It was apparent to me that there was intense fear and hatred of Palestinian youth for Israeli soldiers and vice versa. In Jenin, one of the older sons in a large family was in prison for having killed an Israeli. The youngest son described Israeli soldiers shooting bullets at the ground in a circle all the way around him. As we sat on the couch in the living room of this family, Israeli planes screamed overhead toward Lebanon. For me this was not only deafening but also frightening.

Elsewhere on the West Bank, we saw the scars of injuries to the hip of a man who had been shot with a kind of dum-dum bullet that expands in all directions once it enters the body.

We visited a mother and child in a hospital. A man who was wanted by the Israelis was carrying the child as he ran. Soldiers shot at the man and hit the two-year-old child who would from then on be paralyzed.

We visited a hospital in Jerusalem where I saw a man with a bandage on the small remaining bit of one foot.

We visited a Palestinian refugee camp where Israeli soldiers pointed rifles at our driver, stopped the car, and ordered us to leave.

In another refugee camp, we visited a family who was living in two tents next to their house which had been "sealed" by the Israelis. I talked with the very old woman who lived in the one room of that house that had been left unsealed for her. She said that all her life she had lived under occupation: under the Ottoman Empire, under British rule, and then under the Israeli occupation.

We visited in homes that were scheduled for total demolition due to the accusation that a member of the family had engaged in some sort of security breech. Near the remains of one house that had been demolished, a child's shoe lay on the ground.

We frequently heard about and sometimes saw strips of land that had been cultivated by Palestinians for generations, but had been confiscated by the Israelis for military security zones. Typically, the Israeli settlements were on hilltops overlooking Palestinian villages and fields below. At a wake for a young Palestinian, I sat with the women in one room while Staughton was with the men in another part of a house. I asked one of the women, "What is it that you want?" Her answer was simply, "We want our land!"

At a refugee camp in Gaza, wide areas had been cleared of houses to make dirt roads so that Israeli patrols could move through and make security checks. When an alarm sounded, I went with the women and children into a bedroom. Later, we peered through bullet holes to see whether the Israelis had left the area. That evening, we went out at dusk when masked Hamas demonstrators were scrawling graffiti on the walls, and others, unmasked, handed out leaflets. We stayed in a home that was scheduled for demolition because one member of the family was thought to have been involved in a security offense.

At another location in Gaza, I climbed over a pile of rubble and picked up a fragment of a beautifully painted tile, probably from a kitchen or bathroom of a home that had been demolished.

We listened to a Palestinian young man who fingered his gun as he talked, saying he was ready to "throw his life against the wall." Later, we talked with a man whose brother had intended to give his life in a suicidal mission. The man with whom we were speaking said he understood why his brother felt that way but that was "not a very mature idea."

We talked with a doctor who worked in one of the health centers. We learned that Hamas, and other groups that have militant wings, provide much of the health care, child care, and training programs for women to help them learn survival skills.

We drove past flourishing Israeli *kibbutzim* (collective farms) along the Jordan River. We could see efficient irrigation systems in use and productive crops and fruit trees. But on the other side of the road there was drought and desolation where Arab families were denied water. We visited the home of a man who could not obtain a permit to add an additional room to his house when the son married and brought his wife to live with the family. He had had to sell his animals. He anticipated that he would lose his land and be able to support himself and his family only as hired labor for Israelis.

In Hebron, we climbed up what was left of stone steps to an upstairs room where an old man lived. Most of his large house that had been the home of an extended family had been destroyed by the Israelis. And just across the barbed wire fence from his house was a large water tank with an Israeli six-pointed star on it. Israelis and Palestinians were living under very different conditions within a stone's throw of each other.

We met with labor union organizers who were restricted in travel, were in and out of jail, and were able at best to get Palestinian employers to allow their employees to participate in one-day strikes against the occupation without losing their jobs or being disciplined.

In Jerusalem, we saw a couple of plays in which the actors were both Israeli and Palestinian. All I recall of one play was the effort of prisoners to nurture and preserve a single flower growing in a small pot.

We met with a woman who participated in human rights demonstrations sponsored by Women in Black. We met with a man from Yesh G'vul, an organization of Israelis who refused military service in the occupied territories. We went to Tel Aviv and a small town near Tel Aviv where we stayed in the home of Arab Israelis one time, and non-Arab Israelis another time. We went to the Church of the Nativity in Bethlehem and walked on stones that were smooth and worn down by pilgrims for centuries.

In Nazareth, we visited a man who showed us his grandfather's deed to the land: land which the Israelis had ordered him to strip of its ancient olive trees at his own expense.

We went to the Golan Heights where only five out of more than a hundred villages were still standing, the rest having been demolished during the 1967 war. We saw signs along the road in Hebrew and English, but not in Arabic, warning not to leave the road because of the danger of land mines. We went to the no man's land between the Golan Heights and Syria where family members, who had been separated at the time Israel annexed the Golan Heights, could shout to each other through megaphones (mail and phone service being prohibited). On our way back from the Golan Heights, we passed through areas where the Jewish population had watered lawns and swimming pools. In El Bireh where we were staying, Palestinians were not allowed to water their squash and other vegetable plants.

Back in the States, we interviewed a man who had grown up in Bethlehem and who had wanted to be a school teacher. "Occupation is bad," he said. "If you were angels and you tried to administer an occupation, it would still be bad."

More than fifteen years later, these impressions are still vivid. I don't have to look at our photograph albums or anything in writing to recall them. I came away from the second trip wishing we could focus on and accomplish one thing: stopping house demolitions. Since then, I often ask, What are we doing that makes people hate us and do "terrorist" acts?

I am inclined to think that there are good reasons why people on both sides of the Israeli/Palestinian conflict hate and fear each other. But destroying life and the means to sustain life only makes matters worse.

We talked with elderly people who remembered a time when Palestinian and Jewish neighbors lived together in peace. They assisted each other and comforted each other in times of grief. They recalled Palestinians lighting the fire for their Jewish neighbors on the Sabbath when labor was forbidden, and Jews baking special bread for their Palestinian friends on special occasions. "Why couldn't it be that way again?" they asked.

Staughton

We do not wish to be understood as simplistically pro-Palestinian. The following seem to me to be true:

1. Palestinians have thrown away the opportunity to enlist world public opinion behind the demand to end Israeli occupation of the West Bank by suicide bombings of Israeli civilians. Such indiscriminate killing is always and everywhere wrong.
2. So long as it extends many civil privileges only to Jews, the State of Israel cannot describe itself as democratic. The approximately one-fifth of Israeli residents who are forever barred from full equality with their Jewish neighbors exist in a state of *de facto* apartheid.
3. Unless and until Israelis are prepared to give up their occupation of the West Bank, a "two-state solution" is no longer possible. The settlement of hundreds of thousands of Israelis in the West Bank, on sites of their own choosing often seized from Palestinians, with superior access to water, and in communities connected by a network of roads for Israelis only, as well as the protection of these unlawful colonists by the Israeli army, prevent the creation of a geographically coherent and potentially self-sustaining Palestinian state.
4. Prophetically, tragically, but also hopefully and never to be forgotten, the ethical vision underlying protest against current Israeli policies derives from the most ancient books of the Old Testament itself: each of us must welcome the stranger, protect the widow, and periodically equalize the fortunes of rich and poor. We are all fellow citizens of the world.
5. Remote as its realization may seem at present, the single, secular, and bi-national state advocated by Jews such as Martin Buber and by the Palestine Liberation Organization when it was founded, seems in the long run the inevitable solution for all concerned. Any demographic disadvantage that might be experienced by Israelis in such a single nation would be slight when compared to the minority status of previously dominant whites in the new South Africa.

When we went to the Golan Heights, we visited one of the few remaining Arab villages. Growing apples appeared to be the principal means of livelihood in the area. We were invited to a barbecue in an apple orchard. A form of Syrian white lightning called "arak" flowed freely. It was decided that each group—Arabs and Americans—should sing to the other. I was nominated for our group, and decided to sing the song "Joe Hill" about an organizer for the Industrial Workers of the World who was executed by a firing squad in Utah during World War I.

I was concerned that Joe Hill might appear to be one more p
American. So, before I began to sing, I tried to explain that Joe Hill had
been born in Sweden, that he is thought to have taken part in the Mexican
Revolution led by Emiliano Zapata. . . .

Our host held up his hand. "You don't have to explain," he said. "We
understand. Joe Hill was with Spartacus in ancient Rome. Joe Hill was
in Chile, and in Guatemala. But right now," he paused, "Joe Hill is a
Palestinian."

NOTES

1. Archbishop Oscar Romero, *Voice of the Voiceless: The Four Pastoral Letters and
Other Statements* (Maryknoll, NY: Orbis Books, 1985), 155 (following or companionship), 127 (accompanying in their political options), 140 (never justify misconduct by the poor).

2. To date we have co-edited or co-written the following:

Rank and File: Personal Histories by Working-Class Organizers, 1st ed. (Boston: Beacon
Press, 1973); 2nd ed., illustrated (Princeton, NJ: Princeton University Press, 1981); 3rd
ed. (New York: Monthly Review Press, 1988);

Homeland: Oral Histories of Palestine and Palestinians, with Sam Bahour (New York:
Olive Branch Press, 1994);

Nonviolence in America: A Documentary History, rev. ed. (Maryknoll, NY: Orbis Books,
1995);

Liberation Theology for Quakers, Pendle Hill Pamphlet 326 (Wallingford, PA: Pendle
Hill Publications, 1996), reprinted in Staughton Lynd, *Living Inside Our Hope: A Steadfast Radical's Thoughts on Rebuilding the Movement* (Ithaca, NY: Cornell University Press,
1997);

"'We Are All We've Got': Building a Retiree Movement in Youngstown, Ohio," in
Gary Bellow and Martha Minow, ed., *Law Stories* (Ann Arbor, MI: University of Michigan Press, 1996);

The New Rank and File (Ithaca, NY: University of Cornell Press, 2000).

3. Michael Ferber and Staughton Lynd, *The Resistance* (Boston: Beacon Press,
1971), xi.

4. A. Lynd and S. Lynd, *Rank and File,* 88–89.

5. A. Lynd and S. Lynd, *Rank and File,* 99–100.

6. A. Lynd and S. Lynd, *Rank and File,* 118.

7. See A. Lynd and S. Lynd, *Rank and File,* 111–14.

8. A. Lynd and S. Lynd, *Rank and File,* 261–78.

9. A. Lynd and S. Lynd, *Rank and File,* 202–3.

10. A. Lynd and S. Lynd, *Rank and File,* 203.

11. A. Lynd and S. Lynd, *Rank and File,* xix.

12. Staughton Lynd, *The Fight Against Shutdowns: Youngstown's Steel Mill Closings* (San Pedro, CA: Singlejack Books, 1982), and "The Genesis of the Idea of a
Community Right to Industrial Property in Youngstown and Pittsburgh,

1977–1987," *Journal of American History*, vol. 74, no. 3 (Dec. 1987), 926–58, reprinted in *Living Inside Our Hope: A Steadfast Radical's Thoughts on Rebuilding the Movement* (Ithaca, NY: Cornell University Press, 1997).

13. *Local 1330 v. U.S. Steel*, transcript, 322, quoted in S. Lynd, *Fight Against Shutdowns*, 170–71.

14. *Local 1330 v. U.S. Steel*, transcript, 175 (Roesch), 240–41 (Roderick).

15. Jules Lobel, *Success Without Victory: Lost Legal Battles and the Long Road to Justice in America* (New York: New York University Press, 2003), chap. 6: "Plant-Closing Litigation: 'Youngstown Sure Died Hard'."

16. Ed Mann (1928–1992) was a leading spirit of the Workers' Solidarity Club of Youngstown. For more about him, see Ed Mann, "I'm Going Down That Hill," in Lynd and Lynd, ed., *The New Rank and File* (Ithaca, NY: Cornell University Press, 2000), 95–110.

17. See Staughton and Alice Lynd, "Labor in the Era of Multinationalism: The Crisis in Bargained-For Fringe Benefits," *West Virginia Law Review*, vol. 93, no. 4 (Summer 1991), 907–44.

18. See Alice and Staughton Lynd, "'We Are All We've Got': Building a Retiree Movement in Youngstown, Ohio," in *Law Stories*, ed. Gary Bellow and Martha Minow (Ann Arbor: University of Michigan Press, 1996), 77–99.

19. Most of this account of VNS first appeared in *Impact*, a monthly newsletter edited by members of the Workers' Solidarity Club of Youngstown.

20. We spent thirty years in day-to-day association with rank-and-file workers in Chicago and Youngstown. In this chapter we recount episodes or aspects of experience that did not find their way into books. Among the books are: Alice and Staughton Lynd, ed., *Rank and File: Personal Histories by Working-Class Organizers* (New York: Monthly Review Press, 1988); Staughton Lynd, *Solidarity Unionism: Rebuilding the Labor Movement from Below* (Chicago: Charles H. Kerr, 1992); Staughton Lynd, ed., *"We Are All Leaders": The Alterative Unionism of the Early 1930s* (Urbana, IL: University of Illinois Press, 1996); Staughton Lynd and Alice Lynd, ed., *The New Rank and File* (Ithaca, NY: Cornell University Press, 2000).

21. See Staughton Lynd and Daniel Gross, *Labor Law for the Rank and Filer: Building Solidarity While Staying Clear of the Law* (Oakland, CA: PM Press, 2008).

22. Staughton Lynd, Sam Bahour and Alice Lynd, eds., *Homeland: Oral Histories of Palestine and Palestinians* (New York: Olive Branch Press, 1994), 121–22.

The Worst of the Worst

MAMA BEAR, *ALICE LYND*

We lived for years in one of the ten highest crime areas in Chicago. We used to wonder whether it would cost less to leave our doors unlocked rather than replace the windows broken by thieves who came into the house. Unless I was on the way to the grocery store, I rarely carried more than $5.00 with me.

One dark winter evening as I was walking from the train to our house, I became aware that a couple of men were quietly following me. I turned the corner toward our house. So did they. I figured I could not get to our house before they would jump me. I turned around and said, "Good evening!" They asked me for bus fare. I took out my purse, expecting them to grab it but they did not. I gave them a couple of dollars. They then turned around and walked toward the bus stop. I was trembling as I entered our empty house, got the stroller and went out again to get Martha from the babysitter.

A few years later, walking home from the bus stop on a summer afternoon, I suddenly found myself being dragged along the sidewalk by the strap of the bag across my arm. The next thing I remember is seeing a man carrying my pocketbook into an apartment house across the street. A woman was looking out the window of the apartment house. I called to her and said, "Whoever took my pocketbook can have the money but I need the bag back." About a half hour later, I was on the phone reporting the robbery when the operator interrupted the call saying there was an emergency phone call for me. She connected me with someone who told me that if I came to a certain corner near our house someone would give

Jason Robb was condemned to death for his alleged role in the prison uprising at Lucasville, Ohio, in 1993. As one of the prisoner representatives in the lawsuit concerning Ohio's supermaximum security prison, he sat at the counsel table in court with the Lynds and other lawyers. At one such hearing in August 2005, Jason, who had learned that morning of the Court of Appeals decision against Alice (see chapter on "Mr. X"), thought Alice looked sad. He drew this rose, wrote "Smile" underneath it and passed it across the table to her.

me my bag. I went to the corner and a man, who looked quite different from the one I had seen entering the building, handed me my pocketbook. (What was most troublesome was that my eyeglasses had been taken and it took a week to replace them. Meanwhile I strained to do my bookkeeping job without them.) The police called me that evening and asked me to come to the police station and view a line-up of possible suspects. I refused. I said I did not want to finger the wrong person.

It never crossed my mind that I would end up working with prisoners.

How We Got Involved in Prison Work

When Lessley, one of the founders of Workers Against Toxic Chemical Hazards, was imprisoned only a half hour drive from where we live, Lessley asked us to do the "paperwork" necessary to be placed on his visiting list. For six years, until Lessley was transferred to a distant prison, we visited Lessley nearly every month. Every visit led us to new questions and new insights.

On one occasion, Lessley told us he had just had his annual TB test. He wondered aloud whether prisoners coming to the new private prison in Youngstown, from a prison in Virginia where the incidence of TB was high, would be tested before being transferred to Youngstown. I inquired and learned that the answer was no. In fact, hundreds of prisoners were transferred without their medical files, and without continuing their medications for diabetes and other potentially serious conditions. Another time, Lessley made us aware of "prison labor" doing work that could have been done by unionized workers.

We began to go to statewide conferences sponsored by students at Oberlin College. As a result, when Ohio decided to build a supermaximum security ("supermax") prison in Youngstown, we were contacted by staff of the American Friends Service Committee telling us someone was needed to monitor what went on inside that facility. Furthermore, a national campaign against control units was planned for April 1996 and we were asked to plan an event in Youngstown.

What Is a Supermax Prison?

We knew nothing about "supermax prisons" or "control units" where prisoners are kept in solitary confinement for twenty-three or twenty-four hours a day for years, and where physical and mental abuse is sometimes rampant. I began by reading all the articles I could obtain on conditions in supermaximum security prisons and the psychological effects of prolonged solitary confinement, not only on the prisoners but also on the guards in such prisons.

I was determined that if I was going to do anything about the new supermax in Youngstown, it had to be together with people who lived in or near Youngstown, not just students from outside. I drafted a paper called, "What Is a Supermax Prison?" and I invited people on the mailing lists of the Workers' Solidarity Club of Youngstown and the Youngstown Peace Council to a meeting. Fifteen people came. I read my paper and then asked, "Does anyone want to do something about this?" Yes. "What?" "Plan an educational forum."

A woman who lived near the site arranged for us to hold the first forum in a chapel on land within sight of the cranes that were building what was later named the Ohio State Penitentiary (OSP). At the same time, the Corrections Corporation of America was preparing to open a new private prison in Youngstown, so the forum focused on both new prisons. Nearly a hundred people came.

First Contacts with Men Condemned to Death

I wanted one of the speakers at the forum to be a person who had been held in prolonged solitary confinement, or a close relative of such a person. I found both. One of them was Jackie Bowers, sister of George Skatzes (pronounced "skates") who had recently been sentenced to death for his alleged role as a leader of the prison uprising at Lucasville, Ohio, in April 1993 (otherwise known as the "Lucasville riot").

Jackie put us in touch with the lawyer who would handle George's appeal. The lawyer told us that someone needed to read the entire record and then look for information that should have been in the record but was not. We first visited George in the fall of 1996 and ever since then we have tried to visit him every month.

George introduced us to other prisoners sentenced to death for their supposed roles in the Lucasville disturbance, Jason Robb and Keith LaMar. Jason and Siddique Abdullah Hasan, a Muslim imam alleged by the State to be the principal leader of the uprising, lent us papers from their trials. We began to correspond with them as well.

Beginnings at OSP

In April 1998, the fifth anniversary of the Lucasville uprising, tours of the unfinished OSP were offered to the public. We went, as did students from Oberlin College. Various students were given conflicting information about how long prisoners would be required to stay at OSP and other questions. We arranged to go with one of the Oberlin students to meet with the warden and his assistant.

In early May 1998, we received letters from Jason and Hasan. They said that they had been awakened one morning at four o'clock and told to pack their personal property, they were going to Youngstown. They were among the first prisoners to arrive at OSP. They described the trip and the treatment they received en route and upon arrival.

A week later, George Skatzes was sent to OSP. Staughton and I made the first visit by anyone to any prisoner at OSP. George was in a booth where he sat for two hours on a fixed stool with his feet chained and his hands cuffed behind his back. A glass partition separated him from the booth in which we were locked. A correctional officer sat just outside George's side of the booth.

On our next visit, George was wearing a "black box" that held his hands and arms in a rigid position, with one hand above the other, the upper hand facing up and the lower hand facing down, so that it was impossible to use the hands in coordination with each other. It was years before we were able to get the administration to stop using the black box routinely during visits.

Initially, the property restrictions were very severe: no socks, no T-shirts, no books other than one soft-cover holy or devotional book, no newspapers, no magazines, no radios, no TV except for institutional programs for several hours during the day. I recall George saying, "Never before in my life have I been in a place where I could not have a bar of soap!" At that time there was also no outdoor recreation, and no exercise equipment in the very small individual indoor exercise spaces. Each "pod" had one exercise area where outdoor air could come in through a grating. All of those conditions changed during the course of our advocacy for prisoners.

Beginning in the summer of 1998, I began efforts to find lawyers for individual prisoners at OSP. Nearly all such efforts failed. The law is written in a manner that makes it very difficult for prisoners to win, attorney fees are limited, and great deference is given to prison administrators to run prisons as they see fit. We were retired, we had no office or anyone to look at the mail or to take phone calls in our absence, and I refused to let Staughton bring a lawsuit without the active participation of younger experienced practicing attorneys.

Suicides

Early in 1999, a prisoner newly transferred to OSP committed suicide. In July 1999, I received letters telling me that another prisoner was suicidal, had been released from suicide watch and was being taunted by guards. I sent an inquiry to the Warden's assistant. A week later we got a phone call from the Warden's assistant telling us, "He's dead." The Warden's assistant asked us what we thought OSP could do to give the prisoners more of a sense that life was worth living. Staughton and I responded for about an hour.

After the phone call, I said to Staughton, "They should ask the prisoners rather than us." I drafted a form that said, "If someone asked you, WHAT COULD OSP DO TO MAKE YOU FEEL YOUR LIFE IS MORE WORTH LIVING, what would you say?" I wrote a covering letter in which I said, You don't have to respond if you don't want to, you don't have to sign your name if you do respond, but say only what it is OK for me to submit to the administration. I sent the form and the letter to 100 prisoners at OSP. Not everyone responded, but I received 110 responses! In a manner that would not disclose who wrote what, I typed up what the prisoners said on a variety of topics and I sent copies to the prison authorities.

I also sent copies to the American Friends Service Committee, Human Rights Watch, and others concerned about supermax prisons. A lawyer from Human Rights Watch contacted me. In her opinion, litigation was not the way to go. She suggested I contact the state's legislative oversight committee. Furthermore, she said, if we could get a member of that committee to agree to inspect OSP, she would volunteer to go with him and to prepare requests for documents prior to the inspection. I spoke with a state senator from Youngstown who happened to be on Ohio's Correctional Institution Inspection Committee (CIIC). I suggested documentary information to request, such as how many suicide attempts had occurred at OSP. In December 1999, the Executive Director of the CIIC, the state senator, and the lawyer from Human Rights Watch did an inspection of OSP.

The report issued by the CIIC included some very significant conclusions. Ohio did not need a supermax prison; it had a block of supermax cells in its maximum security prison that were never filled. What Ohio needed was a maximum security prison in the northern part of the state. Of more than four hundred prisoners at OSP, arguably as many as two hundred had committed offenses while in prison that might justify their placement at OSP, but the others were there on questionable, flimsy, or insufficient grounds.

One evening, not long thereafter, the sister of a prisoner phoned me saying her brother at OSP had sent her a letter that she understood to be a suicide note. I told her I could call the prison, but if I did they would put her brother on suicide watch in a cell with no property. She said, No, don't do that. But would I call the next morning and ask the chaplain to see him? I agreed.

At about 5:00 the next morning, she phoned me again. Her brother had been found dead. From then on, I have told prisoners, if I think you are seriously considering suicide, I have to notify the authorities. And several times, my reading was correct and my intervention made a critical difference.

Filing a Lawsuit

Our friend, law professor Jules Lobel, has written a book about what he calls "prophetic litigation." It is necessary to raise some issues even if you lose again and again. Over time, the attitudes of the public and of the courts will change. For example, there were many unsuccessful cases brought before *Brown v. Board of Education* declared that "separate but equal" schools were not equal, and that segregation in public schools was unconstitutional.

Jules knew that we were concerned about the plight of prisoners at the OSP. He asked me to draft a memo telling him how I thought we could demonstrate that incarceration at OSP is "an atypical and significant hardship" when compared with "the ordinary incidents of prison life."[1] Jules was then ready to work on a case that everybody assumed was a loser but needed to be brought. He contacted the Center for Constitutional Rights (CCR), and CCR got a grant for enough money to cover initial costs.

CCR was in New York, Jules was in Pennsylvania, and we needed local counsel in Ohio. Staughton and I went to Cleveland and spoke with lawyers at the American Civil Liberties Union (ACLU) of Ohio Foundation. The legal director was intensely interested. The ACLU of Ohio agreed to take responsibility for the "due process" issues (what procedures should be used for selecting or retaining prisoners at OSP). Volunteer lawyers associated with CCR and the ACLU of Ohio joined the team. Initially, CCR took responsibility for the mental health, medical, and outdoor recreation issues. But over the course of time, all of us worked on all the issues.

On January 9, 2001, we filed a federal lawsuit. The lengthy "complaint" was packed with details supported by documents provided by prisoners. I believe those details were the key to our success. Before the filing of the lawsuit, we had corresponded with more than three hundred OSP prisoners. (Between January 2001 and January 2008, we corresponded with more than six hundred of the approximately one-thousand and sixty prisoners who were incarcerated at the OSP at some point during those years. The information and papers they provided were critical.)

When the lawyers first met with the judge, the State's attorney asked the judge to put the case "on the shelf" while the State made necessary changes. The judge replied, "You'll still be making plans when this case goes to trial." He put the case on the "expedited" track.

Soon after the lawsuit was filed, Staughton and I went to visit OSP prisoners, one a week, whom we had reason to believe were mentally ill. We soon noticed that a psychiatrist or psychologist from "Central Office" would subsequently interview those same prisoners, whereafter they were transferred out of OSP. One day, when we were meeting with one such prisoner, the new warden came to the visiting booth and told the prisoner in our presence that he was going to be transferred!

In the fall of 2001, the State proposed and the prisoners accepted a partial settlement that provided for monitors of medical and mental health care at OSP, and the building of outdoor recreation areas. But the State regarded the decisions about who should be at OSP and what procedures would be used as going to the core of their mission. A few days before the trial on those issues was to begin, the judge met with the lawyers to see whether a trial could be avoided. I recall saying to the judge, "The prisoners have confidence in you." "Then we'll go to trial," he replied.

Early in January 2002, the judge opened the trial in one of the living areas or "pods" at OSP. The individual prisoners named in the complaint as representatives of the class of OSP prisoners were placed in separate cells within that pod. As the prisoners peered through the food slots in the steel doors of the cells, the judge listened to opening arguments by the lawyers.

Then, in the judge's courtroom later that day and all the next day, Staughton questioned thirteen prisoners about conditions of confinement in the Ohio prisons from which they had transferred to OSP as compared with conditions at the supermax. "Why," the judge wondered aloud, "would anyone rather be on Death Row than at OSP?" Many prisoners were sent to OSP without being given any reason. One prisoner had been in the chow line when another prisoner hit him over the head with a huge spatula. The blow caused serious injuries requiring hospitalization. Upon release from the hospital, this victim was sent to OSP, despite the fact that he had not fought back.

After the trial, another judge was asked to try to "settle" the case. The State made a proposal. We, the lawyers for the prisoners, met with prisoners from different parts of OSP, once again in a pod where all we could see through the food slots were pairs of eyes, and sometimes a hand. One prisoner said that what the State was offering would probably help him but would not solve the problem. The prisoners were unanimous in rejecting the State's proposal. Another prisoner suggested that we offer a counterproposal. These prisoners, who for the most part did not know each other, came to consensus. Staughton called for a show of hands. All voted yes. Then he called for anyone voting no. One hand appeared. Staughton asked the man, "Didn't you vote yes?" From across the pod, someone called, "That's what happens when you get hit over the head with a spatula!" Uproarious laughter!

We resisted intense pressure to make the prisoners accept the State's proposal. We said it was up to the prisoners and they had made their decision. They knew they were gambling: there was a possibility that the court would rule against them, but they preferred to take that chance rather than accept less than they believed was needed. A few weeks later, the court ruled wholly in favor of the prisoners.[2]

The Court of Appeals[3] and the United States Supreme Court[4] later agreed that incarceration in high maximum security at OSP is "an atypical and significant hardship." Prisoners have a "liberty interest" in avoiding placement there, the federal courts ruled. Adequate specific notice of the conduct believed to require supermax placement, a hearing, and a brief statement of reasons, are constitutionally required.

During the following months and years, the population of OSP dropped to less than half its capacity. Many prisoners were reduced from high maximum (supermax) to maximum security. OSP became predominantly a maximum security prison within a building designed for supermaximum security. Prisoners in southern Ohio who wanted to be in the northern part of the state were permitted to request transfer to OSP, knowing that it would be more restrictive, but closer to home so they could have visitors. One of the first prisoners to arrive at OSP told us that we had changed the place from being intolerable to a place that is tolerable.

Nearly ten years after the OSP opened, the class action was terminated. It is making a difference in other states. Courts are citing the Supreme Court's decision in the Ohio supermax case and providing similar relief to prisoners in other supermax prisons.

Also gratifying is that some of the men who came forward to serve as named plaintiffs are out of prison and have done well on parole; others remain in prison and have maintained good behavior at much lower security levels. I recall one such man, a man who is serving a life sentence for murder and armed robbery, who said he had promised his mother and me that he would not use violence anymore. But, he wrote, it takes more strength to act nonviolently.

Whenever I speak publicly, I urge young and old to do whatever they can—teach preschool, or run after-school programs, whatever—to keep our youth from ending up in supermax prisons!

The prisoners gave us nicknames. Staughton is "Scrapper." I am "Mama Bear."

LUCASVILLE, *STAUGHTON LYND*

I have always hated both prisons and the death penalty. On those occasions when I was imprisoned for a few hours, and heard the metal doors clang shut between myself and freedom, I felt anguish. As for the death penalty, I became aware how strongly I felt about it when Alice and I visited the cemetery for indigent death row prisoners at the Jubilee Partners community in Georgia early in 1991. The cemetery is a small green clearing in the woods. When we laid eyes on the place we had an immediate feeling, "This is where we belong." We transplanted daffodils from the Macedonia Cooperative Community and asked the Jubilee members for permission to have our own ashes buried there.

I like to say that I became an advocate for prisoners in the manner of Osama Bin Laden's driver. Salim Hamdan, one of the men apprehended by U.S. forces and labeled an "enemy combatant," defended himself as follows. "I was unemployed," he told his captors. "This guy offered me so-and-so many dollars a month if I would drive for him. Naturally I accepted. I'm not a terrorist, I'm just Osama Bin Laden's driver."

It's the same way with me, I like to say. When Alice and I retired from Legal Services in 1996, she became interested in the new, "supermax" prison being built on the east side of town. Alice doesn't drive. As one thing led to another, she needed someone to drive her around. "Your Honor," I imagine myself telling the judge, "I'm just her driver."

But I am also a historian. Alice has explained (in her chapter entitled "Mama Bear") how we came to meet George Skatzes. We formed a strong initial impression of his innocence and offered our services to the lawyers representing him in his death penalty appeals. Alice spent three years reading and cross-indexing the more than six thousand pages of trial transcript in *State v. Skatzes* before she became immersed in the supermax class action. We visited many witnesses to the events for which George was convicted. I read the almost equally long transcripts of the other men sentenced to death for the murder of hostage Officer Robert Vallandingham. As I write in 2008, there are several other men found to be guilty of crimes during the Lucasville uprising whose cases I am investigating. I frame hypotheses and, sometimes with one man, sometimes with two, assess with these convicted prisoners the accuracy of my conjectures and what must be done to test them further.

The Lucasville Story

The Lucasville story is a tale of predominantly black prisoners from Ohio cities confined in a rural all-white community from which the prison's guards were recruited. It is a story of a "long train of abuses," of a protest that got out of control, and of ten cruel and unnecessary deaths. Finally it is a story of a negotiated surrender, followed by prosecutions based on the unreliable testimony of prisoner informants, in turn followed by the long-term solitary confinement of many human beings, and one day, perhaps, five more deaths.[5]

George Skatzes made us aware of certain particular pitfalls of capital litigation in the United States. One is the so-called death qualified jury. When a jury is chosen in a trial for which the prosecution seeks a death sentence, persons opposed to the death penalty are excluded from the jury. How can the resulting body be a representative jury of one's peers?

Another abomination is the use of "snitch testimony." During the eleven days of the Lucasville disturbance, physical evidence such as bloodstains or fingerprints was destroyed or contaminated. There was no physical evidence linking any suspect to any weapon or linking any suspect to any victim. Therefore, in nearly fifty Lucasville cases, prosecutors relied almost entirely on the testimony of informants, or "snitches," who typically received something of value in exchange: the dropping of some or all charges, a sentence that ran concurrently rather than consecutively and added no time to the prisoner's confinement, transfer to another prison or out of state, or a letter to the parole board. It was inherently unreliable evidence.

But the story has another side. Members of the labor movement like to think that they are building a movement in which "an injury to one is an injury to all." Yet in a layoff, low-seniority workers—often members of a minority or women—may be put on the street with no work at all, while other union members not only continue to hold full-time jobs, but even work overtime. Similarly, in strike situations, the no-strike clause that is standard in most union contracts may cause one group of workers to cross the picket line of striking members of another union. The labor movement sings about "solidarity forever" but in practice falls short.

Accordingly we in the so-called free world may have something to learn from prisoners: not from all prisoners, of course, but from those who refuse to turn state's evidence—to snitch—even when the refusal may cost them their lives. In the song "Kevin Barry," when the British soldiers said to their captive, Turn informer and we'll free you, Barry proudly answered no. Likewise the five men condemned to death after the Lucasville disturbance may go to their deaths because they refuse to be snitches. What is most remarkable about this culture of solidarity is that it crosses racial lines.

Black and White Together

The five men sentenced to death as leaders of the uprising at the Southern Ohio Correctional Facility (SOCF) are three blacks (Siddique Abdullah Hasan, James Were, and Keith LaMar) and two whites (George Skatzes and Jason Robb). Moreover, in 1993 both Skatzes and Robb were members of the Aryan Brotherhood. Yet these five men not only cooperated during the eleven-day rebellion, they have refused to become witnesses against each other during the years of solitary confinement that followed.[6]

It was Alice who brought to my attention the remarkable testimony of Sergeant Howard Hudson in the trial of George Skatzes. After the prisoners surrendered and the Ohio State Highway Patrol entered L block (the area the prisoners had occupied), they found a variety of graffiti on the walls. Sergeant Hudson, the State's principal investigator, identified a photograph taken in the L block corridor.

> Q. On the wall on the right there appears to be something written?
> A. Says, "Black and White Together."
> Q. Did you find that or similar slogans in many places in L block?
> A. Yes, we did, throughout the corridor, in the L block.
> Q. Including banners that the inmates produced?
> A. Yes, sir.

Further:

> Q. [What is photograph] 260?
> A. 260, the words, "Convict unity," written on the walls of L corridor.
> Q. Did you find the message of unity throughout L block?
> A. Yes. . . .
> Q. Next photo?
> A. 261 is another photograph in L corridor that depicts the words, "Convict race."[7]

"Convict race" is my favorite! Evidently the cultural creation of racial identity can work in more than one way. Among the Lucasville rebels, the process appears to have operated not to create separation of the races, but to overcome racism. The one thing about which I am certain is that not since the early 1960s in the south have I experienced as much interracial solidarity as I have among convicted prisoners whom the State of Ohio considers "the worst of the worst."

Fact-Finding as a Historian

As we came to know the Lucasville defendants, I became a fact-gatherer for all of these death-sentenced men. Alice and I collected documents and affidavits. We interviewed witness after witness. Together with a broad spectrum of those considered by Ohio to be the "worst of the worst," we became guerrilla historians regarding a prison uprising and a situation of severe confinement in Ohio's supermax prison. It was very much like doing any other history, except that with regard to what happened in 1993, how well we did the history might determine whether a person spent the rest of his life behind bars or was executed.

The supermax lawsuit went well, surviving a trip to the United States Supreme Court. Beginning in 2001 and continuing for seven years, we were allowed one or two plaintiff representatives in the courtroom during hearings. One of the representatives was Jason Robb, a member of the Aryan Brotherhood. He insisted that African-Americans needed their own spokesperson. That second person was for a long time another of the Lucasville capital defendants, Keith LaMar, or as he calls himself, Bomani Shakur (Swahili for "thankful mighty warrior"). Together with Jason and Bomani, Alice and I reviewed draft pleadings and discussed legal strategy.

So I have devoted more than a decade to painstakingly sapping and mining the judicial proceedings against the Lucasville defendants, especially those sentenced to death. I have made evidence available to defendants' counsel. I have written friend-of-the-court briefs, articles in periodicals like *Monthly Review* and the *Catholic Worker*, a law review article, and a book about the Lucasville uprising. I have also coauthored a play that was produced in seven Ohio cities in April 2007.

It is the most demanding, at times the most frustrating, and overall the most rewarding work I have ever undertaken as a historian.

MR. X, *ALICE LYND*

Crises can bring out the best and the worst in us. They can challenge us to find strength we did not know we had. They can reveal our weaknesses to us. They can lead us to clarify what is most important to us, and they can plunge us into confusion.

In writing about Mr. X, I have drawn on letters and notes that I wrote during moments of clarity and confusion, hope and despair, anger, resignation, inner strength and self-doubt. This is the story of what I at one point called "backbone strengthening exercises," and of my recognition that I was not the tower of strength that people gave me credit for being. For the sake of the reader, I do not mention all of the episodes and procedural tangles that left me feeling as if I were at the end of a yo-yo.

Central to this story is our belief that as lawyers we cannot serve the interests of only one individual heedless of the effect on others. I experienced firsthand, in minuscule, some of the shortcomings of the practice of law that have been an intense source of grief for many of the prisoners with whom we work. During this litigation I faced frustrations that prisoners face routinely: struggles with my attorneys; not being kept informed, or being misinformed by my attorney; inaccurate statements of fact by my attorney (and more typos in corrected drafts than in first drafts); misrepresentations of fact by the prosecution that my attorney declined to rebut; attorneys not doing what they said they would do; and my having to make consequential decisions without enough time.

The August 2000 Affidavit

In August 2000, Staughton and I went to see a prisoner at the OSP, whom I refer to as "Mr. X." We first met Mr. X when he was at another prison in

1998. We knew that he had been in the area when some of the murders took place during the 1993 "Lucasville riot." Mr. X told us in 1998 that George Skatzes had nothing to do with the murder of Earl Elder, one of two murders for which George had been sentenced to death. Mr. X also asked for our assistance with some of his own legal problems, and I did a number of things for him during the summer of 1998.

Sometime thereafter, Mr. X was transferred to Ohio's supermaximum security prison in Youngstown. In the spring of 2000, Mr. X heard that we were preparing a class action lawsuit concerning conditions of confinement at the supermax, and he expressed interest in participating. Once again, he also asked for assistance with some of his immediate problems.

I obtained some information for him. We also wanted to ask Mr. X more questions about the murder of Officer Robert Vallandingham during the "riot" in 1993. So we set up an appointment and went to see Mr. X.

We talked about his immediate concerns. We asked him about the murder of Officer Vallandingham. Mr. X brought up the Elder murder. "George should not be punished for being innocent," he said. He told us that three people had killed Earl Elder. He named two. I then asked him, "Do you want to tell me who the other guy was?" "It was me," he blurted out. He turned to his left, bent over, and sobbed. In seven years he had not told anyone. He wanted to be at peace with himself.

I was stunned, dismayed. In the car on the way home, I asked Staughton, "Now what do we do?" We decided to contact a very experienced, out-of-state, criminal defense lawyer. He advised us that our primary duty was to write an affidavit, to preserve as evidence what we had been told in as much detail as possible. By that time, we had looked at documents, such as the coroner's testimony concerning the wounds that killed Earl Elder. The documents corroborated some of the facts that Mr. X told us. I wrote the affidavit, concluding that we found Mr. X's disclosures to be highly credible but we believed further investigation needed to be done.

I kept the affidavit until a meeting of the team of lawyers representing George Skatzes. I sought out the lead attorney on the team, took her aside, and handed her the affidavit in strictest confidence. I think we told Mr. X during the interview in August that we would have to tell George and his attorneys, but Mr. X does not remember that.

Several years went by. The attorneys who had originally been working on George's case had all left the large law firm that was representing him, and a newer attorney was now the lead attorney on his case. She phoned us in September 2003, a few days before George's petition for post-conviction relief had to be filed in court, to say that she intended to file my August 2000 affidavit. We protested. Once again we sought legal advice but the alternative we proposed was rejected by George's attorneys. With the consent of George Skatzes, but without consulting Mr. X or obtaining his consent, my affidavit was filed on October 6, 2003, as an e - hibit in support of George.

Staughton and I promptly went to see Mr. X. We told him that an affidavit by me, disclosing the information he had told us in confidence, had been filed by George's attorneys. We then asked a criminal defense lawyer in Cleveland to represent Mr. X.

March 2004, Grand Jury Subpoena

On March 11, 2004, Staughton was in New York and I was home alone when the phone rang. It was an Ohio State Highway Patrol trooper. He said he had a subpoena to serve. I said Staughton was not here. That's OK, he said, the subpoena was for me. A few minutes later he came to the door with two subpoenas, one to appear and testify on April 2, 2004 (a day when Staughton was scheduled to be in Iowa). The other subpoena required me to bring with me all documents and records I had relating to contacts with Mr. X. With the two subpoenas was a letter from the Lucasville Special Prosecutor offering to take my deposition in the county where I live instead of requiring me to travel to southern Ohio. I immediately notified the attorney who had agreed to represent Mr. X, and then began making phone calls to find a lawyer to represent me.

An attorney in Cleveland returned my call and I talked with him for two hours on the phone. I asked him, "What if I refuse to testify?" "You could go to jail," he said. He explained that I could be held in jail until the term of the grand jury expired, and then I could be subpoenaed again to appear before the next grand jury, and be jailed again. The process could go on indefinitely.

That was Friday night. He told me to be at his office Monday morning, and be ready to tell him what I wanted to do.

Saturday night, our son Lee called. He asked me what I was going to do. "I don't know," I replied. He wished me "strength and clarity." During the night I came to a sense of clarity.

By Sunday evening when Staughton returned home, I had prepared a lengthy document for my attorney. The first heading was, "The Big Question: What Do I Want to Do?" It began:

> 1) I want to file a motion to quash [throw out] both of the grand jury subpoenas. . . . I would like to litigate and, if necessary, take the matter up on appeal. I think we need a brief that puts forth sound legal argument, supported by facts that are true to the best of our knowledge. Staughton and I want to be involved in developing the legal theory and in deciding how it will be presented.
>
> 2) If ultimately ordered to testify, I expect to refuse and I am willing to take the personal consequences of refusing.

Among the reasons I gave were these:

> Mine would be like "snitch testimony." As a lawyer, I have opposed the use of snitch testimony.
>
> I do not want to get into the morass of trying to decide what is and what is not within the permissible scope of inquiry. I do not want to open the door. This is the simplest, clearest path, and the best way to maintain my integrity.
>
> I am a Quaker. I oppose the death penalty, as have Quakers traditionally. Quakers, other Christians (such as Martin Luther King, Jr.), and people of other persuasions (such as Gandhi) have taken upon themselves the consequences of standing firm on matters of faith and principle. If that means I have to spend time in jail, the longer the stay the more difficult it would become physically. If I am disbarred or reprimanded, so be it.
>
> I would explain to George Skatzes that I want to do as he did: When George was told that if he did not cooperate with the State he would be faced with three capital murders, George told the State's investigator, "I can't help you."

Staughton and I went to Cleveland on Monday and retained counsel to advise and represent me. The lawyer said I looked "like anybody's grandmother." We agreed that his associate would do the research and would write and file a motion to quash the subpoenas.

Staughton and I also did some legal research. We learned that the attorney/client privilege belongs to the client. What matters is whether the client reasonably believed that an attorney/client relationship existed. It is the attorney's job to assert the attorney/client privilege on behalf of the client, but only the client can give it up. We found a frequently cited case which said that an essential element of an attorney/client relationship is whether the information discussed is so obviously confidential that it is covered by the attorney/client relationship. We asked my attorney to make this argument. The motion to quash was submitted on March 31.

I also began to prepare for the possibility of going to jail. Anticipating that my dietary needs would not be met in jail, I talked with friends who had spent time behind bars and had fasted. I talked with women about how to get along with the other women in jail. Staughton and I read aloud a biography of Margaret Fell, a Quaker who was sentenced to life in prison and forfeiture of all of her property because she would not take an oath of allegiance to the king of England and would not promise to forbid Quaker meetings in her home.

Being a Client

At the end of April, I received an e-mail from my attorney's associate telling me that the prosecutor's office had filed a response to our motion to quash two weeks earlier, and had contacted him to schedule a hearing on the motion. I was digging a flower bed by the mailbox when Staughton came outside and told me. I was so angry!

I replied within an hour, telling the associate I could not understand why he did not notify us and send us a copy as soon as he received a written response from the Special Prosecutor. Staughton and I had done additional research that we had expected to use in a reply brief and it was probably too late. I asked for a copy of the prosecutor's brief. The associate sent it to me with a note saying it was not his practice to send copies to clients, and he thought the prosecutor's argument was not worthy of a reply. I disagreed. I thought the State's brief discredited me, and that we needed to present the case law on which I was relying. I drafted a reply in the form of an affidavit and asked the young man to file it. He did.

The hearing was scheduled for May 21. I was determined not to let this case rule my life, and not to let it interfere with my work for prisoners at the supermax prison. But it interfered greatly with my ability to sleep. I brooded during the nights over how I would answer every conceivable question, and in the daytime, Staughton would quiz me as if he were the prosecutor.

I needed letters from doctors describing my medical needs. One of them said I was showing signs of "situational anxiety," such as high blood pressure. He prescribed some sleeping pills but told me it was possible that no medication would work.

In preparation for each of what turned out to be three hearings, I wrote statements that I expected to read in court to explain why I was refusing to disclose information that had been given to me during an attorney/client interview. Here are excerpts from the first such statement, written in the spring of 2004:

[M]y reasons for refusing are based not only on law but also on conscience. The former is subject to change. The latter is not.

I oppose the death penalty. It was on behalf of George Skatzes, a man on death row, that I initially contacted Mr. X. I cannot imagine myself cooperating with an attempt to put another man, Mr. X, on death row.

I oppose the use of snitch testimony to get convictions. I was not present when the criminal offense was committed. I do not have personal knowledge of what occurred. I am not willing to be a snitch.

For centuries, Quakers and others have suffered incarceration rather than compromise deeply held beliefs and principles.

I pray every day, "Help us to be instruments of thy peace." That means to me, among other things, taking suffering upon oneself, not inflicting it on others. Sometimes it means remaining silent, as did George Skatzes who, as a result, is now on death row.

Three days before the hearing was to take place, my lawyer phoned saying it would be rescheduled for some time in July. Recalling a comic movie that we had seen at our son's house, I wrote to family and friends: As is said in *My Cousin Vinnie*, "There's nothing to worry about until there's something to worry about!"

July 23, 2004 Hearing

I first appeared before the Scioto County Court of Common Pleas on July 23, 2004, in Portsmouth, Ohio. As we drove south from Columbus, it became apparent from signs and billboards along the road that this was hillbilly country. We were below the Mason-Dixon line, and entering a county where petitions had been collected calling for the death penalty after the Lucasville "riot."

We met my attorney in the hallway. He asked me questions about my family background. I told him there were lawyers and doctors on my mother's side. There were judges and ministers on my father's side. Neither of my parents were lawyers, but I had a strong sense of my father's integrity.

My lawyer and two prosecutors went into the judge's chambers. When my lawyer returned, he told me that after meeting the judge he had concluded that the purpose of this hearing was to make a record for appeal. He would ask for time to file post-hearing briefs so that I would not be jailed that day!

Staughton, although a lawyer, was not permitted to stay in the courtroom during the hearing. The State took the position that since he was present during the interview with Mr. X they might want to call him as a witness. I could see him peering through the window in the door from time to time, and we had several friends inside the courtroom. I felt I was able to maintain clarity and dignity throughout the hour and a half of questioning. The judge gave us more than a month before we had to file a brief.

Staughton and I drafted the post-hearing brief and the Cleveland lawyers added a section concerning the significance of the issues for other lawyers in the future.

On October 14, 2004, the court denied my motion to quash the subpoenas, ordered me to testify before the Scioto County Grand Jury, and declared (contrary to law) that this was a final appealable order. I terminated the services of the Cleveland lawyers, and notified another lawyer who had agreed to take my case on appeal *pro bono* (without charging me for his services).

October 2004, Second Subpoena

On Monday, October 25, a trooper came to our home and served me with a subpoena to testify before the grand jury on Friday, October 29. I immediately contacted my new lawyer. I told him I wanted him to try to arrange for my case to be handled the way the cases of some news reporters who refused to reveal their sources were being handled. The prosecutor agreed that, with the permission of the court, I would tell the court I was refusing to testify, there would be a finding of contempt and a sentence, and the sentence would be suspended until the appeal was decided. But the judge did not agree. The hearing was rescheduled for November 5.

I drafted another statement that I expected to read in court, saying I was convinced that Mr. X reasonably believed his communications with me were protected by the attorney/client privilege, that he had not waived his privilege, and that I was obligated to protect it. Mr. X could be indicted with death penalty specifications if I disclosed the information. I planned to say:

> I think this Court recognizes that the fundamental underlying issue for me in this case is the death penalty.
>
> I am a Quaker. Quakers believe that the light of God is in every person. In times past, when it was against the law to do so, Quakers protected runaway slaves who came across the Ohio River from the south. It is part of our religious faith and practice also to oppose the death penalty.
>
> I believe that the law grows through the willingness of individuals to engage in acts of civil disobedience. The law no longer condones slavery. I hope that, sooner rather than later, Ohio will abandon the death penalty.

Nothing went as expected on November 5. We arrived at the courthouse an hour before the appointed time. My attorney was already there and we talked. He indicated that the court of appeals was a very conservative one and there was no assurance that the Ohio Supreme Court would hear the case. Now that I was under a court order to testify, if I refused I could be jailed for criminal contempt. Although he was prepared to get the sentence stayed while the appeal was pending, he wanted to know what I was going to do in the long run.

I told him that we thought Mr. X might agree to a plea bargain if he would not get the death penalty. My lawyer immediately discussed that with the prosecutor.

The next thing I knew, the Special Prosecutor testified in court that Mr. X's case had been reviewed and a decision was made that they would not seek the death penalty for Mr. X. Settlement possibilities had opened up that might benefit everyone. There was hope.

But Mr. X did not agree to take a plea bargain. I had to return to court on November 19. The commitment of the prosecutor not to seek the death penalty was a major victory. But I still felt that I could not betray the trust of the man who had confided in us.

Our daughter Martha was coming for a few days to celebrate Staughton's seventy-fifth birthday with us on November 22. Fortuitously, she arrived the day before the hearing. But, given the uncertainty, we planned nothing for Staughton's birthday.

The three of us got up early in the morning and drove for nearly six hours to Portsmouth. In the car, Martha sang us a song called "Love is the Key" by Tuck and Pattie. I told Martha that one of the things I imagined doing in jail was to sing, but I didn't know how the other women would feel about that. I recalled that during the 1960s jailed civil rights workers would sing. "Do it," she said.

I appeared before the Grand Jury on Friday, November 19, 2004. I was asked to take an oath to testify truthfully. I affirmed: "Whatever I tell you will be the truth, but I do not intend to testify." The prosecutor asked me my address. Where is Niles? Northeast Ohio. Was I served with subpoenas? Yes. *Duces tecum* [bring documents]? Yes. Did I bring documents? No. What was my employment? I am not answering any further questions. I was in the grand jury room for no more than five minutes.

Very hurriedly, before I went before Judge Marshall, my lawyer told me that the prosecutor was offering me a deal: accept whatever the Court of Appeals rules, testify if the Court of Appeals so rules but give up the possibility of appealing to the Ohio Supreme Court. I had to decide instantly. I said, "No."

I had prepared yet another statement and this time I read it in court. I said that I felt bound not to testify unless and until either Mr. X gave me his express consent or he had a plea agreement and my testimony would not hurt him.

Judge Marshall asked me, "If the Court of Appeals affirms this decision, as I feel strongly they probably will, are you going to refuse to testify again?"

I started to reply, "My feeling is that . . ." He cut me off: "That is a yes or a no. Are you going to refuse to testify if the Court of Appeals orders you to testify?"

I responded, "May I remain silent?" Judge Marshall: "I would really like her to answer that question."

I replied, "Your Honor, I don't feel able to give you a yes or no answer."[8] And again: "One last opportunity, Ms. Lynd, will you testify before the Grand Jury today?"

I replied: "Under the present circumstances where 'Mr. X' has not been willing to come forth himself—" The Court: "Is that a 'No'?" I replied: "That is a 'No.'"

The Court: "I am ordering that you be incarcerated until you agree to testify before the Grand Jury."[9]

Being in Jail

As we were waiting for the elevator to go up to the jail on the fourth floor of the courthouse, the officer of the court who was escorting me said in a very courteous manner, "I don't think I've ever taken a lady of your age to jail before."

When we arrived at the jail he announced that he had "a female." The gates were unlocked and I entered. I was not booked or fingerprinted or searched as I had expected. I was told, "sit there," or "come this way."

While I was in a tiny cubicle across from boxes marked "grievances" and such like, a woman who must have been in the courtroom came by. She kept saying, "You should take the Fifth!" She concluded, "Sometimes the judge is overbearing." On her way out a few minutes later, she gave me a thumbs up sign.

Most of the time I was in a cell with nothing but a narrow bench—no toilet, no water—across from the kitchen where I watched supper being prepared. These are some of the thoughts I had while in jail on November 19, 2004:

1) How long until I get out? My lawyer said the grand jury is impaneled until December 31. That's six weeks. I can make it if I have medications and if diet is not a problem. I have to be able to make it on my own: Let me be an instrument of thy peace.

2) Let go, there is no point in planning. Those letters I was going to write don't have to be written. If I don't buy or make Christmas presents, so be it. Staughton will say whatever has to be said to the press and to people who ask. Staughton will do our Christmas message. But what will Staughton do if he has trouble with the computer?

3) Some of those female prisoners look like they wouldn't like me. Will I be put with them? One has scars on each cheek. Most prisoners are wearing tennis shoes. One is wearing sandals. They must wear their own shoes. They are wearing white socks.

4) Medical care. There is a doctor seeing prisoners late on Friday afternoon. If I stay here, will he see me? Are these routine examinations or sick call?

5) Food. They are preparing some form of pasta with canned tomato sauce. I can't have that. They are opening large cans of pears and pouring off the juice. I can have pears. I wish they would save the juice for me. They have large bags of salad. I could eat that. But no, they are pouring on some salad dressing. Would there be any way for me to wash off the salad dressing?

6) What time is it? I can still see daylight outside in a high corner of the kitchen window. It seems like it should be dark by now but it isn't. It must still be before 5:00 or so.

7) Rest. I'm keyed up. I'll see if I can lie down on this narrow bench. The noise is just background noise. It doesn't bother me. There's nothing to do. I can just let the world pass by me. This must be why George sleeps so much.

Meanwhile, my attorney had taken off for the Court of Appeals, some sixty miles north of Portsmouth. He left his cell phone number on a card for Staughton. Staughton turned to the dozen or so supporters and asked, "Does anybody have a cell phone?" A friend from Youngstown did.

It was a race against time to get a stay from the Court of Appeals before the weekend. When word came through on the cell phone that the Court of Appeals had granted a temporary stay, there were problems with the fax machine in the clerk's office. Then the stay had to be taken to Judge Marshall's office. And when Staughton went up to the jail to get me, the officer had the order that I was to be jailed but no copy of the temporary stay. Finally, the stay arrived at the jail on the fourth floor.

"That's Staughton's voice!" I said to myself. "In such a short time?" I called his name. No answer. I tried putting my shoe between the bars at the bottom of the door. No response. I waved my hand under the door. No response. I remembered Martha encouraging me to sing. So I began singing things that Martha or Staughton would recognize but no one else would know. I began with a song I used to sing to Martha when she was a baby. Then I sang "Dona Nobis Pacem," and then a Quaker song that has a line to the effect that no storm can shake my inmost calm.

Waiting with a crowd of supporters outside the gate to the jail, Staughton turned to Martha: "Is that your mother singing?" Martha didn't hear it. But Staughton was sure it was I!

When I was let out, I could not believe so many people who had come so far had waited so long, standing by me. A friend from Pittsburgh took us out to dinner, and then we drove home. Martha and I were free to invite friends to a birthday celebration for Staughton!

A Letter from Mr. X

In retrospect, December 2004, was the most difficult period for me. The cat and mouse game continued with the Special Prosecutor. From day to day I didn't know whether the stay of my imprisonment would be continued so that I could celebrate Christmas with our daughter Barbara and her family, or whether I would have to go back to jail. I had no question about the decisions I had already made, but I was receiving conflicting advice as to what legal strategy to pursue. If it were not for some things I wrote at the time, I would be writing now only of confusion, bleakness, and a sense of being lost.

After my appeal was filed (and when Staughton was again out of town) a letter—totally unsolicited—came from Mr. X addressed to Staughton. It said, in part:

> [O]ut of great respect for your wife "Alice," I'm going to go ahead and grant her permission to just say enough to the "grand jury" to keep herself out of

jail. I just wouldn't be at peace with myself, knowing that she was behind bars because of me. So please try to say as little as possible.

On December 19, Staughton and I went to see the spiritual leader of the Muslim prisoners at the supermax. He had sent us a message that he wanted to talk with us before the temporary stay of my sentence expired. He had discussed my case with two other Muslims and two Aryan Brothers. If I went to jail, he told me, they would go on hunger strike and boycott the commissary! We discussed the convict code. He said: 1) You don't snitch, but 2) If you have consent, you do testify. Mr. X should come forward so that I don't go to jail, he said. This reaching out to me, and the reassurance that prisoners would understand if I did testify, meant a great deal to me.

I also received a huge card from George Skatzes that he and another death-sentenced prisoner had made. A cut-out pasted on it said, "Give me the strength to make stepping stones out of stumbling blocks." As I meditated on this letter, it seemed clear to me that I had done all I could for Mr. X and it was now time to help George.

Appeals

The brief to the appellate court in my subpoena case imposed an overload on me at a time when Jules Lobel, Staughton, and I were drafting a brief to be filed in the United States Supreme Court to defend very significant gains we had previously won for the prisoners in Ohio's supermax prison.

I could not sign the Supreme Court brief in the supermax case because I was not admitted to practice before the Supreme Court. Although I had done the initial work on that case and had put more time into it over the years than any other attorney, there was no point in applying for admission to the Supreme Court: I would be disqualified for having recently been cited for contempt of court. Tears rolled down my cheeks as I sat in the back of the courtroom at the Supreme Court on March 30, 2005, waiting to hear Jules argue for the due process rights of prisoners against attorneys representing the State of Ohio, the Federal Bureau of Prisons, and nineteen other states!

On August 30, 2005, the day before a major hearing was to begin on whether or not Ohio could move Death Row to the supermax prison, I was trying to comply with a last minute order from the court when my lawyer phoned and faxed to me the decision of the Court of Appeals in my subpoena case. The Court of Appeals had ruled against me and the Scioto County Common Pleas Court was told to order me to return and testify before a new grand jury and face the same judge! Once again, my subpoena case came as overload at a time when I was already under very great stress.

The Court of Appeals agreed with Judge Marshall that I was representing George Skatzes when Mr. X spoke with us about the Elder murder, and what Mr. X had told us was not protected by the attorney/client privilege. In addition, the Court of Appeals found technical procedural grounds for denying my appeal. My lawyer filed papers asking the Ohio Supreme Court to take my case. But if the Ohio Supreme Court agreed to take the case, we would have to win on procedural grounds before the court would even consider whether Mr. X should be protected by the attorney/client privilege.

Third Subpoena

In mid-September 2005 (when Staughton was out of town), I was served with a subpoena to testify on October 7. It said in capital letters: "YOU ARE FURTHER INSTRUCTED THAT FAILURE TO APPEAR AS ORDERED BY THIS SUBPOENA MAY RESULT IN THE COURT ORDERING YOUR IMMEDIATE ARREST." That met the condition in Mr. X's letter.

Staughton and I had previously talked about how I could testify in a manner that would be protective of Mr. X. I had decided: If I testify, I will tell it as straight as I can. The courts have told me that I represent George. My testifying is what he needs, and that is what I have to do.

At chorus rehearsal on Monday, October 3, 2005, we were learning the first chorus in Bach's *Christmas Oratorio*. We worked for a while on one particular part, learning the notes and the rhythmic pattern. After some minutes, I became conscious of the words I was singing: "Cease to be fearful." Suddenly, the words penetrated. They were a message. It was a message I needed. These words sustained me through the coming days and nights.

During the week I also felt sustained by my mother and father. I thought often of words my mother used to say to me from the Bible, Isaiah 30:15, which I remembered as saying, In calmness and confidence shall be thy strength. And from Psalm 91:1, 11 and 12, He that dwelleth in the secret place of the most high shall abide under the shadow of the Almighty. . . . He shall give his angels charge over thee, to keep thee in all thy ways. They shall bear thee up in their arms lest thou dash thy foot against a stone.

I testified. Two days later, Staughton and I went to see Mr. X to tell him that he could soon be indicted. And two days after that, the indictment was issued.

I worried that my having cooperated with the authorities might feed animosity toward us on the part of prisoners. I was apprehensive that the publicity might make it harder for us to represent prisoners in the supermax class action. But one of the Lucasville defendants to whom we spoke a few days later said, Maybe this would be the thread that when pulled will unravel all the Lucasville cases that were based on unreliable evidence.

I wrote the following statement and sent it to prisoners who expressed interest or concern.

To Whom It May Concern

Questions have been raised as to why I disclosed information that resulted in a man being indicted for murder. I offer the following by way of explanation.

1) I fought the grand jury subpoena in court for nineteen months. I claimed that the information I had was protected by the attorney client privilege. It was my duty to assert the client's privilege, but I did not have the right to waive (give up) the privilege without the express consent of the client. The Court of Common Pleas ruled that there was no attorney client privilege as to the particular subject matter. I was subpoenaed a second time to testify. I went before the grand jury and refused to answer their questions. I was then found in contempt of court and briefly jailed. The Court of Appeals affirmed the Court of Common Pleas and, although I had an appeal pending in the Ohio Supreme Court, I was subpoenaed for a third time to testify before the grand jury.

2) Initially the State indicated that it would seek the death penalty. During the course of this litigation, the prosecutor went on the record saying the State had decided not to seek death penalty specifications. Given the length of sentences already imposed, a life sentence might be less than the maximum number of years to which the prisoner was already sentenced. The only likely effect would be on parole.

3) The man who was later indicted gave me his express permission that if it came down to my testifying or being jailed, I should testify. The third subpoena stated in capital letters that if I did not comply I would be subject to immediate arrest. I would surely have been jailed with no grounds for being let out of jail until I complied with the court's orders, because the legal issues had already been decided by the courts. Being jailed for more than a day or two could have had serious consequences for my health.

It has been and is troubling that I have lost the trust that some prisoners might otherwise have in me. Fighting this case was very costly for me not only in dollars but also in stress. I believe that the kind of information that was disclosed to me should be protected by the attorney client privilege and I did all I could to assert that. But I also have obligations to another man who was convicted and sentenced to death for an offense that he did not commit.

Outcome

The trial of Mr. X was set for the week of June 5, 2006. I was subpoenaed to testify against Mr. X on June 7 unless he accepted a plea bargain on June 6. On the evening of June 5, the court-appointed attorney who was defending Mr. X phoned me and asked me whether I would be willing to take a phone call from Mr. X to discuss a plea bargain. I said yes. In the course of conversation with Mr. X's lawyer, I asked whether the prosecutor had offered a term of years that would run from 1993, rather than 2006. "Can they do that?" he asked in surprise. I said I had heard of such sentences in other Lucasville cases.

The next morning, as I was preparing to leave for southern Ohio, a phone call came from Mr. X. I told him I agreed with him that I should not be required to testify against him, but the courts had ruled against us. If I testified against him I thought a jury would be likely to convict him. "I ain't takin' no plea bargain," he replied. So I continued to pack my suitcase and prepare to leave for my court appearance.

Within half an hour, Mr. X's attorney called and told me Mr. X had agreed to a plea bargain. Then the Special Prosecutor phoned me. Mr. X was pleading No Contest to the charge of Murder. His sentence would be fifteen years to life with credit for time served since 1993. A letter would be sent to the Parole Board from the Special Prosecutor minimizing Mr. X's role in the Lucasville riot. And I was no longer under a subpoena.

The Special Prosecutor relied on my grand jury and deposition testimony to convict Mr. X, but not to exonerate George Skatzes. Mr. X had a very good institutional record at the supermax prison. In 2007, his security level was reduced below maximum security and he was transferred to another prison. He will come up for parole consideration in 2010. But in 2008, George Skatzes is still under a sentence of death for the aggravated murder of Earl Elder.

A Postscript by Staughton

As I accompanied Alice on this journey, the fundamental question for me was always: Is there a way to conduct ourselves so as to uphold the principle of solidarity, that is, to benefit both men, rather than sacrificing one for the other? Logically this seemed impossible. But in the end, I believe Alice may have achieved that goal. Because of the Special Prosecutor's letter to the Parole Board, Mr. X may be paroled earlier than he would have been if he had never spoken to us in August 2000. As for George Skatzes, the State, through its plea agreement with Mr. X, accepted as true Mr. X's confession to one of the murders for which George was sentenced to death. According to Mr. X, George had nothing to with the murder of Earl Elder. Some court, someday, should exonerate George Skatzes.

THE DEATH PENALTY AND THE PRISON SYSTEM

Ohio's Death Row was moved to the OSP in 2005. We were already representing a class defined as all prisoners incarcerated at OSP. We now represented approximately 150 additional men who were sentenced to death.

We came to know many of the death-sentenced men as individuals. We believed that some were not guilty. But some also admitted to unimaginably horrible crimes. The question remains whether either killing these men, or locking them up for the rest of their lives without the possibility of parole, is an appropriate response.

Attorney Jeffrey Gamso, Legal Director of the ACLU of Ohio, begins speeches by reading the definition of aggravated murder in the Ohio Revised Code: "No person shall purposely, and with prior calculation and design, cause the death of another. . . ." He goes on to say that these words precisely describe the death penalty.

Farrakhan

Some unlikely voices appear to believe that people can change and that our society should be much more prepared to forgive. We were surprised and enormously impressed by the content of Louis Farrakhan's speech at the Million Man March on October 16, 1995, and most particularly his eight steps. This is Alice's summary of the steps Farrakhan proposed:

> Not hating the person who points out what you are doing wrong;
> Recognizing what you have done that was wrong;
> Confessing it to the person wronged;
> Feeling regret deeply enough so that you won't keep repeating it;
> Making amends;
> Asking for forgiveness and forgiving others;
> Settling differences and reestablishing relations with former enemies; and
> Being relieved of the burden of guilt that weighs down the soul.

Lessley

When our friend Lessley was in prison, we had a conversation with him about Minister Farrakhan's speech at the Million Man March.

Lessley said he thought atonement and reconciliation were the most important steps. Alice replied that she had been thinking how difficult it would be for prisoners to do anything by way of atonement and reconciliation as long as they are locked up. Lessley said yes, that was very true, and then he continued.

He had had a cellmate who said something like this: "Lessley, you'll never know what it is like to have killed a man. I would do anything to breathe life back into that man. I can't talk to that man. If only there were some way I could talk to someone who loved that man, to ask forgiveness. But there is no way I can do that."

Then Lessley went on to say that his cellmate was tormented particularly at night. In the morning he would get up and stay busy with activity all day to keep himself from thinking. To see him during the day and to hear him joking you would think he was happy, but as night came on and he had to go into the cell he became sad.

Lessley said he had had seven or eight cellmates who had been murderers and they were all the same in this respect, that they used activity to keep themselves from thinking. Their sleep was fitful. One would wake in the night and scream or sit bolt upright in bed. If only there were someone they could go to and ask forgiveness then they wouldn't have to keep from thinking all the time, he concluded. It was as if Lessley were putting all this together as he talked with us.

Glenn

Nearly ten years later, the two of us sang at the Memorial Mass for a prisoner named Glenn Benner who had just been executed by the State of Ohio. Glenn had asked us to sing the song that we had learned from Nelly and Carmencita in El Bonete, which begins:

> When a group of brothers approaches the altar
> God's smile is there.
> Lord, we are coming today
> To praise you and give thanks
> For so much goodness (*tanta bondad*).

Glenn had been on Death Row since 1986 for raping and killing two young women, one of whom had been a childhood neighbor and friend. We got to know Glenn in 2005 when he was in the "honor block" on Death Row, having had no conduct reports for approximately nineteen years.

One of the speakers at the Memorial Mass was Hilary Hughes from Ireland who became first a pen pal and then a close friend of Glenn Benner.

She read from a letter Glenn wrote to her describing himself before he knew her:

> I needed love, and it just wasn't there. I felt empty inside. Dead inside. Really, I just stopped caring. I experienced fear that I was petrifying and becoming frozen in place as a lifeless object or thing. I felt as though I was dying slowly, by degrees, day after day, from inside myself.

Hilary continued: He felt unworthy of love. Every day he lived with knowledge of the terrible pain he had caused so many people by his actions. He found this very, very difficult to bear. He loved his family and carried the pain of knowing that he had let them down. In his shame he withdrew from them, feeling unworthy of the support and love they offered him. Glenn joined the Catholic Church in 1994. In the latter part of his life it was a joy for him to be able to say to his family, "I love you, and I'm sorry."

The family of one of Glenn's victims did not want Benner to go to his grave without answering questions about the murder that baffled the family. A brother of the victim, Glenn's childhood friend Rodney, tried unsuccessfully to set up a visit with Glenn.[10]

On the night before the execution, Glenn made a phone call to Rodney. They agreed to meet the next morning before the execution, but Glenn was not sure the officials would let him meet with a member of the victim's family. Glenn called Rodney again and they talked on the phone for an hour and a half:

> They talked about their lives. They'd grown up two houses from each other. . . . They'd played bows and arrows together. . . . They talked about the awful details of Trina's death. . . .[11]

Rodney drove something like five hours through the night, arriving at the prison early the next morning. Beginning at 8:00 a.m., Rodney and Glenn talked through the bars while the execution team stood nearby. At their parting seventeen minutes later, "They were calm. There were tears. They shook hands."[12]

As Rodney was leaving the prison, he wanted to say one more thing to Glenn. He tried to phone Glenn but was told that Benner was being readied for his execution and couldn't talk. Rodney said he wanted to tell Glenn, "I forgive you." Hilary, as Glenn's spiritual advisor, was able to convey that message to Glenn before he died.[13]

Glenn Benner was not the only one who changed. Rodney changed too. Rodney gave up his place as an execution witness. He does not believe in the death penalty anymore. "People can change, he now believes. After all, his sister's killer did."[14] As a deputy warden said of a prisoner executed in

Alabama, "the man who died tonight is not the same man that came here 13 years ago. It makes me wonder about the death penalty."[15]

Life without Parole

Many persons opposed to the death penalty accept life without parole as the most politically feasible alternative. We oppose life without parole.

People need hope. Years ago we talked with a man who was sentenced to life in prison. "Why should I maintain exemplary behavior if nobody cares?" he asked us.

Most murderers are not sentenced to death. Some are given the possibility of parole after serving a lengthy number of years. Why shouldn't that possibility be kept open for all prisoners who, in a tragic moment many years ago, committed an offense of a kind they would never do again? A man whose death sentence was reduced to life in prison told us, "Don't lock us up inside our past."

What about Prisons?

The remaining, ultimate question is: What about prisons themselves? Does the penal system accomplish society's objectives? If not, what is the alternative?

We suspect that most people simply want criminals out of the way, stored out of sight and out of mind like nuclear waste. But most prisoners are ultimately released into society with less chance of earning a living or maintaining a family than before incarceration. And the cost of warehousing people, from $70 to well over $160 a day per person, is robbing state governments of money needed for education and health care.

It seems to us that what drives the creation of prisons is the problem (for the capitalist system) of surplus human beings. Generations of Africans were brought to the United States in chains to do the dirty work of building up this country's economy. Impoverished workers from China, Ireland, and Eastern Europe were lured to come to the United States, and the same is true of Hispanic "guest laborers" today. But when the railroad has been built, the steel has been poured, the lettuce and grapes have been picked, what is to be done with the superfluous children of those who did that labor? Incarceration, we think, is a system of social control of redundant or potentially dangerous elements of the population.

So what is the alternative? Staughton has found it provocative to challenge audiences in the middlewestern heartland with what he calls "the prison program of Jesus of Nazareth." That program has three elements, he suggests.

First, visit prisoners. See Matthew 25:31–46. Unless one has face-to-face contact with the people under discussion, discourse will remain abstract and academic. In our experience prisoners are like other people. Some will try to take advantage of you; some won't. Some will tell you what they think you want to hear, or what serves their purposes; some will tell you what they believe to be true. Some are easily provoked to act on the spur of the moment; some are very thoughtful. Not all prisoners are criminals, and not all criminals are behind bars.

Second, oppose the death penalty. See John 8:2–11. If Jesus could tell the gathered lynch mob, "He that is without sin among you, let him first cast a stone at her," it would appear he was opposed to the death penalty, especially as he then told the accused woman, "go, and sin no more."

Third, and most controversially, free all prisoners. Jesus' first reported public remarks were at the synagogue in Nazareth, when he "stood up to read" the words of the prophet Isaiah: "The Lord hath sent me . . . to proclaim liberty to the captives, and the opening of prisons to them that are bound." Isaiah 61:1 (what Jesus read), Luke 4:16–21 (description of his reading). How can these words mean anything other than the abolition of all existing Bastilles, Abu Ghraibs, Guantanamos, supermaximum security prisons, and other prisons and jails of every kind?

But we would add one very important qualification. Prisons cannot be abolished without changing society as a whole. Prisons cannot be abolished in a society that does not have jobs for young men and women who manage to graduate from high school. Prisons cannot be abolished as long as more money can be made from selling drugs than from working. Prisons cannot be abolished by a society in which the most highly approved career path for the young is to become soldiers, that is, to learn and practice a socially accepted kind of killing. The "opening of prisons to them that are bound" is inconsistent with the maintenance of what Karl Marx called a "reserve army of the unemployed" from which criminals will forever be forthcoming. Abolition of the penal system will only come about in the context of creating "another world" that we continue to believe is possible.

NOTES

1. *Sandin v. Conner*, 515 U.S. 472 (1995).
2. *Austin v. Wilkinson*, 189 F.Supp.2d 719 (N.D. Ohio 2002). See also, *Austin v. Wilkinson*, 204 F.Supp.2d 1024 (N.D. Ohio 2002).
3. *Austin v. Wilkinson*, 372 F.3d 346 (6th Cir. 2004).
4. *Wilkinson v. Austin*, 545 U.S. 209 (2005).

5. I tell the story both of the uprising and of the judicial proceedings that followed in my book *Lucasville: The Untold Story of a Prison Uprising* (Philadelphia: Temple University Press, 2004).

6. For greater detail, see *Lucasville*, chapter 7.

7. Testimony of Sergeant Howard Hudson, transcript, *State v. Skatzes*, 1922, 1930–45, 1950, 1978, 1993–94.

8. *In Re: Grand Jury Subpoenas Issued to Alice Lynd*, Case No. 04 CIH 089 (Ct.Com.Pl., Scioto Co., OH; Nov. 19, 2004), transcript, 4–5.

9. *In Re: Grand Jury Subpoenas*, transcript, 6.

10. The following account is extracted from "Meeting cools sting in heart, Man no longer believes in death penalty after seeing change in Glenn Benner II," by Carol Biliczky, *Beacon Journal*, Akron, OH, Feb. 18, 2006; and conversations with Glenn Benner's friend, Hilary Hughes.

11. Biliczky, *Beacon Journal*.

12. Biliczky, *Beacon Journal*.

13. Biliczky, *Beacon Journal*, confirmed in conversation with Hilary Hughes.

14. Biliczky, *Beacon Journal*.

15. Richard M. Kerger, Esq., "Hatred Wins," unpublished manuscript [1997], 53.

Afterwords

"OCTOBER, OCTOBER," *STAUGHTON LYND*

More than fifty years ago, just before we joined the Macedonia Cooperative Community in Georgia, Staughton wrote this poem:

> October, October,
> Fall-furthering copper month,
> Are we ripe that you come for us?
> Moments of our lives
> Lie in mounds like leaves,
> Awaiting.
> With what stillness you touch us!
> Why do you come so gently?
> Is there something
> You are afraid to say?

RETROSPECTIVES

Alice

It took me a long time to become a loving person.

When I was no more than three years old, we were living in an apartment building that had a supervised play area for children behind the
building. There was a wooden ledge above slanting doors leading to the
basement. Children would climb up onto the ledge. Sometimes one child
would push another child out of the way and off the ledge. One day, I did

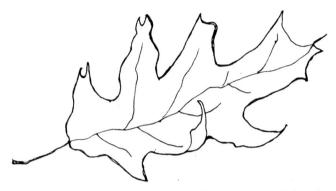

Staughton drew this leaf and had it printed on greeting cards for Alice.

that to a smaller child. I was scolded and sent home. I remember crawling up the stairs to our apartment, feeling completely humiliated. I also took from that incident the lesson that other people may be able to get away with doing bad things, but I can't.

As a teen-ager I recall feeling that I cared about people in the abstract, but individuals annoyed me. In high school, the other girls told me to wear more lipstick. If what I was wearing wasn't enough to please them, I decided, I won't wear any! (I still don't.)

Later, in college, I read a book by Rudolph Dreikurs that gave me a sense that I could be a more loving person. If I could be a more loving person, I had to do something about it. I made an appointment and became a patient of Dr. Dreikurs.

Shortly before I graduated from college in 1953, I decided that I did not want to teach. As I saw it, teaching young children requires that you give love on demand. I did not want love demanded of me. I got over that after I had children of my own!

When we went to the Macedonia Cooperative Community in 1954, members who had been there for years spoke of giving up our "last inch," and "being vulnerable." I resisted. I did not want to be vulnerable. But trust grew and deepened. We did become vulnerable. We did give all.

After Macedonia, when we were living in Atlanta, I was a teacher of two-year-olds at a day care center. I liked to hold a child in my lap as I tied his or her shoes, because that was a moment of establishing a relationship with the child.

In 1963, when our son Lee was five years old, he fell out of a window and fractured his skull. I learned to pray while he was undergoing hours of surgery. That he survived at all was a miracle, and for the doctor too it was a triumphant success that Lee suffered no permanent brain damage. "Now and then they toss you a bone to keep you going," the doctor commented. During the coming weeks, I recalled the mother of a child who was killed at the age of ten telling me, "You don't have the strength within you to deal with something like that. You have to breathe it in from the air." In the short run, pressure of the skull on Lee's brain produced episodes of psychotic behavior. Lee would physically attack me. For his own safety, I had to hold him. Here I was, loving my attacker. Martin Luther King's words were helpful, reminding me of Jesus telling us to love those who hurt you.

Years later, I worked as a paralegal, developing claims for Social Security disability clients. I was frustrated by the fact that their needs were so great and the most I could get for them was money. Staughton described my feeling to a colleague who replied, quoting from the Gospel of John, "Feed my sheep." So I continued.

I myself had been disabled from 1970 to 1972. Doing Social Security disability claims, I could use my own experience of pain to help others. I realized that what I was doing was expressing love to people. I was perhaps the only person who took the time to hear them tell what had happened to them, what their life had been like before they became disabled, and what they could no longer do because of their impairments. I needed that information to demonstrate disability. But it also became a process of discovering the person hidden behind the mask of disability. I was amazed by the resourceful ways individuals would find to adapt to their impairments: for example, one woman would place a large pot on the stove and fill it with small amounts of water so as not to have to lift a heavy pot; a disabled man would put groceries into the basket of his disabled wife's motorized wheelchair and she would drive up the ramp into the house with the groceries.

When my job was suddenly terminated, I told the lawyer for whom I was working that he could take away my job but he could not stop me from finding some other medium to express love to people.

Since retirement from employment, my work with prisoners has become a very rewarding opportunity for expression of love. Many of the prisoners have had horrendous childhoods and traumatic experiences as young men, and have endured years of deprivation and mostly negative feedback day by day. It is difficult for many of them to trust. But the best in them comes forward when you respect them as human beings, listen to their legitimate concerns, and respond frankly.

Protecting one prisoner who made a grave confession to me caused me very great stress and the prospect of remaining in jail unless and until I would betray his confidence. I jotted down a note while in the midst of that turmoil. It says: "Love is the only way to deal with [Mr. X]; wanting to express love is a way to recover my own balance, healing me." (See the chapter on Mr. X.)

These were stepping stones for me.

Staughton

If another world is indeed possible, how do we get from here to there? I have had a persistent need to imagine an answer to this question.

Earlier I described how, as a teenager on the New York City subway, I encountered what I came to call "Burnham's dilemma." The European middle class was able to create the institutions of a new society within the womb, or shell, of feudalism. How can there be created within capitalism institutions that prefigure another and better world?

As a teenager I had only the barest glimpses of an answer. I recall a moment during several weeks that I worked in a Toledo factory when I thought, The only thing I know that I really care about is the way the wind turns upside down the leaves of that birch tree. Another time I was hitchhiking around the country and spent a night alone in the middle of nowhere. I walked along a country road in the dark singing at the top of my voice the few songs that seemed to express fully what I believed, such as William Blake's "Jerusalem."

At the time I met Alice I deeply appreciated the example of the New England town meeting. I still love the novel *Look to the Mountain* by LeGrand Cannon, Jr., about the years of the American Revolution and Mt. Chocorua in New Hampshire, a mountain that I climbed many times as a child and as an adult.

I have experienced some more complete anticipations of another world. The Macedonia Cooperative Community was the first. Then the southern civil rights movement, the Workers' Solidarity Club of Youngstown, and as I write, the prisoners sentenced to death after the Lucasville uprising.

But none of these groups have been permanent. After the collapse of SNCC and SDS amidst recriminations and backbiting, I experienced something resembling Post-Traumatic Stress Disorder. National gatherings, and proposals for national organizations, frighten me.

During the past several years, inspired especially by the Zapatista rebellion in Chiapas, I believe that I have found a partial answer to Burnham's dilemma. It is the idea that our Movement for change should not attempt to take state power. Rather, we should create a horizontal network of self-governing institutions, strong enough that whoever holds the highest offices of government will be accountable to what Subcomandante Marcos calls "the below," that is, to us.[1]

There is a recollection of Myles Horton, one of the founders of the Highlander Folk School, that well expresses the endless capacity of ordinary people to create self-governing community from below. As a teenager from a very poor Appalachian family, and at the time, as a Christian, Myles taught a vacation Bible school in a remote hamlet called Ozone. It was the depths of the Depression. About halfway through the summer he decided that something more than the Bible was needed. He let it be known that on a certain evening there would be a meeting at the schoolhouse to consider the crisis in people's everyday lives.

People walked across the mountains barefoot to get to that meeting, Myles Horton recalls. As the gathering was about to begin, he realized that he had nothing to propose that might be immediately helpful. In desperation, Myles remembers, he said, "Why don't we go around the circle and see what ideas people brought with them?"

They did so. A communal program emerged. The Highlander style of education, which, to a considerable extent, became the organizing approach of SNCC, was born.

Alice

We have been asked to describe in *Stepping Stones* how we keep going in the face of discouragement and defeat. For me the answer is, take the initiative, focus again. What remains to be done? What is the next step? Or, if I need to distance myself from the present situation for a while, I go outside and work in the garden, or sit by a sunny window and sew. The kaleidoscope then begins to show a pattern. Things begin to fall into place.

Years ago Staughton and I saw a movie based on the life of Mahatma Gandhi. We recall a scene in which Gandhi is lying on the ground after being beaten by police in South Africa, beside a waste container in which the hated identification passes were being burned as a protest to that aspect of apartheid. In the movie, one sees Gandhi's arm reach out, his hand pick up one more pass and thrust it into the fire.

Whether fact or myth, that image often comes to mind. I find it unimaginable that I would have such defiant courage as he did in that situation. But that image inspires what I do.

We have on the wall in our kitchen some words attributed to a group known as KOR[2] in Poland during an era of totalitarian governmental repression. Although I am more cautious and do not consistently live up to their high standard, these words give me inspiration and guidance:

> Start doing the things you think should be done.
> Start being what you think society should become.
> Do you believe in freedom of speech? Then speak freely.
> Do you love the truth? Then tell it.
> Do you believe in an open society? Then act in the open.
> Do you believe in a decent and humane society? Then behave decently and humanely.

Alice and Staughton

We should say a final word about nonviolence, to which we remain firmly committed, and which continues to manifest itself in our lives.

In his Third Pastoral Letter, Archbishop Romero considered the relationship between the church and the popular political organizations that were proliferating in El Salvador. People in the countryside asked Romero: "Does being a Christian mean one has to join some popular organization seeking radical changes in our country? How can one be a Christian and accept the demands of the gospel and yet join some organization that neither believes in nor has sympathy with the gospel?"[3]

In his Third and Fourth Pastoral Letters, Archbishop Romero answered, Where people are the victims of kidnappings, murder, torture, threats, and arson, violence is often regarded as necessary and consciences can lose their sensitivity. He wrote about different kinds of violence: structural or institutionalized violence, repressive violence, terrorist violence, spontaneous violence, and what he regards as legitimate self-defense. But, to avoid retaliation and even greater violence, he says, violence used in self-defense must not be greater than the need, and must be used only after every possible peaceful means has been tried.[4]

We still struggle with the question of whether what Archbishop Romero called "legitimate self-defense" is ever the solution. Just as Staughton has found it difficult to find an answer to "Burnham's dilemma," so he has thus far not been able to imagine a way in which slavery in the United States could have been ended peacefully. Alice responds, Yes, and a hundred years later that war is still being fought! As is said in the Old Testament, the sins of the fathers are visited upon the children's children unto the third and fourth generation.[5]

Who would have believed that people gathering in the streets with candles, night after night, could have thrown off Soviet domination of Eastern Europe? Equally impressive is the transition to democracy in South Africa. Before his imprisonment, Nelson Mandela was in charge of the guerrilla or terrorist component of the African National Congress, an entity named "Spear of Africa." He traveled all over the continent to absorb the lessons learned by violent insurgencies in many countries. Yet when imprisoned for twenty-seven years, in a time of ever-escalating brutality by the apartheid government, the message he apparently broadcast to colleagues not behind bars was to attack property, not human beings. There followed the nonviolent creation of a single multiethnic state.

For ourselves, and in our own lives so far as we are able to imagine them, we believe that a nonviolent and just society cannot be created by violent means.

An Affair of the Heart

As we were about to put the finishing touches on this book, Staughton came very close to sudden death and was saved by open heart surgery.

The most puzzling part of the experience was that we had so little warning. An alert physician told Staughton that what Staughton assumed were respiratory symptoms might in fact indicate heart problems, and advised a stress test. The cardiac diagnostician who administered the stress test said that there appeared to be a serious blockage of one artery and recommended heart catheterization. (This is a procedure whereby doctors obtain a picture of the arteries that supply blood to the heart.) Everyone's expectation was that if they found a blockage, the doctors would insert a stent (a tube) and Staughton would spend one night in the hospital before returning home.

Instead, catheterization produced a picture showing almost complete blockage of the flow of blood to the heart and Staughton was taken directly to surgery. A triple bypass was performed.

As Staughton partially regained consciousness, he imagined himself inside a large metal cylinder. With very great difficulty he made his way up one side of the cylinder's inner wall. Other people seemed to be present but he could not communicate with them: he was entirely on his own. It was the hardest thing he had ever done.

At first, Staughton thought, "Well, maybe this is what it's like to come out of very heavy anesthesia." On reflection it seems to him that he was fighting for his life. Alice responded that prisoners nicknamed Staughton "Scrapper" for a reason: he *is* a fighter.

For six weeks after surgery Staughton could not drive, and our daughter Barbara picked up prescriptions at the drug store and did all our shopping. The heart surgeon told Staughton that he had come about as close as it was possible to come to dying and still "stay vertical." The surgeon also said that it was a mystery how God spared one person and not another. Barbara quietly commented: "Well Dad, now you need to think about why God saved your life, what task He still has for you."

We do not believe in a supernatural deity. Yet, hopefully without too much solemnity and pretentiousness, we have tried to discern our "task" at every stage of our journey. This book invites you to take that journey with us. Perhaps you will see some possibility that did not occur to us, or otherwise feel strengthened in finding your own way.

Meantime, we feel enormous gratitude. As Staughton convalesces, we leave our house only for short walks. This time together has given new depth to the words from the common marriage vows, "to have and to hold, to love and to cherish." Or as we said to one another at our Quaker wedding in 1951:

> In the presence of God and of these our Friends, I take thee [Staughton/Alice] to be my [husband/wife], promising to be unto thee a loving and faithful [wife/husband] as long as we both shall live.

A LETTER TO MARTHA, *ALICE LYND*

The following was written in answer to a question by our daughter, Martha, in Guatemala in 1998. Alice read it at Martha's wedding to Horacio Enrique Altán on July 10, 2005.

What I want for You in a Husband
That he will be someone who will always want to be with you and who you
will always want to be with;
That he have a strong "will to love," and that he be able to live it;
That your love and appreciation for each other grow deeper and stronger as
the years go by;
That he nourish your soul, and that you nourish his;
That you find the perceptions of each other helpful and leading to more than
either of you alone would have thought of;
That the give and take be roughly equal and that this be expressed both in
major life decisions and in day-to-day activities . . . ;
That he be a person whose influence on our grandchildren we would welcome;
That he have a practical sense of what is and is not within the limits of
your combined abilities, energy, and resources, so that he does not ask too
much of you;
That he give you space and quiet and fun and beauty as you need it;
That he always treat you with respect and truthfulness, that he be able to
forgive you, and encourage you to be your better self when you fail to be
all you could toward him.
Our love is always with you. May you be held in the light and protected from
harm. These are some of my prayers for you.

HAPPY, *ALICE LYND*

When I asked our grandson, Geordie, what he would like us to write about in *Stepping Stones*, he answered: "What makes you happy." Here are a few things that make me happy:

(1) Ensemble singing. In high school I was part of a sixteen-voice "madrigal group" led by a teacher who taught us to blend our

voices so that each part sounded like one voice, to listen to the other parts, to bring out particular lines or balance the parts with each other. I always have preferred singing or playing music as part of an ensemble, delicately balancing the parts.

(2) Spring flowers. One winter not long after we moved to Ohio, I was going through the Burpee catalog ordering seeds. It brought to mind as never before the joy I had in recalling the flowers that bloomed the previous spring. Most joyful of all, I think, are the windflowers. Their faces are so completely open to the sun and they bloom for weeks!

(3) Going on walks and having whoever is with me call my attention to extraordinary beauty: hiking with ten-year-old Barbara through a fairyland high in the Presidential mountains of New Hampshire one morning in June 1966 when everything was glistening with dew; our daughter Martha seeing a hawk or a heron; our friend Katharina being enchanted with how the ice had crystallized above the water along Mill Creek.

(4) Satisfaction in making things: a quilt, a well-made suit or sweater, or an attractive salad.

(5) Sitting at a table with grandchildren and the sunlight pouring in; listening to Lee and Betsy sing, and Geordie or Monica play their instruments; playing at the beach with Marie.

(6) And, since 1950, being at one with Staughton, the sense of peace, and loving the way he touches me.

NOTES

1. Staughton discusses this theme more at length in Staughton Lynd and Andrej Grubacic, *Wobblies & Zapatistas: Conversations on Anarchism, Marxism and Radical History* (Oakland, CA: PM Press, 2008).

2. KOR stands for Workers' Defense Committee. Members of KOR provided financial, legal, and medical assistance to workers and their families who were suffering from government repression. As a consequence, KOR members soon began to suffer loss of employment, arrest, imprisonment, beatings, and in a few cases death. KOR was founded in September 1976 and voted out of existence in September 1981 when its members decided that its role was being filled by Polish Solidarity. This summary of KOR's guiding principles appeared in "Reflections[,] A Better Today," by Jonathan Schell, *New Yorker* (Feb. 3, 1986), 60.

3. Archbishop Oscar Romero, *Voice of the Voiceless: The Four Pastoral Letters and Other Statements* (Maryknoll, NY: Orbis Books, 1985), 88.

4. Romero, *Voice of the Voiceless*, 105–7, 143–45.

5. Exodus 34:7.

Selected Bibliography of Publications by Staughton and/or Alice Lynd

Lynd, Staughton, *Anti-Federalism in Dutchess County, New York: A Study of Democracy and Class Conflict in the Revolutionary Era* (Chicago: Loyola University Press, 1962).

Lynd, Staughton, ed., *Nonviolence in America: A Documentary History* (Indianapolis, IN: Bobbs-Merrill, 1966).

Lynd, Staughton and Thomas Hayden, *The Other Side* (New York: New American Library, 1966).

Lynd, Staughton, *Class Conflict, Slavery, and the United States Constitution* (Indianapolis, IN: Bobbs-Merrill, 1967).

———. *Intellectual Origins of American Radicalism* (New York: Pantheon Books, 1968).

Lynd, Alice, *We Won't Go: Personal Accounts of War Objectors* (Boston: Beacon Press, 1968).

Ferber, Michael and Staughton Lynd, *The Resistance* (Boston: Beacon Press, 1971).

Lynd, Alice and Staughton Lynd, eds., *Rank and File: Personal Histories by Working-Class Organizers*, 1st ed. (Boston: Beacon Press, 1973); 2nd ed., illustrated (Princeton, NJ: Princeton University Press, 1981); 3rd ed. (New York: Monthly Review Press, 1988).

Lynd, Staughton, *The Fight Against Shutdowns: Youngstown's Steel Mill Closings* (San Pedro, CA: Singlejack Books, 1982).

Lynd, Staughton and Alice Lynd, "Labor in the Era of Multinationalism: The Crisis in Bargained-For Fringe Benefits," *West Virginia Law Review*, vol. 93, no. 4 (Summer 1991).

Lynd, Staughton, *Solidarity Unionism: Rebuilding the Labor Movement from Below* (Chicago: Charles H. Kerr, 1992).

Lynd, Staughton with Sam Bahour and Alice Lynd, eds., *Homeland: Oral Histories of Palestine and Palestinians* (New York: Olive Branch Press, 1994).

Lynd, Staughton and Alice Lynd, eds., *Nonviolence in America: A Documentary History*, rev. ed. (Maryknoll, NY: Orbis Books, 1995).

Lynd, Staughton, ed., *"We Are All Leaders": The Alternative Unionism of the Early 1930s* (Urbana, IL: University of Illinois Press, 1996).

Lynd, Alice and Staughton Lynd, "'We Are All We've Got': Building a Retiree Movement in Youngstown, Ohio," in Gary Bellow and Martha Minow, eds., *Law Stories* (Ann Arbor, MI: University of Michigan Press, 1996).

———. Liberation Theology for Quakers, Pendle Hill Pamphlet 326 (Wallingford, PA: Pendle Hill Publications, 1996), reprinted in Staughton Lynd, *Living Inside Our Hope: A Steadfast Radical's Thoughts on Rebuilding the Movement* (Ithaca, NY: Cornell University Press, 1997).

Lynd, Staughton, *Living Inside Our Hope: A Steadfast Radical's Thoughts on Rebuilding the Movement* (Ithaca, NY: Cornell University Press, 1997).

Lynd, Staughton and Alice Lynd, eds., *The New Rank and File* (Ithaca, NY: Cornell University Press, 2000).

Lynd, Staughton, *Lucasville: The Untold Story of a Prison Uprising* (Philadelphia: Temple University Press, 2004).

Lynd, Staughton and Andrej Grubacic, *Wobblies & Zapatistas: Conversations on Anarchism, Marxism and Radical History* (Oakland, CA: PM Press, 2008).

Lynd, Staughton and Daniel Gross, *Labor Law for the Rank & Filer: Building Solidarity While Staying Clear of the Law* (Oakland, CA: PM Press, 2008).

LEGAL CASES

Local 1330 v. U.S. Steel, 492 F.Supp. 1 (N.D. Ohio 1980).

———. 631 F.2d 1264 (6th Cir. 1980).

Austin v. Wilkinson, 189 F.Supp.2d 719 (N.D. Ohio 2002).

———. 204 F.Supp.2d 1024 (N.D. Ohio 2002).

———. 372 F.3d 346 (6th Cir. 2004).

Wilkinson v. Austin, 545 U.S. 209 (2005).

Index